Praise for
FACE TO FACE WITH KATRINA SURVIVORS

"These stories had to come out! The nation will stand up and cheer for Houston's response to the Katrina victims and this marvelous book."

STATE REPRESENTATIVE GARNET COLEMAN
Texas Legislature

"It was fantastic, I couldn't put it down! Two thumbs up! . . . The book truly is an outstanding contribution to help rectify the evacuees' stories so inaccurately portrayed in the news at the time."

BRETT PERKISON MD, MPH
Katrina First Responder
Department of Family and Community Medicine
Baylor College of Medicine

"The stories of survival, hope, and compassion are breathtaking. The true spirit of Houston comes through loud and clear in Dr. Moyé's book."

JOHN EDDIE WILLIAMS
Managing Partner
Williams and Bailey Law Firm, Houston, Texas

"A moving, heart-warming, and dignified tribute to the evacuees and volunteers of Hurricane Katrina."

KIERAN SMART MD, MSC, MPH
Katrina First Responder
Flight Surgeon, Space Medicine Advanced Projects
Wyle Laboratories, Inc., Houston, Texas

"Dr. Moyé captures the human aspects of a natural disaster . . . for both survivors and the people who cared for them."

GUY S. PARCEL, PhD
Dean
University of Texas School of Public Health, Houston

Praise for FACE TO FACE WITH KATRINA SURVIVORS

". . . captivating."

ABDUL J. SANKOH, PhD
Research Scientist
Sanofi-Aventis, USA

"This brought back a flood of memories. I can't sleep . . ."

DOUGLAS HAMILTON, MD
Katrina First Responder
Wyle Laboratories, Inc., Houston, Texas

"Finally, a marvelous departure from the media's focus on the negative aspects of the Katrina catastrophe. Stories of the enduring human spirit—challenged individuals at their best not their sensational worst, remarkable almost unbelievable Katrina survivors and compassionate volunteers—told with skill and mastery by Lemuel A. Moyé."

LOUISE DAVIS STONE
Freelance Editor and Writer
Retired Director of the Publications Division, NC Department of Labor

"What a tour de force! The stories themselves were really moving . . . the pain and generosity of the victims were overwhelming. As a reader, I kept asking myself, 'What would I have done?' or 'Could I have been so brave?' All in all a terrific book—very moving and a real revelation."

JANET WITTES, PhD
President
Statistics Collaborative, Washington D.C.

FACE TO FACE
WITH
KATRINA SURVIVORS

A First Responder's Tribute

"*Then there was Josie herself. She seemed to be the center of the family: always busy at service, or at home, or berry-picking; a little nervous and inclined to scold, like her mother, yet faithful, too, like her father. She had about her a certain fineness, the shadow of an unconscious moral heroism that would willingly give all of life to make life broader, deeper, and fuller for her and hers.*"

W.E.B. DuBois. *The Souls of Black Folk.* 1903.

FACE TO FACE
WITH
KATRINA SURVIVORS

A First Responder's Tribute

by
Lemuel A. Moyé, MD, PhD

OPEN HAND PUBLISHING, LLC
Greensboro, North Carolina
www.openhand.com

Cloth Cover ISBN-10: 0-940880-77-6
Cloth Cover ISBN-13: 978-0-940880-77-1

Paperback ISBN-10: 0-940880-78-4
Paperback ISBN-13: 978-0-940880-78-8

Open Hand Publishing, LLC
P.O. Box 20207
Greensboro, NC 27420
336-292-8585
e-mail: info@openhand.com
www.openhand.com

OPEN HAND
PUBLISHING, LLC

Library of Congress Cataloging-in-Publication Data

Moyé, Lemuel A.
  Face to face with Katrina survivors : a first responder's tribute / by
Lemuel A. Moye. -- 1st ed.
    p. cm.
  ISBN-13: 978-0-940880-77-1 (cloth cover : alk. paper)
  ISBN-10: 0-940880-77-6 (cloth cover : alk. paper)
  ISBN-13: 978-0-940880-78-8 (pbk. : alk. paper)
  ISBN-10: 0-940880-78-4 (pbk. : alk. paper)
  1. Disaster relief--Texas--Houston. 2. Disaster victims--Texas
--Houston. 3. Hurricane Katrina, 2005.   I. Title.
HV555.U62T415 2006
976.3'35064--dc22

    2006026097

Book and Cover Design: The Roberts Group

Front cover photos: Color photo by Ester Fant, University of Texas Medical
School at Houston. Background photo by U.S. Air Force, courtesy of the
Department of Defense

First Edition 2006
Printed in USA

DEDICATION

To the New Orleans evacuees and
the Houston volunteers,
whose generous spirits kept us all connected
in the face of disaster. It was upon this bedrock that
compassion flowed.

Table of Contents

Author's Preface   xi

Publisher's Note   xv

Introduction   1

Chapter 1
Katrina Takes New Orleans Apart and Brings Houston Together   3

Chapter 2
Compassionate Responders *and* Compassionate Evacuees   17

Chapter 3
The Breadth and Depth of the Evacuees' Problems   33

Chapter 4
Practicing Medicine Together and Without a Safety Net   55

Chapter 5
Beyond Anguish   83

Chapter 6
Young Mothers   105

Chapter 7
Husbands, Fathers, and Sons   131

Chapter 8
Katrina Survivors Look to the Future   161

Chapter 9
Above and Beyond the Call of Duty   183

Chapter 10
For Conduct Honoring Humanity . . .   203

Chapter 11
Conclusion   217

Appendix: The University of Texas School of Public Health   229

About the Author   231

Author's Preface

Losing all they owned, suffering in silence, initially denigrated by many others who were in a position to help, and perhaps ultimately set aside by contemporary U.S. culture, most Katrina survivors will never be acknowledged for who they were—American heroes. The evacuees were strong for their neighbors and families not to gain recognition, but because their strength of heart required that they endure. And endure they did—with dignity.

The stories comprising most of this book reveal not just the best of the American character, but the affirmation of the survivors' perseverant spirits. The light generated from their efforts just needed time to shine through the dark mists of prejudice and negativism through which they were initially viewed.

Many clinic workers in Houston volunteered their time, energy, and the best of their spirits and attitudes to first stand for and then stand with the evacuees. These tireless workers didn't just reflect the light from the evacuees; they were their own source of inspiration and revelation. This book revolves around these twin suns which together shine light on us all.

Gripping as many of these stories are, hard documentation for them is impossible. While I was the treating physician for many of these survivors, only their names, their physical ailments, and the treatment of those conditions are recorded in their medical charts. In accordance with the Health Insurance Portability and Accountability Act (HIPAA), I am prohibited under federal law from collecting and transporting any personal information (e.g., patient names and personal information) from health facilities for anything other than official business. Several additional conversations with the survivors were not formal patient-physician interactions at all, but conversations in the general evacuation room, of which there is no official record whatsoever. In addition, as in any emergency room, the treatment circumstances were sometimes urgent, and commonly dire, further precluding any documentation.

Thus it was impossible for me to keep or report any evacuee's real name, characteristics or treatment details in this memoir, and I have no record of the original patient's name. All I could legally do was record in my personal journal at the end of these long clinic shifts my own recollections of these patients, deliberately changing their names, and, sometimes, the details of the treatment of their condition. I have used the actual name of a fellow first responder, only when permitted and when that responder has reviewed my description of our interaction and agreed. These included the following healthcare providers: Ms. Mindy Cox, Dr. Barry Davis, Dr. George Delclos, and Dr. Kristy Murray.

Finally, no one's memory is perfect. Any inaccuracies or omissions concerning the dates, treatments, and details of my interactions are mine and mine alone, and I accept full responsibility for them. I freely admit that, if anything, I have left out many compelling examples of compassion, conviction and strength of evacuees that the urgency and fatigue of clinic circumstances precluded me from recording or re-membering. Fortunately, these omitted examples of heroism and heart strength, equally visceral, intense, and gripping, rest in the minds and bosoms of the evacuees and the volunteers who aided their recovery.

Furthermore, should any evacuees, despite my attempts to shield them, recognize themselves in these stories, I would only ask that you accept my occasionally imperfect memory as my sole excuse. My only intent is to respect and value your sacrifice, and through this memoir, to reveal your honor and valor to the world.

The text did not arise all at once; it developed slowly, gradually taking shape from my querulous recognition of the great schism between the common media portrayals on the one hand, and my personal experiences with the evacuees and the volunteers who cared for them on the other. Unsure what to do with observations that I couldn't ignore, I began sending e-mails to several friends and colleagues across the country. Many people responded sympathetically, but one, and only one, suggested that I begin to write and clarify my observations—Ariela Wilcox.

Ariela Wilcox, a literary agent and book producer in San Diego, California, accepted me as an untested nonfiction writer. Knowledgeable, competent, and approachable, she listened patiently and repeatedly as I ached over this book's early drafts. The perfect counterbalance for my efforts, Ariela kept me in stable writing equilibrium. Sensing the theme of the word-song I wished to create, her deft touch was expert; she knew that if she simply hummed the tune I would write the lyrics. This book would not be in your hands if it weren't for Ariela's solid, sensitive guidance and editing during its creation, and its appearance would have been impossible if she had not persistently sought out the *right* publisher.

If Ariela was the gyroscope, then Richard Koritz, Editor and Publisher for Open Hand Publishing, LLC, was the engine. His consistent enthusiasm for the project, like raw rocket fuel, propelled the book through production and on to market. Richard worked strenuously to settle the book's theme into place, and then, redoubling his efforts, he tirelessly reviewed the book's contents, reading draft after draft of the manuscript, all the while sharpening its message.

Our frequent, almost daily contacts, were both professional and cordial, allowing us to focus on our shared, mutual goal—to get the true story of the Katrina survivors out to readers interested in the survivors themselves—not just their plight. Through his labor, Richard demonstrated the insight of the leader who understands the need to not just "sound the charge," but to "lead the charge."

Ariela, Richard, and I, of different backgrounds, creeds, and races, recognized the quintessential message of the Katrina survivors—strength of heart triumphs over adversity.

I welcome your responses to the evocative themes portrayed in this book. Please email your comments to facetofacewithkatrina@msn.com.

Finally, my dearest thanks go to Dixie, my wife, on whose personality, character, love, and common sense I have come to rely, and to my daughters Flora and Bella Ardon, whose continued emotional and spiritual growth reveals anew to me each day that, through God, all things are possible.

Lemuel A. Moyé
University of Texas
School of Public Health
September 2006

Publisher's Note

When Dr. Lemuel Moyé's agent first sent me the draft of this book, I was astounded to discover that the name of President George W. Bush was not even mentioned! (It still isn't.)

Long before I ever heard of Dr. Moyé and his book, I knew that the people of New Orleans and especially the poor and largely African-American segment of the population had been treated in a criminally negligent way by the U.S. government. Indeed, in a column written for the *Greensboro (NC) Times* many months *before* Hurricane Katrina, I exposed the fact that the only preparation for *Hurricane Ivan* done by U.S. federal emergency officials in New Orleans was to accumulate ten thousand body bags! And they were busy seeking as many more body bags as they could get their hands on. For they predicted that as many as fifty thousand citizens of New Orleans might die as a result of a direct hit of Hurricane Ivan on this major city. According to federal authorities there, it was "impossible" to transport the citizens of this low-lying metropolitan area out of harm's way because so many poor people lacked their own *private* transportation, i.e., automobiles. I contrasted this with the evacuation of more than one million citizens of Cuba from the northwestern area of that impoverished island nation by the Fidel Castro-led government in anticipation of the very same hurricane.

I concluded: "Fortunately, for the poor people of New Orleans, Hurricane Ivan largely bypassed their city, but 'hurricane roulette' is just a tragedy waiting to happen there." (*Greensboro Times*, February 2005)

During and after Hurricane Katrina, in New Orleans and in the

Gulf Coast region, and later in Houston and elsewhere, there were men and women of good will, including local government leaders, who unselfishly helped to rescue and aid their fellow human beings. But the only branch of the *national government* that acquitted itself well was the Coast Guard, whose *local* forces, based in Alexandria, Louisiana, performed heroically. Ironically, the Coast Guard is under the Department of Homeland Security, whose chief, Michael Chertoff, working directly under President Bush, *blocked* federal relief dollars for Katrina victims by refusing to make a declaration of an "Incident of National Significance." Chertoff, along with President Bush, was the key saboteur of the rescue effort, even more than their subordinate and ultimate scapegoat, FEMA Chief Michael Brown or, as President Bush called him, "Brownie."

The scandalous and even criminal treatment of U.S. citizens by their government at all levels, and especially the federal level, is by now well-known. Such comprehensive works as *The Great Deluge* by Douglas Brinkley and *Come Hell or High Water* by Michael Eric Dyson have done a good job documenting the criminal character of the U.S. government response. Nevertheless, Open Hand Publishing, LLC decided that *this* book, with no mention of George W. Bush, still has something important to share with the people of the USA and the world.

Face to Face with Katrina Survivors focuses on the human beings whose lives were most devastated by Hurricane Katrina and the ensuing damage caused by the breached levees, the poorest of the poor who had been stranded and abandoned in New Orleans.

The corporate-dominated mass media described these victims as people who chose to abandon their children and desert their families to steal useless stereos. Dr. Moyé initially expected to meet such people. This book is the product of the *collision* between his expectation and his actual experience with the survivors whom he interviewed and examined at the Houston Astrodome complex immediately after they were bussed there from a devastated New Orleans, Louisiana.

As the author described these evacuees: "[They] operated from a compassionate and gracious strength of heart . . . It was an honor to watch, and even participate in, their reactions as they demonstrated their allegiance to family, to culture, to each other, and, in the end, to us all." Dr. Moyé's undeniably honest narration exposes the fact that the U.S. mass media has taken the heat off of the system by "blaming the victims" in the most vicious fashion.

Elsewhere I have written that the Bush Administration is responsible for *ethnic cleansing* in New Orleans and that this constitutes twenty-first century lynching and land-stealing. In early October, as we are going to press, the *Wall Street Journal* has cited a door-to-door survey in New Orleans indicating that only 41 percent of the pre-Katrina population has returned there in the more than a year that has transpired since then!

From *Face to Face* the reader can learn, in the most personal way, why so many poor and African-American people have gotten the message from the government and the system that they should *not* return to New Orleans. In the wake of the barbaric treatment they received (and continue to receive) from the government, insurance companies, real estate sharks and others, is it any wonder that *none* of the evacuees recounted by Dr. Moyé in *Face to Face With Katrina Survivors* was planning to return home to live in New Orleans?!

What is miraculous about this book is that Dr. Moyé provides a heretofore unparalleled description of the depth of the misery and devastation experienced by the poorest citizens of New Orleans, the main targets of this ethnic cleansing. And yet, he is able to present a book that realistically holds out some hope for the future. This is due to the fact that Dr. Moyé concentrates *his focus*, not on the leaders, the movers and shakers, but on *the people themselves*.

Indeed, the book reveals the startling depth of the "souls of black folk" *in our time* quite similar to that depth of spirit which W.E.B. DuBois discovered and reported so eloquently in his classic work of that name over one hundred years ago. As the publisher of *Face to Face with Katrina Survivors*, I am no doubt prejudiced in its favor. Notwithstanding this fact, I truly believe that chapters such as "Young Mothers," "Beyond Anguish," and "Husbands, Fathers, and Sons" are so beautifully written that, like DuBois' masterpiece, *Souls of Black Folk*, the text begins to soar; it seems transformed into poetry and even music.

The people Dr. Moyé encountered admiringly included not only New Orleans evacuees but also Houston volunteers. This decent and brilliant man allows us to accompany him on his journey of discovery. And what he has discovered is the decency, the compassion and the love shared among *ordinary* people in our society—from New Orleans to Houston and beyond.

Dr. Moyé was ennobled by his contact with the survivors and the volunteers. We at Open Hand Publishing, LLC believe that the reader will be ennobled by his contact with Dr. Moyé and his book.

In the process of editing and publishing this book, I received valuable help and encouragement from a number of formidable women. Along with their enthusiastic endorsement of the book, both Louise Davis Stone of Chapel Hill, North Carolina and Joanne Nyamukapa of Phoenix, Arizona provided a thorough editorial assessment of the book. Chinese-American documentary filmmaker Loni Ding of San Francisco, California suggested the narrative structure for our photo section; and Executive Director Amelia Parker of the International Civil Rights Center and Museum in Greensboro, North Carolina provided constructive suggestions to this section as well. Clara Villarosa, the Grande Dame of African-American booksellers, generously provided straightforward and wise counsel. Minnesota's Sherry Roberts, of the Roberts Group, Open Hand Publishing, LLC's book designer, has once again gone above and beyond her assigned responsibility. And, my wife, Sandra Self Koritz, a partner in Open Hand Publishing, LLC as well as my life-partner, believed, from the beginning, in the strength of Dr. Moyé's narrative and expressed a strong and unwavering desire to have us publish this book.

Finally, it has been a pleasure and a privilege to collaborate closely with the exceptional Dr. Lemuel A. Moyé. A privilege—because the man possesses so many academic gifts, shares them generously, and, all the while, remains open to criticism, welcoming, embracing, and moving with it so as to advance the creative process. A pleasure—not only because all of these sterling qualities are wrapped up in a good man but mostly because knowing such a person is an encouragement for anyone who seeks a better world for humanity.

Our collaboration enhanced our respective understanding of the tragedy of Hurricane Katrina, and reveals the strength two people can bring to each other in a joint effort to get out the truth.

Richard A. Koritz
Editor and Publisher
Open Hand Publishing, LLC
October 2006

Introduction

In August 2005, a tropical wave formed then quietly disappeared in the Atlantic Ocean just west of equatorial Africa. After several days it emerged just east of the Florida peninsula, strengthening to become the hurricane season's eleventh tropical storm. Computers, following their well-rehearsed procedures, routinely generated a name for this typical disturbance in an unusually active season—"Katrina."

The atmospheric powerhouse of Hurricane Katrina detonated directly over the people of the Gulf Coast of Louisiana and Mississippi. However, its aftershocks continue to reverberate throughout the USA. This is especially so in Houston, designated as the new home for many of the storm's survivors.

As a Houston physician, I was called to provide immediate care for the evacuees who were arriving by the busloads just two days after the storm departed New Orleans. Like thousands of other physicians, nurses and volunteers, I turned to television and radio for what to expect. The media's message: "Expect the worst!"

Both network and cable television's 24/7 graphic coverage of the Katrina aftermath in New Orleans was grisly. The media fueled characterizations of the stranded, deserted, and abandoned population that had been forced to go through the storm-related horrors in New Orleans as people who chose to abandon their children and desert their families to steal useless stereos. The media pundits predicted a similar urban crisis for Houston. In increasingly strident pronouncements, New Orleans citizens were characterized as uncivil, untrustworthy, and unwelcome.

Yet, Houston's public health workers, counseled by some to ignore the call, stood their ground. Waiting as the evacuees disembarked the buses in their new home, we chose to offer ourselves to these desperate people, holding our breath for their response . . .

The debacle never happened. My direct experiences with these gentle people over the next ten days demonstrated repeatedly that the survivors operated from a compassionate and gracious strength of heart that endured during this most severe of tests. Their response to our assistance was deepest gratitude, the quietest strength, and steadfastness of spirit. The disaster never occurred, and the stories that fueled it continue to mislead America dangerously.

The actual accounts of strength and character of the Katrina survivors and my interactions with them comprise this book. The stories these evacuees quietly shared with me trumpeted their patience, their pride, and their conviction to embrace life, whatever it held. It was an honor to watch, and even participate in, their reactions as they demonstrated their allegiance to family, to culture, to each other, and, in the end, to us all. This book is my tribute to them.

CHAPTER 1

Katrina Takes New Orleans Apart and Brings Houston Together

On Wednesday, August 31st, my wife and I sat glued to the television screen. Like the rest of the country, we had ringside seats from which to watch the collapse of New Orleans.

Ten days prior, the meteorologists turned their attention to a run-of-the-mill tropical low in the Atlantic. Appearing just off Florida's east coast, Tropical Storm Katrina gradually strengthened. Growing to a Category One hurricane, she grazed the southern tip of Florida, producing substantial rain and water damage in both the Miami and the Tampa-St. Petersburg areas. Americans, consumed with angst over Iraq, new school year activities, and plans for the Labor Day weekend, paid scant attention to the crippled hurricane as she emerged from western Florida into the eastern Gulf of Mexico.

However, Katrina refused to die. With a growing sense of dread, the U.S. Gulf Coast population watched the weakened storm struggle to stay organized. She wobbled unsteadily then gradually strengthened as she drew tremendous quantities of heat from the warm Gulf. These waters, the hottest in memory during the summer of 2005, provided inexhaustible supplies of the raw energy so necessary for the storm's enormous engine.

Two days later, she was back to hurricane strength. After steadying her weaving trajectory, she appeared to take aim at the Florida peninsula, promising to deliver a one-two punch to the weather-beaten Sunshine State. The sympathetic eyes, prayers and support of Gulf Coast residents turned to Florida, the target of so many storms in the previous two years. Of course, nobody wanted Florida to be hit yet again. But, succumbing to the cruel logic of the human-hurricane interaction, nobody wanted to take the hit for her, either.

Naturally, none of this affected the complex relationship of Katrina with her environment, an interaction that still confounds the best meteorologists in the world. As the hours passed, the storm strengthened, gorging herself on the huge reservoirs of Gulf water heat. Pushing her way up from Category Two to Category Four, Katrina changed her trajectory. Slowing her northward movement, she crept to the west, until she positioned herself north in the gulf, three hundred miles west of Houston, due south of New Orleans. Sunday night, the strong beast bared her teeth to strike.

On Monday morning, August 29th, Katrina uncoiled northward as predicted, slamming into the vulnerable Gulf Coast. Like a one hundred mile wide tornado, Katrina tore her way through the populous area where Louisiana, Mississippi, and Alabama come together.

Although the damage was grievous, the first reports out of New Orleans that afternoon were that the Crescent City had been spared the worst of the storm. That singular distinction was earned by Mississippi, whose vulnerable coastal communities were dismembered by the huge storm surge and winds in excess of one hundred miles an hour. New Orleans, it was said, while battered, had survived. Its luck and citizenry intact, The Big Easy had once again avoided The Big One—*if* initial reports were to be believed. No one yet realized the size of the hole the beast was tearing into the heart of this historic city.

At 2:00 P.M. on Monday, New Orleans city officials learned that one of the city's critical levees had breached. The Big Easy, notorious for its insouciance in the face of danger posed by its below sea-level existence, was taken completely by surprise. The city rapidly filled with water as the contents of towering Lake Pontchatrain poured into her.

The resulting flood was predictable, the ineluctable consequence of mathematics and fluid dynamics. But two days later, like the rest of the world, my wife and I watched the destruction of New Orleans with sick horror. It was clear that the survivors would have to be moved, or they would die by the thousands in days. But where would they go?

Discussions to prepare Houston to accept the majority of New Orleans' thousands of evacuees took place in the office of Bill White, mayor of Houston. Under his solid leadership, the city's leaders and workers prepared to accept the ravaged survivors of the Crescent City, just three hundred miles east.

Plans for the clinic took shape at 6 A.M. on Wednesday, August 31st. The vast Reliant Center-Astrodome complex was selected as the best spot. Rods and curtains for sectioning off the exhibition hall were taken out of storage, and like Tinker Toys, were fashioned into rooms for patient registration and physician care.

Meanwhile, a convoy of four hundred and fifty buses headed west out of New Orleans for Houston along I-10. At Reliant Center-Astrodome, medical triage areas and examination rooms were hurriedly assembled. Computers, copiers, and telephone lines were installed. A makeshift pharmacy was rapidly constructed as local businesses donated medical supplies by the score.

At 10:00 P.M., Wednesday evening, the first shipment of cots appeared in the Astrodome, and volunteers, who had been working all day, began setting them up. Ten minutes later, the first buses arrived at the Astrodome parking lot, full of evacuees.

I had been a faculty member at the University of Texas School of Public Health in Houston for eighteen years that summer. I was a physician, but hadn't practiced medicine for years, focusing instead on research. The only time I wrote prescriptions anymore was when a family member had an infection, or a colleague was out of his or her blood pressure or asthma medicine. I was so inactive in medicine that, for the first time, I had considered not renewing my medical license, a cyclical rite for physicians in Texas. However, following my tradition, I had renewed it yet again that summer. It arrived, allowing me to practice for two more years, beginning August 31, 2005.

My mom had just moved down to Houston from New York, and I was with her that Friday before the long Labor Day weekend, catching up on e-mail. At 10:23 A.M., I, along with the thousands of employees of the University of Texas Health Science Center at Houston received the customarily kind message from the university president, Dr. James Willerson, wishing us all a happy Labor Day holiday.

The local news programs preempted the normal TV programming to cover the evacuees' arrival at the Astrodome complex. Some had arrived in the predawn hours, including one bus driven by an "unauthorized driver."[1] During this programming, all Houstonians were asked to donate supplies for these survivors who were arriving with nothing of their own and would be staying indefinitely.

Like many Houstonians, my wife and I pitched in right away. We had donated goods to one charity drive or another over the years. I thought nothing special about this one as we crammed our Explorer full of items we thought the survivors could use. *The need was greater than most*, I thought, *but that was all*.

I was dead wrong.

There were designated drop off points, but these were located miles from the Astrodome Complex where many evacuees would be staying. Our route took us by the Astrodome where we saw a Toys-R-Us parking area just a minute's walk from the new home of the evacuees. My wife and I looked at each other for a moment then I silently turned the car's right turn signal on. In a few moments we slowly rolled into the lot.

The parking lot rapidly filled with cars chock-full of donations, as many others also saw the advantage of dropping off goods within a few moments walk from the new, temporary home of the survivors. Tailgates slammed down, trunks sprang open, and SUV gates swung

---

1. Taking it upon himself to drive, a desperate young man invited several fellow survivors to join him, and he slipped his unauthorized bus into the caravan traveling to Houston from New Orleans. After some discussion, he and his fellow survivors were permitted access to the Reliant Astrodome Complex staging area like all other bus occupants.

wide, displaying all manner of apparel and toiletries for the evacuees. In just a few minutes, every space in the large parking lot was taken by a private vehicle donating something to the Katrina survivors. *It was a Texas tailgate party that gave away clothes, not food.*

We parked, and I got out, walking around the back of the car to open the back hatch, revealing its contents to some of the survivors who I saw making their way toward us. Walking away from the vehicle, I entered the midst of the Katrina evacuees, getting my first real exposure to them.

I braced for the worst. The media was overrun with stories of the desperation and sick, uncivil behavior of the evacuees. By the media's account, these despicably poor people were hungry, ill, and crazed. According to the stories that spread like wildfire, these demented souls were relying on instinct, falling back on animalistic impulses, abandoning their children, giving in to animal-like, carnal desires. The "refugees" as they were commonly referred to in the early days of the catastrophe, were not to be blamed for what they did, we were told. They just couldn't help themselves. Having not eaten for days, distraught by their treatment in New Orleans, we were led to anticipate angry outbursts, gang-like violence, maybe even an urban riot as their anger boiled over into blind rage. The message was that, while they needed care, they should also be feared.

Their appearance was certainly in conformity with what the media depicted. The parking lot rapidly filled with un-groomed people, coated in grime and soot. While some walked in clusters of two or three, most were walking alone. Some merely sat on the hot asphalt of the parking lot. Fearful children buried their faces in the comfortable knees of their parents, turning their little backs to the strangers who were coming in to the parking lot in all of these strange vehicles.

As soon as I walked away from the car, a woman came up to me. (I think she was black, but dirt covered her so completely that I couldn't be sure.) With no introduction, in fact without saying a word, she hugged me. Quietly, she held me close for a second. When she pulled away, I saw tears streaming down her face.

"You don't know what this means to us!" she stammered through her crying.

I gave her my handkerchief, completely taken aback by this total, open-hearted display of gratitude.

"We had no idea what to expect here," she continued, wiping her eyes with the handkerchief. "They just let us off of the bus. We didn't even know where we were going! Somebody said Texas, someone else said we were headed for Arkansas! Then someone said we would have to turn around and go back to New Orleans. Oh! We just didn't know."

"Well, you're here in Houston, now," I offered, struggling to keep my composure. I had never been in the presence of an adult who had broken down so utterly and completely in front of a stranger.

"Houston. Houston! We are so very thankful for being here. You and everyone else here are very special to us. You are the most special people in the world!"

"Would you like to see what we brought . . . ," I tried.

"You can't know what your being out here means to us!" she continued, ignoring what I tried to tell her about our donations. "This makes us feel special! For a week we thought no one cared about us! But your being out here shows how wrong we were. I can't tell you what a difference this day makes."

She didn't care about the shirts, or slacks, or anything else we brought. Looking around, I saw her reaction repeated all over the lot. This woman was not the only evacuee whose spirit had withstood the New Orleans debacle. Not one of the many survivors that I could see at that lot was taking any of the donations! These desperately dirty, unkempt people who had only the tattered clothes on their backs were not rummaging through shoes, picking through jeans, casting about through piles of clean underwear and socks that had been brought for them. The evacuees' primary interest was not in getting clothes for themselves or even for their children, who stood quietly at their sides in their own tattered garb.

Stopping Houstonians who were getting out of cars in the parking lot, the survivors repeatedly said:

"Thank you!"

"God bless you!"

"This means more than I can say."

Over and over again they poured out their gratitude with tears in their eyes, forgetting their own material needs. These people whose lives had been rung out by their four day experience in New Orleans, were intent on expressing their complete and utter gratitude for our presence. They thanked us before they knew what we were giving. Our presence meant everything. To these survivors our material things meant nothing; we could have come empty-handed. The continuous expression of thanksgiving expressed by the Katrina survivors was a consistent theme in my relationship with them over the next two weeks.

"Do you have family here?" I asked another woman, whose clothes were muddy and in tatters.

"My husband and I are the only ones that we know who got out. He's over there," Covering her eyes from the hot sun she pointed to the end of the parking lot about twenty feet away.

Following her finger, I saw she was pointing to an older gentleman. Like her, he was un-groomed. Wearing a beat-up T-shirt that, almost torn into two separate pieces, was barely able to stay on his dirty torso, he squatted down, looking at some shoes. Watching, I noticed with surprise that he wasn't trying any of them on. Instead, he had put together several rows of men's shoes. Going through a pile of shoes that he had gathered, he was studying them carefully. I realized at once what he was doing.

"He's sorting them!" I exclaimed. "He's organizing them for others to go through and choose."

She said nothing. She just watched her husband with me.

"Doesn't he know that they are for him to choose?! We brought these," I said, showing her the clothes in the back of our own car, "for you to take. They are for you to have, not for you to work to organize!" I had given no thought to who would organize the donations, just assuming the job wouldn't be necessary if the evacuees plowed into them looking for what they needed. There were hundreds of pairs of shoes, untold numbers of shirts, piles of new underwear, socks, and toys for children. As I looked around, I saw that other evacuees were involved in converting these heaps of clothes and toys into neat, organized collections.

"I didn't think you would need to do this." I said.

"Why not?" she asked.

"I thought you would be too tired. Too run down." *Too defeated*, is what I thought to myself but didn't say.

"It's been terrible," she said. "The worst week of my life! For days we had no contact with anyone who would help. And then the rumors. There were always the rumors, like the army was coming to take us away, like we were prisoners, like we had done something wrong! All we wanted to do was to survive, and then to leave. And for days we couldn't do that. But, you," she said, "and your neighbors. You have . . .", she struggled for a word, "erased all of that. We are whole again. We are getting better, now that we know that you know that we matter. I think we were forgetting that. Your being here reminded us."

I was overwhelmed in the presence of this remarkable woman, so physically broken down, yet both articulate and emotionally resilient.

"Don't you want to see if you could use any of this?" I insisted.

"No. Not now. Seeing you", and she turned around to point to the other Houstonians being greeted in a similar way by the other survivors, "everybody else who has come out to greet us—to speak with us, to be with us, to want us. That," she finished, smiling again, "is enough. Thank you again."

Returning to the car, my wife and I met several other survivors. Greeting us with the same enthusiastic and warm gratitude, they offered to help us with unloading our donations. Together we carried them to a corner area of the parking lot where other evacuees were busily cataloging and organizing the donations. Not a single one of them was selecting clothes for themselves or their children.

We drove home, discussing nothing else but the astonishing response of the survivors to these gifts. We had both commented over the years, somewhat tongue-in-cheek, that "the media is the worst place to get your news." But that didn't prepare us for the incredible disconnect we had just experienced. The separation between the traits we saw in the steadfast and thankful evacuees on the one hand, and the bawdy, inhuman descriptions conveyed by television and the print media on the other, was jarring.

As we arrived home we both knew that we would do more for these gentle people. We weren't alone. Much later, I spoke to a colleague of mine, Mindy Cox, who described her reaction on that first illuminating day.

"You can't help but want to take care of these amazing people!" Mindy exclaimed. "My husband and I came down here from our home outside the 610 Loop, simply to drop off some clothes and things for them. We heard all of the stories. We planned to help a little, but that's all. We didn't want to stay long and put ourselves at risk.

"But what risk?" she continued. "These survivors mean no one any harm. They pour out their thanks to you. Their gratitude is like a river. You just get caught up in it.

"We meant to stay a couple of minutes, but we couldn't leave that supermarket parking lot. My errands, so terribly important to me earlier in the day, now counted for nothing! These evacuees, these strangers, found doors to our hearts that, once opened, weren't easily closed.

"Others were caught up in it too. They pulled up with their cooking grills, set up shop and started their own small cook-offs. Pretty soon, the air was full of the smell of barbecue and home-cooked sauce. Others among us bought bottles of water and soft drinks from that Fiesta supermarket with our money and just distributed them to the evacuees. And do you know what they did? The evacuees, themselves near the end of endurance, took plates that were heaped high with fresh cooked food, walking it across the huge parking lot to those too sick to get food for themselves. The attitudes you expect to see in the best churches was on full display among strangers in that parking lot.

"I tell you, Lem" she continued, with fierce determination filling her eyes, "we stayed at that Fiesta all day and into the evening. Even when there was no sorting to do, no more food to distribute, we stayed."

"Why?" I asked.

"To share with them. To tell them how sorry we were for what they went through. For how they were treated. To listen to them. But . . ."

Mindy hesitated, in a moment of reflection. Then she said: "What I really wanted was to be among them. To be with them. To show them that the world and the TV was lying and that they do matter!

"You know, lives are complicated and we react to that by separating. In this country we've become experts at disconnecting from our fellow workers, our neighbors. Here, the advice provided by the media was the same. 'Don't mix with this dangerous crowd,' we were warned. 'They're different, because they're black', or 'because they're poor', or 'because they live differently.'

"Yet in this tragedy, the evacuees demonstrated a quality that I want to believe we all have locked away inside. These survivors chose to be *elevated* by the debacle. They have a quiet, spiritual defiance. The storm may have destroyed their belongings and demolished their homes, but did not ruin them. Their hearts were broken—but not their spirits.

"They are made of the best American fabric, and I was so proud of them, and needed to help them. This was as bad as, maybe even worse than, 911," she added, referring to the terrorist attack on New York City and Washington D.C. "But this time, I could make a difference! Right here at home. I wouldn't turn my back on that!"

Neither my wife, nor I knew of the impending crisis as we, along with thousands of other Houstonians met and mingled with the evacuees. Although the Reliant Center Astrodome Complex was spacious enough to handle the thousands of new arrivals, the relatively small number of physicians and nurses who reported for duty the day before had worked several consecutive shifts without relief. By Friday morning, they were stretched to the breaking point. A decision was made . . .

Returning to my workstation and rapidly scanning the morning e-mail flotsam, I came across the following message, received at 11:59 A.M. from the University of Texas Health Science Center e-mail server.

> **TO:** All Faculty, Staff, Fellows, Residents and Students
> **FROM:** Office of Public Affairs
> **DATE:** Friday, September 2, 2005
> **RE: Katrina Response & Relief as of Friday morning**
>
> We are working to keep up with ever-changing requests from relief agencies as their needs and those of the evacuees increase

in Houston. Following is information about immediate opportunities and needs. Please remember that there will also be many opportunities to help in the days, weeks and months ahead if you are not called upon this weekend.

Physicians Needed—As of this morning, physicians in all specialties are needed at the Astrodome. Beginning mid-afternoon, physicians in all specialties are needed at the George R. Brown Convention Center downtown, where UT Physicians will create a new clinic operation for evacuees who will be sheltered at the Convention Center. UT physicians are asked to coordinate their schedules with their chair or supervisor. There is no need to call the command center before reporting for duty.

The Office of Public Affairs would appreciate knowing who is reporting for duty; please e-mail . . .

I read this message several times to make sure I understood. Physicians were needed at once at the Reliant Center Astrodome, and also at the George R. Brown Convention Center, located four miles north and east, closer to Houston's downtown district. That much was obvious. However, as I studied the message carefully, there was one sentence that really caught my attention, galvanizing me to action. It was: "*There is no need to call the command center before reporting for duty.*"

This statement was singularly unique in a university message. In the post 9/11 era, the need for administrative oversight at the University never seemed to end. You needed approval for everything: to enter buildings, to buy equipment. Research red tape was everywhere. To a faculty member, it was stultifying.

However, in this matter, things were different. There was no need to check into a command center! *Vacating the need to check-in was a virtual call-to-arms.* It was university code. What they were really saying was, "Hey, you guys. Things are serious. This is for real. Get over here quick!"

It took only fifteen minutes for me to collect my things. Rummaging around through a first and then a second closet, I finally found a lab coat that I'd used in practice back in the 1980's. Going through my black bag, I couldn't decide what I would need. I just grabbed a BP cuff, a stethoscope, an ophthalmoscope to examine eyes, and a notebook with the treatment plans I used to treat patients in general/family practice twenty years before, jamming them all into the well used pockets of the old white coat. I shoved what I wouldn't take back into my bag, leaving it on the desk. Telling my wife I was finally ready, I got into the passenger seat of her car wearing jeans, boots and above it all, a grievously old and ghastly purple scrub top. She got in, turned the engine over, gave me a curiously inscrutable smile, and we headed to the Astrodome.

The new Reliant Park Complex, within view of our home, is immense. From 1961 to 2002 it contained only the Astrodome and the Arena. However, much had changed recently as the city worked to modernize and upgrade its sports and convention center image. On the spacious grounds where there used to be two buildings, there were now four: Reliant Stadium (home of the NFL team, the Houston Texans), Reliant Center (new convention complex), Reliant Astrodome (the "Astrodome" to the rest of the world), and Reliant Arena (an older, smaller convention center). These huge buildings are all in proximity to each other, on the same grounds, connected by roads and interspersed with acres of parking.

The e-mail instructions were to head to the Reliant Astrodome, so we navigated our way through the long side streets that surround the Reliant Park complex with its multiple entrances and exits. On a normal day, the Astrodome was only a five minute drive from our house. Today, it took thirty.

The streets were jammed with traffic, and as best as we could tell, every car was packed to the gills with donations! A caravan of charity. SUV's, station wagons, sedans, were all full of material. Underwear in one car. Toothbrushes and toiletries in another. Children's' clothes in a third.

"I can't believe all of this!" I exclaimed, my eyes flitting from car to car.

"The TV said that the local Walgreens and CVS are almost out of toiletries because so many donors have purchased them," my wife replied, inching the car forward.

We also marveled at how polite the drivers were. Everyone was confused. No one wanted to be in traffic. Yet patience prevailed. Cars that wanted to edge into traffic were permitted. Cutting into traffic could lead to gunfire at any other time in Houston, but not today. Not near the Astrodome.

So we moved slowly with the hundreds of cars, in three lanes of traffic, each full of donations for the incoming strangers. It was a tie-up unlike any other I had ever seen in Houston. In fact, *it wasn't a traffic jam at all; it was a donation wagon-train.*

We finally arrived at one gate that was closed. Policemen were there to ensure no entries were attempted. I was beginning to wonder how to get to the Astrodome, and was about ready to tell my wife just to stop on the street, and let me walk up to a guard and ask. She (as usual) having a better idea, called the policeman over who had stopped traffic. He stuck his head in and said simply,

"Ma'am?"

"Doctor on board," was all she said.

Instantly stepping back, the officer raised his left hand to stop oncoming traffic, allowing us to turn in front of the traffic he'd stopped, so we could pass through the entrance with no delay. My wife and I looked at each other thinking the same thought. *This IS serious!*

For five additional minutes we followed a police car as it drove across the huge parking lots. This spacious area had become gigantic bus fields where buses stopped, unloading their manifests of survivors. We passed security cars that were rushing off on their own missions, and we drove by the foot and horse patrols that were setting up security perimeters.

Sitting quietly as our car approached the debarkation point, I was of two minds. Half of me was anxious to get in there. To pitch in. To make a difference. *They called for docs. Here I was. What are we waiting for? Let's get to it!*

Nevertheless the other half of me was wary. At fifty-two years of age, caution had first snuck up on and then overtaken me. *Who was I fooling?* I asked myself. It had been over a decade since I had practiced medicine. I was no longer a swashbuckling intern, commander of a hospital ward. I was a mathematician with a medical license, a book worm toting a collection of antiquated remedies and treatments that had no place in the twenty-first century. What was I walking into? What on earth did I think I was doing here?

And what about the stories? I wondered. By this time, my wife and I had heard them all a hundred times: Wild looting in New Orleans. Rampages. Beatings by gun-toting thugs. The Superdome and its own, new breed of ghastly horrors. An orgy of convulsive self destruction in a city's last agonizing hours. Is this what had been transplanted to Houston? Was this what I had deliberately and voluntarily agreed to face? Yet, I couldn't reconcile that television imagery with what I had seen with my own eyes at the donation site less than two hours before.

I didn't know how to think about this, so I just didn't. We came to a stop at one of the Reliant Arena building entrances. Kissing my wife goodbye, I got out of the car and walked in. A passing nurse grabbed my arm . . .

CHAPTER 2

Compassionate Responders *and* Compassionate Evacuees

"**Y**ou're a doctor? Come with me!" asserted a short, determined nurse as she grabbed my arm the very moment I entered the Astrodome to volunteer my services as a doctor. With a death grip on my wrist, the insistent nurse pulled me rapidly through a foyer jammed with people.

"Hey! Hey!" I called out, startled. "Just where are we headed?"

"We need you over here, but, we've got to get going!" she yelled back over her shoulder to me, the words barely audible as her pace accelerated. Already in a half-skip/half-trot, I struggled to keep my balance as we bumped and bullied our way through the crowd.

I was an Astrodome newbie, on the job for all of three seconds. I had checked in with no one, had given my name to no one, and had validated my credentials with no one. The only thing identifying me as a doctor was a twenty year old white lab coat I wore with my name stitched above the pocket in faded red thread, and a folded stethoscope in my pocket.

"We'll be there in just a moment," she called back to me. Feeling my pace slow, she whirled. "Doctor!" she pleaded. "We need to hurry!" Trotting now, we jogged first left then right then left again, finally leaving the sea of people behind and entering a small room.

It looked like a gymnasium with concrete floors. Folding chairs were scattered around its walls. Evacuees who had just completed the seven hour trip from New Orleans milled around in the room we had just entered. The overhead light hanging from a ceiling 100 feet high left no shadows, illuminating with cold light the scene of poverty and despair.

Three hundred people were there. Each was gray-brown, covered with a thick cake of gray dust glued to their skins by old sweat and the hot sun. All were dressed in rags. Some had no shoes. Others wore one shoe. Still others wore shoes from different pairs. To the left was a man with one black and one red sneaker, helping a short woman wearing two large, left men's shoes on her feet. The scene would break the hardest of hearts.

The audible moans of the injured and ill added to the higher-pitched whimpering of the children I now saw for the first time. Offspring and parents were as one, with mothers and fathers holding tightly to their children, who in turn offered no resistance. There was no rebellious twisting and turning, no childish cries demanding to be indulged. Shocked into physical collapse and emotional disintegration, these children wanted their parents close.

Up to four days without water, five days without food, untreated diabetes and hypertension etching its crippling effects on their bodies as plainly as the fatigue lined itself in their faces, coated in sweat and dust, they sat on the concrete floors or walked aimlessly from one part of the crowd to another. The atmosphere was that of an emotionally torn crowd of dirty mourners respectfully attending the death of a beloved family member—*disconsolate dignity.*

The nurse steered me to the left, and we quickly walked through part of this human miasma to a corner of the room, where we stood before a group of fifteen evacuees. These patients were by themselves, separated by several metal gates originally constructed to split up lines of jostling sports fans eager to purchase tickets for a game. Today, these gates were put to a sadder use.

It was this group of patients who the nurse now told me were my responsibility to treat—without instruments, lab support, or supplies.

"What do you mean 'treat them'? With what?!" I demanded, astonished.

"That's up to you, but we need you to get started!" the tired nurse demanded. "You're the only help that these people have now," she continued, the edge in her voice softened by her anguished look as she quickly hurried on to her next impossible assignment.

Standing in the middle of fifteen evacuees in various stages of distress, my heart raged with frustration. Thick layers of dust clung like paint to the desperate evacuees, completely obliterating any sign of their races or ethnicities. Some of the wounded lay on thin cots. Some squatted, while others sat silently on the cold and unforgiving concrete floor in this corner room at the Houston Astrodome complex. Together they grieved. Some moaned softly. Others prayed. One older man hummed an unrecognized song while a younger man leaned against him, crying. Yet, vigilance burned through their fatigue as they watched for the next peril that would confront them, the next threat that would attack them, the next sacrifice life demanded of these wounded citizens who had been treated like prisoners.

I can do nothing for these people! I savagely thought, reviewing the situation again and again in my own mind, straining to see an answer to this unsolvable problem. *No thermometers anywhere,* I observed. *No tongue depressors. No gauze. No cotton balls. No alcohol or soap. No lab equipment. No running water! No IV's. No modern medicines!*

At my wits' end, watching these mysterious, patient survivors watch me, I made up my mind. Walking over to the nearest patient, I knelt down, extending my hand to her. I did not yet see that it was this quiet group, the new American pariahs, who would be both the masters and the teachers of self-control, determination, affection, and endurance.

Welcome to Katrina Clinic—Houston Texas, the Astrodome.

Moving through this small group of patients, I saw two women and a young boy to my right. One of the women sat on the floor, wearing a pair of jeans. One pant-leg was intact, the other was torn off above the knee. On her lap was another, younger woman. Laying perfectly still, this second woman was completely encased in dirt. The only way I knew that she was still breathing was the small swirl of dust her exhaled breath blew free from her upper lip. Sitting at the unconscious woman's head, was a young boy. The child may have been eight years old.

Speaking to the woman who was sitting up, I introduced myself and then asked, "Can you tell me your name, please?"

"Yvonne," she said, looking over at the little boy.

"Is this your son?" I asked, also looking at the boy, who was gently stroking the unconscious woman's hair. "What's his name?"

"John," she said emotionlessly.

"Is this your daughter too?" I asked, gesturing to the young woman lying across her lap.

"No."

"Well, your sister then?" I continued.

"No."

My inept attempt at conversation was getting me nowhere.

"Yvonne," I repeated, "what is your last name?"

"Baker."

"Ms. Baker, will you please tell me if I can do something to help you?"

"Yes, you can."

Moving a little closer on my knees, I asked, "Well, then can you tell . . ."

"But not yet."

I froze in mid-move, staring at her.

"You need to help her first," Ms. Baker replied, nodding down to the still, younger woman in her lap.

"I'll do as you ask," I responded, unconsciously matching her same gentle intonation. Diverting my attention to the unmoving young woman, I asked Ms. Baker, "What is her name?"

"Don't know."

Again, I froze. "Well, what happened to her?"

"Don't know, sir."

"Well, she's in your lap? I just assumed . . . ."

"We don't know her sir."

My approach was all wrong, and I knew it. "Maybe, you can explain what happened. I'm afraid I don't understand," I confessed.

"John and I are by ourselves," Ms. Baker began. "When we got here a little while ago, this girl was lying here. Nobody was around. We stood around for a few minutes, but every time we looked back over, we saw her lying here. Alone. We didn't want her to be by herself, so we came over."

"You mean, without knowing her, you . . ."

"It was John's idea."

"I looked from John to his mom and back, failing to conceal my surprise. After a moment, I scooted the one or two feet across the floor to John. A small child, his physical appearance was like all of the others. His dirty clothes smelled and he was covered with a thick, gray grime.

He made sure to stay close to his mom, but was focused, almost captivated, by the young woman resting on his mother's lap.

"Hi, doctor," he said quietly, still stroking the woman's hair.

"Your mom told me that it was your idea to take care of this lady."

"She didn't have anyone. I thought it was OK if we stayed with her, until her family came. I thought we could help."

"You're right," I said. "I'd like to look at her for a few moments. Can I do that?"

"OK, sir," John replied, withdrawing.

I took a few moments to briefly examine her. Although quiet, the young woman was breathing regularly. I saw that she was arousable, and not in imminent danger of dying. Chronic fatigue and dehydration had robbed her of her consciousness, but I thought she would respond well to water and rest. I signaled for John to come back over. He looked to his mom for approval, and when she nodded, he scooted over to me again.

"I think she'll be OK, John, but it'd be better if we could change her position. Can you help?"

The Bakers and I gently rolled her on her back. I walked over to get some donated clothes, and returning, I placed them under the patient's legs to elevate them. For the moment, that was all I could do. As soon as we were done, John returned to the ill woman's head, gently stroking her mangled hair.

"Some help will be here soon," I said. "But you did a good job. When she wakes up, she'll appreciate what you and your mom did for her. John," I asked, "why did you do this? You don't know her."

"My mom saved me. Lots of times. I just thought . . ."

I drew closer, "Thought what, son?"

"I thought we could help her, like my mom helped me. Can you make her better?"

My throat caught, and I sat there, sharing a quiet moment with them. This young man simply transmitted the loving message his mother had given to him. For right now, it was better than anything I could do.

" . . . In a few minutes. But right now, I need for you to do what you've been doing."

"OK."

"I won't leave this area until either I help her, or I find someone who can," I promised. "If you want me, just call me, and I'll come over. We have a deal?"

"Deal," he repeated, a glimmer of a smile, of hope, emerged through the dirt and made it to his eye.

We shook on it, and I moved on.

Standing, I announced, "is there anyone here I can help?" Something in me instantly regretted my offer, expecting a loud clamor of voices demanding my attention. But the only response to my request was silence for one then two long seconds. Finally, a man in tattered rags sitting next to me, the blood from an oozing forehead laceration crying out for my attention, pointed a long index finger to the back from where I heard a thudding noise for the first time. He said simply, "Better see to Jasmine."

Making my way to the back, I introduced myself to Jasmine Tyler. Thin as a rail, covered with grime, Ms. Tyler sat on the floor with her thin legs outstretched, leaning back against the cold concrete wall, repeatedly banging the back of her head against its hard surface.

Leaning down in front of her, trying to get at eye level, I cautioned quietly but firmly, "Hey, now. You need to stop that." "You've been through so much. Don't make it worse," I finished. Kneeling in front of her, I gently grabbed both of her shoulders. She stopped at once, her head falling forward so hard that, for an instant, I thought she had fainted.

"Ms. Tyler, how old are you?" I asked.

"Sixteen, now," she said, picking her head up, beginning to bang her head again. The terrible fatigue had reduced her eyes to thick, ashy slits.

"Come on, stop that now," I said, putting one hand gently on each side of her face, making it more difficult for her to bang her head. When she stopped, I removed my hands and asked, "where are your parents, Ms. Tyler?"

"It's just me," she whispered, shaking her head ever so slightly in my hands.

"So you left New Orleans by yourself?" I asked, desperately trying to get a conversation going with this puzzling young woman.

Quiet and still, she opened her eyes a hair wider revealing an odd, disconnected expression. The look of . . . *what?* I wondered. *Dazed? . . . . No . . . there was something more . . . Not dazed . . . it's too wild . . . She's afraid.*

No! I thought. *Not merely afraid, but frightened! Paralyzed with fright!* Like a child desperately trying but unable to awaken from a nightmare, Jasmine Tyler was lost in the grip of some inner horror, quaking before its power over her. I pulled back to collect my thoughts when someone behind me whispered quietly,

"We had to make her get on the bus with us."

"Why?" I asked, astonished, turning to face a man wearing half of a sordid T-shirt and jeans stiff with dirt who had slid next to me, "You mean . . . ?"

With his quiet, thoughtful eyes locked on mine, he nodded, saying only, "She begged to be abandoned."

Now utterly confused, I turned to my young patient again. "Ms. Tyler," I began trying to get on track with my first conscious patient, "We'll get you some water and a good meal soon. But first, can you tell me if you hurt anywhere?"

"Nooooo," she responded slowly. The head banging stopped.

"Ms. Tyler, can you tell me why you didn't want. to leave New Orleans?" I asked.

It took thirty seconds for her to start talking. Haltingly at first, she began with awkward phrases and terrible expression, as if every word hurt like a tooth that was being pulled. Gradually, the stammering disappeared and she fell into a monotone. Some of the evacuees quietly gathered closer, never having heard her speak at all, waiting to learn why she had refused to leave a city that others were fleeing.

Twenty minutes later, we all knew why.

"We thought we were all right where we were," Ms. Tyler started, "staying with my man's mother in her house. It was a tight fit because the house was small, but it was a good house. A good home, I mean," she said, correcting herself.

"We knew the storm was coming. It started raining last Sunday, and on Monday it really started coming down hard. Water was building up in the street. My man said that I should take Dee with . . ."

"Who's Dee?" I interrupted.

"Dee is my four-year-old. He said that we should take her and go to the Superdome. He heard that was where everyone was supposed to go. He didn't think his mother could make it, though, so while he was going to stay with her, Dee and me would go to the 'dome'. That way, we'd be safe and he wouldn't have to worry about us being at the house with all of that rain.

"What he says, we do," Ms. Tyler shrugged, acknowledging his authority. "Dee and I got out and started walking. The water was only a couple of inches deep then . . ." her voice trailed off as a memory's pain knifed through her.

"How long a walk was it?" I asked.

"Should've been about twenty minutes," she replied softy. "We'd walked that far before, just never to the Superdome. We walked and walked in that water. Lucky for us there were a lot of people walking along with us, so we just followed them. After a while, the water was higher, almost to Dee's knees. She was playing around in it some, and I had to keep telling her not to walk away. 'Baby, you can get hurt out here,' is what I'd say, and she minded well enough.

"The water got deeper, and as the level rose, the water started doing weird things. Playing tricks on us. It would swirl hard in one direction then without warning, start spinning the other way. Plus there was junk in the water. Wood. Pieces of metal, like broken machine parts. I called to Dee and when she came over, I held her hand. 'Hold on to Mama now,' I'd say.

"Then . . . .then . . . .," she paused, closing her eyes as more pain coursed through her.

"Would you like to . . ."

"We were over where I thought the sidewalk would be," Ms. Tyler suddenly continued. "I noticed an older woman out in the middle of the street, holding on to her grandbaby the same way I was holding on to Dee. The two of them were walking slowly, talking to each other. I can still see that! The grandmother was in front, and the child, a little bigger than Dee, walking next to her. The water was thick now, really starting to swirl. Just pushing and pulling at you.

"Suddenly, the old woman cried out. It was a terrible sound! A sound that froze my heart with pain! Turning, I saw that the woman had jerked around, looking back in horror as her granddaughter slipped from her grasp. It happened so fast! That fast moving water just picked that child up and carried her away! I didn't hear any sound from that child; she was just turning over and over in the water, getting pulled further and further behind. The woman called out in terrible pain again, I cried out too, taking a step out toward them into the street.

"Suddenly, a wall of water smacked me right in my chest, almost knocking me down. I heard 'Mama! Mama!' and tried to stand up, tightening my grip on Dee. But my hand squeezed down on only water! Dee was gone! Just like that!

"I can still see it happening," Ms. Tyler said, her voice thick with emotion, reliving the fright. "That dirty, filthy mess had my baby now! She screamed and shouted for me. Then, the water smashed her into a building. I yelled, trying to run in the water after her. I didn't feel like it was getting me anywhere; that water just kept hitting me all over, turning me around. But, I fought against it, had to fight, shrieking and shouting Dee's name, as the rain drove into me. But," Ms. Tyler said, her voice thick with emotion, "it didn't matter what I did because my Dee was pulled away even farther."

"The water took her around a corner. I just picked my feet up off the ground and let it carry me around the corner too, but it smashed me into a broken fence. I wanted to throw-up after swallowing that filth, but I couldn't stop looking for my Dee. I didn't care. I felt like I was drowning, but my blood was on fire. I shouted! I was dying inside. And I was mad. Furious! That devil-water had torn part of me out when it took my Dee, and I had to get her back." Ms. Tyler abruptly stopped talking.

"What did you do?" I softly asked.

"I went half-walking, half-drifting through the water all down that block. And the next one. And the one after that, calling out her name 'Dee . . . Dee baby!' I called again and again all that afternoon and that night."

"You stayed out at night!" I asked as gently as I could, trying to keep the surprise out of my voice. "Didn't you get your husband?"

"No," she replied. "Going back to the house wasn't going to find my Dee! I had to find her right then, or I'd lose her forever.

"Finally, it got so dark I couldn't see any more. I just called 'Dee! Dee! Up one block, and down another. I called and called. Even when I had no voice I called with all the others."

"Other people?" I asked.

"Yeah. They were calling out other names. People that they'd lost. That water broke up a lot of families that day. Parents, husbands, wives, were calling out in the night. And crying. It was pitch black, and all you could hear was that crying. I missed my Dee so much, but the hurt and the pain in those voices showed me that other people had lost their babies too."

Suddenly, this young mother cried, "THIS WORLD'S NOTH-ING BUT PAIN!" so loud that people on the other side of the room looked over at our group. She stopped for a minute, surrounded by several evacuees who murmured prayers for her.

"Once," Ms. Tyler finding her voice, continued, "I heard a lot of noise, and suddenly someone called, 'I found a child.' I splashed over to that voice as fast as I could, my heart in my throat! It beat hard, and I was feeling the rush of relief as I stumbled through the water. I wasn't paying any attention to where I was going. I could have walked off a cliff for all I knew, but I just knew my Dee had been found!"

"Was that her?" someone in the crowd asked behind me, hopeful.

"The child was dead," Ms. Tyler dead-panned. "And, it wasn't her. Wasn't my Dee.

"Next morning, as I walked through the water, I saw a car up ahead turning round and round in the water. As it moved, I saw an arm and leg sticking out a window as the car twisted its way down the street. 'Dee!' I yelled. I was exhausted, but I couldn't let that car with my Dee get out of sight. I chased that car, calling 'Dee! Dee!' Once I saw the arm move, and I knew it had to be my baby! The car was pulling ahead of me, but there was no way I wasn't going to get to it. My legs were banged up from running into things as I worked my way through the water, but I had to get there. Had to.

"The car was pulling away, and I cried out. 'Dee! Dee-baby!' full of fear and full of anger. Suddenly the car stopped. It moved forward for a few more feet then it stopped again. In a few moments, I caught up to it.

"I didn't wait. And I wasn't careful. I was afraid the car would move away from me again. I didn't check if it was my baby, I just climbed on in through the broken windows.

"But," Ms. Tyler continued, "it wasn't my Dee. The little boy was dead. His neck moved back and forth on his head like it wasn't connected right. My heart burst in my chest and I just cried out. Cried out for all of the pain of that day and night! For the children who had died. And who would die. And for my baby.

"Wednesday, I didn't know what to do. I headed back home. I knew it would hurt my man deep in his heart to know Dee was gone. But I didn't know what else to do! I worked my way back to the house, and knocked, but nobody was there. My family was gone.

"Where did they go?"

She shook her head. "I don't know. Haven't seen them since. I don't know where they are, or what they're doing. I just went back to looking for Dee."

"Didn't you feel unsafe looking for her like that by yourself," I asked.

"Nobody bothered me. Nothing mattered," she stated, shrugging her shoulders. "Safety didn't matter. Eating didn't matter. Nothing mattered but finding my Dee.

"I walked and walked that next day. Crying with the other mothers.

27

Looking for my baby. Finally, these two guys found me. They told me I was in a real state! One waited with me, and the other went to find a boat. I didn't want to get in, but they said I had a better chance of finding Dee if I did. I got in and they took me to where the buses were. That's when they tried to make me leave.

"I yelled, I cried. I didn't want to leave without Dee. They told me that there were police and soldiers looking for lost people now and that they would find my baby. I didn't care. I had to find her! I passed out, and when I was awake on the bus, a woman stopped to speak with me." Ms. Tyler continued. "She told me that I had done everything I could, and called me a 'mother among mothers'."

"What do you want to do now? What can I do, we do, to help?" I asked.

"I don't know where my man is, I don't know where my baby is. There is nobody here for me, and my baby's not here for me to love . . ."

Finally, at long last, she broke down. Helpless before the power of her own anguish, she gave in, her body wracked with sobs only mothers who outlive their children know. There was only one thing to do here, but I needed permission. I looked at all of the evacuees who had gathered around, and they silently dropped their heads in assent. I then cradled this young woman in my arms, providing the only comfort I could give. In a few moments, another survivor, yet one more dirty child-woman, maybe a mother herself, came over and held Ms. Tyler, my first awake and aware patient.

I took a few moments to speak with each of my patients, learning briefly about their medical histories. I heard the same ideas repeated in their own words:

"High blood pressure."

"The diabetes."

"Breast cancer."

"Blood pressure problems."

"Breathing problems."

"My sugar runs high."

"Some fluid in my lungs."

"The HIV."

"I had a growth in my neck glands."

"I can't see so good because of my sugar."

"Gout and some pressure problems."

"Some cancer in my brains."

"I have trouble breathing when I don't have the medicine I inhale."

With no blood pressure cuff, no ability to check blood sugar, and no diagnostic equipment, only a few of these statements could be confirmed. Yet, each of the evacuees knew at least something about the chronic diseases they had, paid attention to its effects, and understood the importance of taking the right medication. None of them had been able to take their medicine for over a week, and each wanted to get back on their medication as soon as possible.

They all were tired to the point of nervous collapse. The storm had struck late Sunday night lasting into Monday night. This was Friday. When asked when they slept last, the answers were:

"Sometime last weekend."

"Sunday night, I think."

"I'm not really sure. Not since the storm hit, I guess."

"The night before we got to the Superdome."

"Don't have a clue."

While some had been able to get sleep on the bus during the long ride to Houston, many had not.

Water had been available beginning Wednesday night in New Orleans, and I had just learned that some water was available on the buses that transported them the three hundred miles to Houston. However, they were all dehydrated. As hot as it was, none of them was able to sweat, and some were dizzy when they tried to stand, both signs of acute dehydration. Not a single survivor in that group could remember when he or she had last eaten.

Stress was the great multiplier, amplifying the effect of their chronic diseases, magnifying the damage caused by their dehydration, acute starvation, and fatigue. The dangerous combination of stress, chronic high blood pressure out of control, blood sugars grossly elevated, and the absence of sleep eroded their judgment, and destroyed their decision-making ability.

So I watched, astonished to see that, despite the fraying of their ability to think and act clearly, civility was not a casualty in their fight with the storm's effects. The evacuees' conduct this day was remarkable not for an absence of kindness but for the gentle compassion shared among them.

There were neither angry outbursts nor threatening gestures from these desperately ill survivors. Not one of them demanded something for himself or herself. They weren't arguing over when they would get food, and lodged no complaints about delays in getting showers. These evacuees appeared strikingly stoic to the casual observer who might have expected them to be consumed with their own urgent needs.

Clearly fatigued, this small group nevertheless demonstrated remarkable patience, quietly waiting their turn for attention. When I approached one of them, the others who were nearby moved aside to make room for me, and when I spoke to a particular patient, the survivors who surrounded us lowered their voices out of respect. When evacuees needed help e.g., trying to stand or moaning as they dealt with an inner agony, a survivor nearby would attend to them, working to make them comfortable. Or, if incapable of providing tangible assistance, a survivor provided the intangible, placing a hand on a shoulder or stroking their hair while uttering a gentle word.

These had been strangers before the tragedy, utterly unknown to each other during the storm. Yet they emerged with bonds that revealed an emotional closeness that one expects to see only among good friends and relatives. To quote W.E.B. Du Bois[1]

> "... *there was among us but a half awakened common consciousness, sprung from common joy and grief at burial, birth, or wedding; from a common hardship in poverty, poor land, and low wages; and above all, from the sight of the Veil that hung between us and Opportunity.*"

The storm had driven this family even closer together.

I had only been in the arena for about thirty minutes, and, unwittingly, completed my orientation training at the hands of these gentle, changed people. The message, clearly etched in my psyche by these

---

1. Du Bois W.E.B. (1903) *The Souls of Black Folk.* New York. Barnes and Noble Classics.

brave evacuees was that bold, selfless action is ignited by the spark of compassion. I would see this again and again over the next ten days.

I bent over to talk to another patient, ready to learn another lesson . . .

CHAPTER 3

The Breadth and Depth of the Evacuees' Problems

Suddenly, I felt a sharp rap on my shoulder. "You can't see those patients yet, Doctor!" a voice said behind me.

"What?" I replied, instantly resenting the intrusion as I stood, turning to face this new and insistent stranger who demanded my attention.

"We need to take these patients to the clinic," this new nurse replied evenly, stepping back for a moment as she carefully gauged my reaction. As she moved, I could now see a cadre of volunteers, all with wheelchairs ready to load and transport the patients to the other side of the Arena where the new clinic was being created. It looked like things were becoming more organized now, and I confessed to myself that it was time for me to just get out of the way and let their medical care begin.

Standing up, I said, "Then let's do it quickly. Are there doctors there yet?"

"Yes," she offered. Then smiling, she added, "and you'll be one of them once you check in."

Saying goodbye to this first group of survivors, I turned and let myself be led through the brief administrative process required for me to become a Katrina Clinic doc.

After checking in (which consisted of giving my name, medical license number, and being assigned a provider number that I had to use on every prescription that I would write while on duty), I found a volunteer who amiably agreed to show me to the new clinic area.

We turned to leave the cramped doctor and nurse check-in room, with its huge paper sheets taped on concrete walls. Blank now, there were expectations that they would be filled with the names of physician and nurse volunteers for the duty shifts. Turning left, we walked through a series of six doors adjacent to each other that controlled the flow in and out of the huge evacuee check-in area where each survivor waited to be logged in by computer. Moving rapidly through this check-in area, we walked through another series of doors that opened into the main area itself.

Like any huge modern day Arena, it was cavernous, with bright fluorescent lights glaring out of a dark gray-black ceiling hundreds of feet above me. The area would typically be packed with raucous fans during a sporting or other special event. Not today, though.

There, laid out before me across many acres, were thousands upon thousands of cots. All colors, they extended in semi-neat rows out in all directions. Victims of Katrina were streaming in from the side doors into this living area, choosing cots that would serve as their home for the foreseeable future. Approximately ten percent of the cots were already "taken," holding either evacuees or the trash bags that contained their personal effects waiting to be "unpacked." While most victims were either standing talking to their families or sitting, almost no adult was lying down. Also, although many had not yet eaten in Houston, and water as well as food was becoming available, a large number of evacuees were not yet availing themselves of the fresh supplies.

As we made our way through one of the many aisles that helped to separate the cots into rows, I noticed again, as I had when I first saw survivors in my earlier "clinic," how quiet many of the evacuees were. All were able to walk, but many limped along in either ill-fitting shoes or on badly cut and swollen feet. T-shirts that were supposed to be white were brown, and jeans that were originally blue were now a slick, muddy gray. Some evacuees actually shied away from us as the two of us walked among them. Slowing down to pay more attention to these survivors, I let my volunteer-guide pull ahead of me. I tried to study face after face as I went by. While many of the faces appeared white, and a few of Asian and Hispanic descent (one could not be sure because of the ubiquitous dirt covering them), the vast majority were African-American. Some faces were masked in pain, while others were completely expressionless. However, two things were immediately apparent. These survivors were tired. They were also frightened.

The storm's victims, still in shock from their experiences, could not yet appreciate they were at long last safe and would be well cared for. I had never been in a room so full of fear and uncertainty, and was moved to speak to them. As I slowly made my way though this living sea of frightened survivors, I worked to find the words that would allow me to begin a conversation with any one of them.

Pushing on through the aisle, now congested with more evacuees as they continued to stream into the Arena, I was impressed by the number of evacuees scanning the room. The heads and eyes of many survivors were moving rapidly, never settling on anyone, always moving. Ignoring their own debilitating physical conditions, they were restless, anxiously looking for something.

Not something, but some *one*. They were looking for their families.

One young woman who appeared to be no older than a teenager walked toward me. She cried as she looked first left, then right, then left again across the large arena. She appeared to be straining to identify every single person in the cavernous room, so anxiously did she stare at them. Not watching where she was going, tears blurring her vision, she stumbled into me.

"Oh!" she exclaimed, recoiling at once.

"Hello ma'am." I said, introducing myself. "What's your name?"

"Dawn?" she said more as a question than a statement.

I had never been trained to address a patient by his or her first name. "I'm sorry. Can I have your last name, please?"

"Oh!" she replied, looking at me with questioning eyes. "Dawn Traylor. My last name is Traylor."

"Ms. Traylor, what are you looking for?" I asked, noting that she had no acute medical problem.

She looked up at me for a long moment. About 5'5", she was dark skinned and covered with thick gray dust. It was in her hair, her face, and her eyes. Ms. Traylor constantly wiped her mouth and chin as the tears picked up and carried the dust into her mouth. The same gruel coated the dirty T-shirt and cutoff jeans that she wore. She had a small child with her, also dirty, and like her mom, eyes full of pain.

"I know they're here," she said, her young face etched by the hard lines of fatigue.

"Who are you looking for?" I asked, moving her out of the aisle.

"My other daughter and her father," she replied, her tears flowing more freely now.

"Didn't they come over on the bus with you?" I felt that my own questions were just flatfooted, even dumb, but I didn't know the answers. I had to ask.

She looked quietly at me for a moment. Then she said, "No. No. You see, we were together. My daughter's daddy was one of the people who helped to control who was permitted to board the buses. The police needed help, and he agreed to do it. That meant," she was rushing her words now, her eyes once again scanning the people in the arena, "he and my baby would have to come later. Catch a later bus." Then, she fell silent. Her right hand, holding an old, filthy Kleenex, came up to her mouth, and she started crying again.

"My daughter has seizures," she whimpered, "and he's with her, and I don't know where they are," she finished. She sat down on an empty cot, losing herself in the grief of their separation and fear for her family's fate.

"Ms. Traylor. Please listen to me," I began, sitting down with her now out of the aisle traffic. "These people that you see working here are working for you. They're here to help you and your family when you find them. They're good at finding folks, and they'll get even better over the next few days. If you give them your name, and the name of your daughter, they can find her for you."

I looked back at Ms. Traylor. She gazed at me with a sense of curious puzzlement. I didn't know what else to do but to finish.

"Every New Orleans survivor has to check in here," I said. Recalling one of my brief conversations with the nurses earlier that day, I silently thanked the administrators for having a check-in process. "If you speak to one of the volunteers, they can take your name, and the name of the father and your daughter."

Again she silently stared at me, making me feel that she was surprised I could speak English. She had a look of quiet perplexity. I was really confused by it now, but continued anyway.

"If your family is already here," I finished, "the volunteers will let you know. If they're not here, then when they check in, you can be notified." The PA system was already announcing the names of family members. "If you listen to the overhead," I added, taking her by the shoulder and pointing to one of the big speakers, "they are beginning to call out names. That's to help you find your family."

"Thank you. Y'all would do this for us?" she asked, hands clutching the shredded, dirty Kleenex in her lap.

"Ms. Traylor. We are only here to help. That's all we want to do. Good luck." I wanted to say "I'm sure you'll find them," but I kept silent, because I just didn't know if she would.

"Er, hey. Can I ask a question?" It was from a tall African-American man. His true height may have been 6'3" but, bent by the twin burdens of fatigue and emotional trauma, he appeared no taller than 5'10". He was talking to me.

I stopped, turning to my right to face him. His eyes, cheeks, and chin were streaked with dirt and mud, all topped by thick, uncombed hair, stared back at me. His damp, mud-sodden clothes were much too big for his slender frame. I noticed that a shorter woman and a young child, about six years old, positioned themselves directly behind him. They both pressed tightly against his back, anxious to both hide from view and stay within the protective hold of this man. All appeared to be in good medical condition.

He asked again "Is this the Astrodome? They told us we were coming to the Astrodome."

"Uh, it's part of the Astrodome complex . . . One of the buildings . . ." I stumbled over my answer. It was actually the Reliant Arena and not the Reliant Astrodome, but I managed to not make this unhelpful distinction.

Our abortive conversation sputtered to a halt, but I wasn't willing for it to end. "I'm Dr. Moyé. What's your name, sir?"

"Uh, hello Doctor," he said at once. "I don't mean to stop you from where you were going," he began apologetically. Then, "I'm John."

"No sir," I replied. "I mean your last name." A first name alone would not do.

He looked at me for a long moment. Like Ms. Traylor, he seemed momentarily puzzled by my request. Then, he said, "Jamison. John Jamison."

I stepped out of the aisle, anxious to continue our awkward conversation. "Mr. Jamison, can you tell me where you're from?"

"New Orleans. But the last few days we had to stay there at the Superdome." His voice had started to shake a little, and his family pressed even harder into his back.

The Superdome. I hadn't heard everything about the horrible experiences of the New Orleans Superdome this first Friday after the storm, but I'd heard enough.

I took a chance. "Mr. Jamison. I'm glad to meet you today. You're in Houston, now. This isn't the Superdome."

He looked at me, but not with a sense of relief, which is what I expected—but with new, fierce determination. "We're not staying here!" he declared.

"I think I understand, sir." I answered. "This is a huge building like the Superdome," I continued, "but it's really very different. You, Mr. Jamison, and your family will be safe here. Not like before." I thought about looking at his family, maybe smiling at his daughter, but thought better of it, keeping my gaze on Mr. Jamison, who continued watching me carefully. "You and your family are free to stay inside, or walk outdoors if you like. You're not prisoners here. You can leave the building if you want to, even tour Houston, if you'd like."

Mr. Jamison continued his quiet, firm stare, so I continued. "Plus, there're lots of police," I said, pointing to the large number of uniformed officers easily visible in the huge building. "They are here to protect you and your family. Plus, there's food and water for you here. You can get as much as your family needs. The bathrooms are clean, and they work. And," I pointed to one of the ceaselessly moving people who had the volunteer vests on, "these people in the red vests are here to help you. I'm here, we're here, to help you, not to abandon you. You'll be OK with us, sir."

"You asked for my last name?" he asked, puzzled, his facial expression softening for the moment.

"Yes sir" I replied. "I have to address you properly. You deserve that. We all deserve that."

We shook hands. "If you need to see me," I said, "I'll be in the clinic."

"Really?" he asked. Where's that?"

"Good question," I responded with a smile, not really knowing the answer. Pointing in front on me, I answered, "In that direction, I think. I'm heading there now. Remember, we'll provide anything that you and your family need. Thanks for taking a second to talk to me."

I said goodbye, then hustled to catch up with the volunteer who himself had paused to speak with someone. As I caught up to him, I thought that I had guessed right, and my comments about this not being the New Orleans Superdome had made a difference, if only for a few minutes, with the Jamison family.

Walking on a little further, I saw a young couple on a cot. The woman was lying down on her back, one hand at her side, the other across her forehead. The young man sitting on the same cot ran his hand softly up and down her stomach. They were both quiet, but, as I walked by, the young man asked, "Can you tell me where we are?

"Sure." Introducing myself, I continued, "You're in Houston, Texas, now. What's your name, sir?"

"What?" he asked a little bemused. *The same look*, I thought. Three times now.

"This is Houston. What's your name?" I repeated.

"David, David Stones," he said.

"I hope things work out for you, Mr. Stones," I said. "Is your wife all right?" I asked, looking at the young woman. Neither appeared injured.

"Oh yes, she's fine."

"How'd you do during the storm?" I inquired.

"Not so well, actually. We're not from New Orleans at all!"

"Really," I reacted, surprised. "I thought everyone was from New Orleans."

"No. We're from South Carolina. Ever hear of 'The Plain Truth?'"

"What?" I responded. "Well, I'm always looking for it, but never found it," I replied.

Smiling back, he said, "We get that all the time. We're from the town. The Plain Truth, South Carolina."

"Ah...no, never heard of it."

"Well, her parents," he said, pointing to his wife, "live in New Orleans. We had been planning to get down and see them. We got there four or five days before the hurricane. You know," he continued, "we asked them about the storm, but they said, it wasn't heading for New Orleans. That it was going to Florida. So we thought it'd be safe enough."

"Well, that sure wasn't their fault," I replied. No one knew where Katrina was actually headed until it was almost too late. "How are they?"

"As soon as we arrived and called, we learned that my wife's mom was in the hospital, and my wife's father was staying in the hospital with her most of the time. In fact, that's where we did most of our visiting with them, right there in her mom's hospital room.

"When the storm started forcing people out of the city, the hospital decided not to evacuate her, and her husband chose to stay with her. The last we saw of them was Monday morning when the storm started, there at Charity," he said referring to the major public hospital in New Orleans.

"Did your wife's parents get out OK as well?" I asked.

"I don't know," the young man replied, dropping his voice a little. "I heard people talking on the bus about 'Charity'. It sounded like things got bad there fast. Both her parents are in their seventies. I just don't know . . ." his voice trailed off.

"We stayed right near where the buses came on Wednesday," he continued after a moment. "Caught one on Thursday, and, well, here the three of us are." His wife, who had been quiet for most of the conversation, smiled now.

"Who else is here?" I asked, craning my head to see who I missed.

"Nobody," Mr. Stone replied. "Just us. She's pregnant! Learned it just last week," he said. His hand went to her abdomen again, her hand coming up to cover his.

"Congratulations," I said, excited at the chance to celebrate, if only for a moment. "Is this your first child?"

"Sure is," the new and proud father-to-be replied.

"Did your wife's parents know?"

"No, and they were overjoyed when we told them," he said, standing up in the rush of the moment. "We surprised them with the news on Sunday and, for a few minutes, they were just out of their minds with joy! They hugged us, and then hugged each other. For a few moments, we forgot all about the storm, all about her mom's illness, all about our troubles. We all lost ourselves in our new baby.

"We spent a lot of time last Sunday with them at the hospital, just talking about names," he continued, sitting down again. "They suggested the name 'Faith' for a girl and 'Richard' for a boy. We," he paused for a second, looking at his wife, who started crying, "didn't think much of those names at first. But now, we don't know if we'll see her folks ever again." After a moment, he finished, "We've decided we'll take their suggestions."

"Good names," I agreed. "Tell me though," I continued, "After all that you've been through, are you glad you chose this week to visit from South Carolina?"

Without hesitation, in unison, they both clearly replied, "Yes!"

I left the new-parents-to-be, and stopped to speak to another couple, Mr. and Ms. Liu. They sat together quietly on their cot. Making no attempt to speak to me, they were looking at nothing, looking at everything.

I stopped, introduced myself, and said simply, "How are you today?"

"We're better here, sir," Mr. Liu replied. Short and thin, he appeared to be about sixty years old. "We have showered and have some fresh clothes. Soon we will get a meal. Things are much better here for us now," he finished in soft, precise English.

"What did you do in New Orleans?" I asked.

"We own a small grocery store. It is all that we have," Mr. Liu began. "My wife and I moved to America from Vietnam. We lived in Mississippi for several years, and tried to make a living fishing. It was too hard. We never had luck there, and then we lost our boat in another storm a few years ago. We decided to move to New Orleans. I borrowed some money and we started a small grocery store. We never made much, but we made enough to live on. Until now."

"We lived in the back rooms of our store," he continued, "and stayed as long as we could. Finally, we left on Tuesday to go to the convention center."

"Why was that?" I asked.

"We hated to leave home, but the water was getting higher. We got to the convention center before there were too many people. It was OK and we could be comfortable. My wife packed a suitcase for us, and since we also brought some food, we did fine that first night.

"Many more people arrived on Wednesday and it got too crowded. There just wasn't enough food. So many of the people were hungry," he continued, "that we decided to share our food with them, especially the children. There were children who didn't have anything to eat, so we tried to help them out.

"When we ran out," he continued in precise, quiet English, "my wife and I argued about whether we should try to get back to the store. But," he said, looking over at her, "new people who were just coming in said that the water was too deep in our neighborhood. We decided to stay." Ms. Liu started to cry and her husband stopped talking for a moment, gently putting his arm around her.

"Do you think your store is still there?" I asked after a moment.

"Still there?" he repeated softly. "Yes. It's probably there, but most of the food has either been taken or is ruined now. With no air conditioning or refrigerator, it spoils fast."

"I heard there were some break-ins and stores were robbed," I said.

"I heard this as well," Mr. Liu quietly replied. "I don't know a lot about these things. But," he continued, "there were break-ins before the storm as well. People are who they are. Most people who were good people before the storm, continued to be good afterwards."

Then he asked "But why shouldn't they break in to stay alive?"

"Well," I responded, perplexed, "many people are upset about the idea of looting."

He looked at me, curiously, asking, "People shouldn't break in to take food from a deserted building where there is food that will spoil anyway? Is that the idea? Should they just let it waste while their family goes hungry? Is that how it should work? The people who were stealing just to steal, well, those people have always been around and will always be around." He shook his head, adding, "They'll get what they deserve. But, the others are different. They had to break-in because they thought their families would die if they didn't. That's not stealing what somebody else is going to use. That's taking what others won't use so that your family can stay alive. Isn't that different?

"People who never stole before did it last week because they had no choice," he finished, shrugging his shoulders.

"Did you see any violence at the convention center?" I asked.

"Why do you ask me that?" he asked, genuinely surprised.

"I wasn't in New Orleans," I replied, "and all I know about what has happened has been what is reported on the news."

"No," he answered. "I didn't see any violence. I heard about it from some of the others. I didn't see it though."

As I got up to leave, I asked, "Since you and I both just arrived here, what advice do you have for me as I begin to get to work?"

Mr. Liu looked out over the people coming in to the Arena to find cots in their new temporary home. Then he looked at me.

Finally, he said "We are all different here, yet we are also all the same. We are not wild savages to be caged up. We want to go on with our lives. We want to learn about our families. We want to worship again. Many people here have children. They want them to go to school. We want things to be normal again. You have to understand that."

For the first time, Ms. Liu spoke. "We just want to be treated like people. We matter."

Next, I came across three young male adults. I guessed that they were in their late teens. Each was African-American, lanky and strong, with a sullen look in his eyes. They had pulled three of the cots close together. None of the three appeared to have any personal belongings—just the clothes on their backs.

I asked their names, learning that they were John Mason, Anthony Land, and Michael Sims. I saw that their clothes were in terrible shape. Mr. Mason wore a dirty T-shirt. Mr. Land had on a long sleeve shirt that was missing a sleeve, and Mr. Sims had on a T-shirt that was torn down the middle, gaping, exposing his stomach. Their pants were equally wretched. In fact, everything was dirty about them except for their shoes. Each of them wore new, bright white, spotless sneakers. Clean from the ankles down, they were a remarkable sight.

After introducing myself, I asked, "Why did you only get new sneakers? I just got here, but I understand that there are lots of clothes for adults. You guys could've picked up some clean shirts and pants if you wanted."

Not one of them spoke for several seconds. I feared that I had offended them in some way, and was preparing to apologize when Mr. Mason laconically replied, "We don't really need 'em."

Inspecting these young men more closely, I was again struck by the terrible shape that their clothes were in. Their jeans had holes in them, and their T-shirts were stained and covered with dust.

"Wouldn't you like some clean clothes?" I persisted.

Mr. Mason and Mr. Sims were eager to talk, but Mr. Land remained quiet.

"We know they're dirty," Mr. Sims replied, "but we just don't need them as bad as others do."

"We may look bad," Mr. Mason summarized, "but others had it worse. Except for our sneakers. They were really torn up."

"Torn up?!" Mr. Sims interjected. "They were gone! Ruined! They had no bottoms anymore," Mr. Sims finished. Mr. Land remained quiet.

"That's not how it started, but by the time we were done walking, the sneakers were ruined," John Mason added.

"Walk? How far did you walk?" I asked.

"Best as we can figure, about fifty miles," Michael Sims replied.

"Fifty miles?" I exclaimed. "How'd you do that?" I just couldn't see how that was possible.

"Well, it wasn't what we planned. We had a car, and got out of New Orleans on Monday morning when it really started raining. But wouldn't you know that it broke down just a few miles out from the city! We didn't get more than ten miles out of town!" he declared with frustration, shaking his head but curiously not raising his voice. "We stayed in the car Monday night, trying to ride out the storm.

"It was awful!" Mr. Sims added. "The wind was bad and it would move the car around. We were, well, scared, but we thought getting out of the car would be worse, so we stayed inside. Tuesday morning, the rain stopped and the wind died down. We got out, and didn't know the best way to go. So we just walked along I-10 west, heading away from town."

"Why west?" I asked, noting the words they used. "Scared" was not part of the typical male teenager's lexicon.

"There were a lot of people on the road, walking west," Mr. Mason replied. "Trouble was, nobody knew where they were going."

"We walked with them all day," Mr. Sims joined in. "I think we walked twenty miles that day. After awhile, people started dropping out. Many were just too tired to go on."

"Others just . . ." Mr. Mason added, then interrupted himself, looking over at Anthony Land.

"Well, there was no water out there," Michael Sims interjected. "Nobody had any food. After the storm ended and the sun came out, it was hot as blazes."

"Where were you all walking?" I asked.

"It wasn't where we were walking to," Mr. Sims responded. "It was where we were leaving. New Orleans! We needed to get as far away from that place as possible."

"We walked all Tuesday afternoon and half of Wednesday," Mr. Mason added. "We assumed we'd find help along the way, but no luck. On Wednesday, buses started coming. But, they weren't headed in our direction, but instead heading east, back to New Orleans. We were stuck! We didn't know where we were going, and somebody said the buses were heading back to town to get the people out.

"We had a choice," John Mason continued. "Either keep walking who knows where for who knows how long, or turn around and hope to get on one of those buses. Our feet were already killing us, but we decided to turn back to New Orleans."

"What else could we do?" he asked, bending over for a moment as he wiped away some new dust that had fallen from his filthy slacks onto his new sneakers.

"The walk back was the worst," Mr. Sims offered, dropping his voice some. "Our sneakers were already ruined by sloshing through water back in town. The long I-10 walk just destroyed them."

"But we soon forgot about that," Mr. Mason added.

"People were dead, lying on the side of the road!" Mr. Sims said. "We hadn't seen anything like that before. It was . . ." He fell silent, unable to finish.

"It was awful, that's what it was," Mr. Mason interjected.

"At first we thought they were sound asleep, but their positions were so strange," he continued. "We'd never seen people asleep like that, not even drunks. Finally, we noticed that some of them had their eyes open. And they were stiff, like they had been frozen. Sometimes we saw bugs coming in and out of their mouths and noses." He paused for a moment, shaking his head. "I thought I'd seen it all, growing up in town, you know? But I never saw anything like that."

"Never want to again," Michael Sims added sadly.

"That's when Anthony stopped talking," Mr. Mason concluded.

"It's been two days, and he hasn't said anything?" I asked, looking over at their silent friend.

"Not a word," Mr. Mason responded. "Nothing for most of the way back to the buses, and nothing on the bus ride here."

"We picked his sneakers out for him, and helped him with the laces," Mr. Sims added.

"You know he might really need some help," I responded, looking at the quiet young man who had kept his head down during our entire conversation. "Actually, you all have been through a horrendous week. Listen," I continued, "you might want to talk to somebody about this."

"Well, I actually feel better, just talking to you now," Mr. Mason said. Mr. Sims nodded agreement.

"But, what about Mr. Land?" I asked.

Michael Sims said, "Don't worry about Anthony. We know him.

He'll be OK because he's with us. It'll come back together for him as long as his 'homies' are nearby. The three of us need to hang tight until this whole mess is over with." Putting his arm around his shell-shocked friend, he said, "We can do that. We have to if we're going to make it."

———————————

Continuing to make my way across the huge arena floor, new evacuees arriving by the minute, I shook my head at this education I was getting. The survivors who had spoken with me revealed dimensions that hadn't come through in the media depictions. The evacuees were capable of helping themselves when given the opportunity. Furthermore, I witnessed again what I had observed in my first meeting with a Katrina survivor earlier that day—these people were not takers—they were givers. They had been deprived, soaked, and starved, but had not yet been pushed beyond the ability to be compassionate. The feeling of sympathy that I had been feeling was replaced with a sense of wonder. And admiration.

I came across a man sitting alone on a cot. Like many of the other men, he was dressed in rags. However, he didn't appear tired at all. In fact, this was the first *really* alert evacuee I met. After introducing myself, I asked,

"Mind if I sit down?" indicating the space on the cot next to him.

"Sure, no problem," he replied. After a moment, he said. "I'm Pfc. James Tenyon."

"You're in the army?" I asked, wondering what someone in the U.S. Army was doing as an evacuee.

"That's right," he crisply replied, "Discharged last year."

"Well, if you were discharged," I queried, "then why introduce yourself as a private?"

"I just started that this week," he replied. "It's the only way I get a little more . . . respect. When I just give my name, people who arrived to help me tend to talk *at* me, not *to* me. The 'Private' part gets their attention."

"Well, how's it going so far?" I asked.

"It worked in Louisiana," he answered honestly. "I can't say if it's working here yet."

"Tell me how you're doing?" I asked. A new thought was rumbling around my mind, but I pushed it aside for a few moments.

"I need to get cleaned up and head back as soon as I can," he said, looking around at his surroundings.

"You can't go back for awhile," I explained. "It'll be too unsafe."

"I don't mean back to New Orleans," he replied instantly. "Back to Louisiana. I have a wife and three sisters. When the storm came, I saw to their evacuation. It's time I get back to them now," he answered purposefully.

"Some people didn't take the threat of terrible weather to heart," I replied.

"Well, being in the army helped me with that," Mr. Tenyon answered, "so I took them seriously. My wife did too, though I guess that comes from being with me. I had to fight with my sisters about it, though," he said, smiling a little.

"Where have you been stationed?"

"All over the country, although I never traveled overseas any," he began. "After I was discharged, I worked as a pool cleaner for a year. Thought I was on track to being a manager for them, and one day owning the company. I believed it was possible. But, that's all on hold right now," he finished, a trace of sadness slipping into his voice.

"Where're your sisters?" I asked.

"I arranged for my wife and two of my sisters to fly to Baton Rouge on Friday before the storm," he replied, taking his eyes off me for a moment as he scanned the crowd. My other sister wanted to go to Shreveport where her fiancé was. That took a little work to arrange, but she finally left on Saturday afternoon."

"Have you heard from them?"

"Yep," he said, nodding. "Last Sunday, just when the rain started falling. They called me to let me know they arrived and that they were OK. I think now they're a little worried about me. I need a cell phone," he asserted.

"What'll you do for money?" I asked.

"Well," he said, fishing out a limp wallet-like object with damped and smeared pages in it, "I brought my checks with me, but I can't write anything on them." We both laughed at the sad shape of his checkbook.

"Besides," he said, "the bank's probably gone under along with everything else in that town."

"I'm confused," I said, struggling with his story. "You took this storm very seriously."

"Yes."

"So seriously that you decided to evacuate your family. Yet you yourself didn't try to leave when you had the time, instead waiting to be evacuated. Why wait?" I asked.

"Well I was ready to go after I got my last sister out of town. But the more I thought about it, the less convinced I was that it was a good idea to leave. Somebody needed to look after the property. We had two houses right next door to each other. There wasn't much to them but somebody had to watch them."

"It was that important?"

"It was," he replied laconically, looking me in my eyes. "You have to remember two things. First, we've had bad storms before. There was never any need to leave because of them. Why leave now? Also, as best as I can tell, we didn't need to leave because of Katrina."

"What?" I asked, totally blown away by this comment.

"That's right," he asserted. "It wasn't Katrina that forced us out. It was the levees. If they had held like they were supposed to, we wouldn't be here now. Without the levees breaking, Katrina would have been like any other New Orleans hurricane, and we'd have weathered it."

"Also," Pfc. Tenyon continued in a softer tone, "evacuating sounds good and all, but in reality, it's difficult *and* expensive. My wife's in a hotel in Baton Rouge right now. She and my two sisters are paying every single night to stay there. They're forking over real cash for each of their meals. That's expensive. And they're not working.

"Don't forget," he added, "abandoned homes are easily damaged by the storm. Small problems, like leaks, can become larger problems if nobody's there. But, if you can stay, then you can do things like move furniture, block water from coming under doors, that kind of thing. That's all the houses would have required if the levees hadn't busted. Now though," he finished, "after the levees were gone, nothing matters. The houses are ruined."

"So," I asked, intrigued by this young man's assessment, "where'd you go?"

"Well, I thought the Superdome'd be crowded, so I went to the Convention Center. Got there on Wednesday morning, and stayed through yesterday."

"You know," I added, "I heard the Convention Center had gotten pretty bad."

"Yes. That's right," he agreed. "The main problem was that we couldn't keep it clean. When I got there on Wednesday, the toilets were already overflowing, yet more people kept coming. We had no food and little water, but still the people came. The Convention Center wasn't about violence. It was about broken promises, and frustration. I didn't see anyone hurt due to violence, but I saw plenty hurt by neglect. Some died."

Then Pfc. Tenyon added, "You know, today is the first time I've seen a TV since the storm hit. These things some folks are saying about us just aren't right! They say that we got angry and made a mess of the convention center because we didn't know how to act."

Looking right at me, he asked, "Do you really think rich, white people would have acted any better if they were the ones stuck there?"

Not having considered this question, I simply looked at this angry young man quietly.

"Think about it," he challenged me. "Suppose you destroyed their homes, split up their families and threw them in the street. With no electricity, their credit cards wouldn't get approved. There was no food or water to buy, so their cash money wouldn't help them. Now, if in the midst of this, they heard stories and rumors about help being available at the Convention Center, wouldn't they go there? Any way they could? And, if they went, they certainly wouldn't leave their families behind to fend for themselves against the flooding and the filth, right? No. They would have brought them to the Convention Center too.

"And when they arrived," he added, "suppose they learned that things were no better there. No meals. No good sanitation. Dead bodies lying on the street. Wouldn't they see that their families were threatened? That their lives were in jeopardy? And if the first police they saw trained guns on *them*, do you think they would react calmly, accepting their confinement quietly?"

"No, they wouldn't," this angry young man continued, answering his own question. "They'd get mad. In fact, they would probably get madder than the poor. The poor have come to expect that they won't get much. In New Orleans, they got used to how things were. But the rich, they wouldn't take that lying down.

"Maybe it wouldn't happen to the rich," the private finished, "but, if it did, they would react worse than we did, because they would've thought they deserved better. Yet when we react better than they would have, we get criticized for it," he finished, shaking his head.

"What will you do now?" I asked him, changing the subject.

"Get a job here to make some money. Then as soon as I can, get back to Louisiana to pull my family together. If," he continued, "that's what they want. Leaving your hometown has a way of changing you."

Looking up, he stated matter-of-factly, "Well, I could use some lunch."

We shook hands, and he moved on.

"Can you help us please?" Two women stopped me after I continued my walk through the open area where the evacuees were settling in. Unlike the other survivors that I'd seen so far, these two evacuees had showered and were groomed. However, each of them, like most everyone in the room, looked very tired.

"I'd be glad to," I replied. "How can I help you?"

"Well, we'd like to know how to check in?" one of them asked.

"Oh!" I responded. "Check-in's back over there," I said, turning and pointing, wondering how they got in without going through the administrative, introductory process.

"Not that!" one exclaimed. "We've already been there. We're looking to *volunteer*! How can we become volunteers?" asked the woman on the right, a dirty handkerchief tied around her neck, "I'm Clair Bonet, and this is my sister, Carla."

"Volunteers?" I was astonished. *They were the ones that needed help, after all they'd been through*, I thought.

"Sure."

"Don't you need to rest first?" I persisted. "You know, to eat and get restored."

"All of us need as much help as possible," Carla Bonet responded. "Don't get us wrong. We're glad we're out of New Orleans. That was terrible! But, just because we had to leave doesn't mean we're helpless." Waving her hand out to the growing crowd, she said, "Many folks really want to help out some here. You'll see. As people get rest, and get to eat and clean up, you'll have a lot of new volunteers on your hands. You'll see."

"In the meantime," Carla Bonet interjected, "the two of us can help now. Just tell us where to go." They both quietly but insistently stared at me, awaiting my response.

Astonished, I turned around helplessly to find some assistance. A volunteer passed, and I called her over, saying, "These two women are from New Orleans, and they want to volunteer. Do you know where they can go to start working?"

The volunteer said, "Sure. There are many who want to help out. None of us actually considered that, but they're welcome to help." Turning toward them, she said, "Please come with me."

The one official volunteer took her two new recruits and walked away. The concern of these evacuees was not for themselves—their concern was to serve others.

I navigated my way back to the main thoroughfare. As I continued my walk along the arena floor, I tried to sort out what I had learned.

For days, these evacuees had been dealt two blows in Louisiana; one was natural and predictable, the second was unpredictably inhumane.

The first of course was the fury of Katrina. This storm had shattered their homes, neighborhoods and surroundings. It shredded communities and families. These people had miraculously survived that.

However, not one of them was prepared for the second attack; the evacuees, having survived the brunt of the storm, emerged into a world that didn't care about them. The laggard response to their desperate pleas for help, especially from the government officials and agencies responsible for the ecological and man-made problems that had exacerbated Katrina's impact upon them in the first place, conveyed the new and shocking message that the survivors didn't matter. Nobody on the outside seemed to care. The evacuees had been given the destructive message that they just weren't worth a lot of trouble and effort, and like corrosive acid, this message ate its way into the psyches of these Americans. This was not an attack on their bodies. It was an assault on their spirits. While starved for water and food, they also hungered for dignity and respect.

My conversations had unwittingly conveyed the message that they were important enough to stop for and to help—that they mattered. This is what these evacuees absorbed from my words. It was as though each of these survivors couldn't help but first soak up the message that they and their families were substantial again. Their sense of worth was revalidated. Once the evacuees absorbed this, they would be able to listen to advice. But they first needed to feel valued and validated, to know that they counted.

This was something I could provide for them, regardless of how much rust had settled on my medical capabilities. This also helped me to understand their gracious reactions at the Toys-R-Us parking lot that morning. The most important response to them was not to what we brought, but to our very presence.

So far, I had only a sixty minute experience, but had already learned a critical message from the evacuees that I chose to absorb. I resolved that any conversation I had with any survivor would be conducted in an atmosphere of respect and dignity. That was the required environment for me to practice any medicine that I remembered.

CHAPTER 4

Practicing Medicine Together and Without a Safety Net

I finally completed my slow walk across the main floor of the Arena where the evacuees would stay. I walked into another, small foyer, and then through some doors into what was clearly one of the biggest warehouses I had ever seen.

The open area was colossal, measuring about one-eighth of a mile on a side, with a huge ceiling that seemed as tall as the room was wide. A solid concrete floor slab ran in all directions to the walls, which towered gray and dull above everything. Huge flood lights hung from the ceiling, leaving no room for shadows anywhere. I had entered what appeared to be a titanic, gray, fluorescently lit cube.

This was where the huge trucks commonly arrived, bringing the tons of equipment necessary for the various shows and events regularly scheduled at the Arena. There were three enormous trucks inside this cavernous room now, well off in the distance. They were large machines, but the great size of the room appeared to swallow the trucks up, making them appear like small digestible morsels in a mammoth, ravenous stomach used to consuming far more than it currently contained. Along its floor, people were scurrying in various directions as they prepared for the arrival of patients.

Entering through the doors into this expansive area, I saw that, while much of the room was wide open, parts of it were being curtained off. The part that I walked through now contained several long rows of computers staffed by volunteers whose job it was to check patients into the clinic. Evacuees were already standing in several short lines waiting to receive a medical record number and a hardcopy chart, formally entering them into the Harris County healthcare system. The survivors would give the chart to a nurse who would walk them back to a long corridor that I now saw began after the last row of computers, heading away in the distance. It was toward this corridor I began to walk.

Finally reaching this makeshift hallway, I joined the stream of people walking through. The corridor was compressed, made narrow by the rows of yellow curtains on either side. Above me was only the huge ceiling hundreds of feet away. Looking left and right, I saw the curtains had been drawn back every twenty feet or so, exposing a curtained off area that contained tables and chairs. The first large area off on the left said "Pharmacy," presumably where patients would get the prescriptions filled that doctors would be writing. Patients were already there, winding serpentine-like through the area; apparently physicians were already seeing them in some unknown area up ahead. On the right was a sign that simply said "Labs." To the left, one said, "Counseling." Another one a few feet down said simply "Psych."

Another twenty feet further down on the left the curtains ended, creating a space in the huge building that was taken up by a row of clean white sinks on the left, with paper towel dispensers on the right. Just to the right of this bank of clean sinks was yet one more drawn back curtain. A piece of printer paper had been taped on the curtains, and on it was printed "Family Medicine, Pediatrics." I had arrived.

Walking in, I saw what looked more like a base camp than a clinic. To the right was "Peds" a collection of about ten "rooms," i.e., small, closed off areas composed of aluminum poles on which orange curtains had been strung. To the left was "Family Medicine", another collection of ten rooms. Turning and walking in the direction of family medicine, I saw in the center an open area with five rooms on the left and five on the right. The rooms extended no more than eight feet high; above them was the seemingly infinite space of the warehouse. The overhead fluorescent lights flooded everything with light. In each room were two cots, just like the cots that were out in the arena. The open section between them formed a "hall" that separated the two rows. In the middle of this hall was a long table. Barren today, it would over the next few days be filled with saline bottles, gauze, tongue depressors, prescription pads, and the makeshift patient charts.

The noise was terrible. There was a lot of construction going on in the open warehouse area on the other side of the "rooms" not thirty feet away. Volunteers were busy unloading huge eighteen-wheelers that were full of supplies. Hammers were driving steel nails into hard wood, creating makeshift platforms. Plumbers were installing banks of sinks with running water. Computer wires snaked their way along the floors in huge bundles on the way to the pharmacy. Wheeling drills, wailing saws, and coughing engines all added to the background cacophony. Hardly the best place to see patients, but, it would need to do. It wasn't a medical center, but a makeshift clinic.

Each pediatric and family medicine section had a charge nurse. This was the nurse who had overall responsibility for the nurses, supplies, and the general flow of patient treatment in her section. The charge nurses were the ones who would be in the thick of it, managing the flow of patients. They were by definition the people who knew what was going on.

The charge nurse for family practice was in the process of orienting new nurses to their responsibilities. One of her new nurses asked the question I wanted to ask.

"Where are our patients?" the young lady asked. She was young enough to be in nursing school.

"They come in waves," the charge nurse, Glenna Whitney, responded. "Many of the evacuees are sick on the bus. It takes about forty minutes for the buses to unload their passengers and get them checked into our system now." She paused for a moment, checking her watch. "I would guess we can expect a new group of patients in about fifteen minutes," she predicted.

"How many buses are on the way now?" I interrupted, after introducing myself.

"Hundreds, Doctor."

Several other doctors were also arriving this afternoon. As I and other new doctors arrived, the doctors who had reported the night before began to leave. There was no "changeover", i.e., they didn't talk to us about what patients they had seen, what medicines were available, or the patients who might come back during our shift. Worn out and run down, they weren't interested in any conversation, but were understandably focused on getting off their feet and getting some sleep.

"They treated the first busloads of survivors," Glenna added as I watched this group of physicians leave. "We didn't have very many physicians last night, and they were overwhelmed. But," she continued, stifling a yawn herself, "we didn't know what to expect. How many patients we'd see. How many would have to go to the hospital. How many doctors and nurses we would need. We just learn as we go," she finished, shrugging her shoulders.

I headed back to the corridor that divided the narrow corridor of patient "rooms," and was approached by one of the last doctors who had worked the night before, but hadn't left yet.

"How are you..?" I started, introducing myself to him.

"I'm David. Can you sign my chart," he asked. He was a little wild-eyed.

I looked at him curiously, wondering *why I should need to co-sign his chart and check his signature.*

Reading my mind, he answered my question. "I'm a fourth year medical student—a tired one."

That explained it. As a fourth year medical student, he had earned the right to see patients, take their histories, do physical exams, and make notations in patients charts. However, in order to ensure proper supervision, he was required to have all of his chart notes, nurses' orders, and prescriptions supervised and co-signed by a licensed physician.

I spent a minute or so with him reviewing his notes on the patient he had just finished with. Seeing that all was in order, I co-signed for him, asking, "What's your reaction to these patients?"

"Their medical problems are straightforward enough," he responded immediately. "They're all so tired, some so run down, that they can't say very much. You have to coax their complaints out of them. I honestly don't know how they can stay awake. But," David added, "the real problem is prescription writing."

"What do you mean?" The prescriptions I just checked seemed perfectly appropriate to me. *What was I missing?* I wondered.

"There's no PDR!" he exclaimed.

"What?"

"That's right. No reference for medications," he said, shaking his head.

This was a glaring problem. Most doctors have their favorite medicines that they like to prescribe. We know the doses, beneficial effects, and adverse effects of these compounds and skillfully use them. However, when doctors see new patients who have been on other medications with which they are not familiar, or have to treat problems that they don't commonly see, we have to use medications that we have no real experience using. In this case, we need access to information, and the most common source for information on all approved medications in the U.S. is the Physician's Desk Reference. It contains a description of the medication, what it does, in whom it should be used, the most commonly used doses, and, just as importantly, the patients in whom the medicine should not be used. When physicians have any question about medication, they turn to the PDR.

We would begin seeing hundreds, if not thousands, of patients shortly, patients who we hadn't seen before, and who wouldn't be arriving with their complete medical history in an organized medical chart, and we didn't have a single PDR! These books were on every ward of every floor of every hospital. They're so ubiquitous that I didn't even think to bring one! Now, none were to be found.

"Many of these patients know the medication they would like to have," Dave added, "but they don't know the dose. If it's a medication that I don't usually prescribe, then I don't know for how much to write."

"Well, I don't have a PDR with me," I added, looking around fruitlessly to see if one had miraculously arrived in the last few minutes.

"I didn't bring mine either," a young Indian physician interjected, approaching us. "My name," she added, "is Nitda Jahami."

"I'm Rose Letters," another new physician added. "Neither did I. I didn't even think about bringing one."

"Well, I don't even have one back home that's up to date." Dr. Lance Jacobs interjected. "We're in a real fix here."

"Patients will be here in a few minutes," Nitda pointed out, watching the nurses continue to check in.

"I should have thought about bringing one," Lance stated, shaking his head in self-recrimination.

"Well, you can't blame yourself," Rose interjected. "Nobody thought of it. Why would we?"

"Let's just buy one at the local bookstore," I offered. "The medical center's only ten minutes from here. Actually, regular bookstores carry them now."

"That's a strategy that will work for the next shift, but not for us. It's too late to leave," Rose reminded me.

"Look. I'm dead on my feet," David confessed after working the previous night. "I need to leave."

"See you around," we all said. He waved goodbye as he rapidly left the clinic.

"Well," Lance offered, watching David leave. "The first shift didn't have a PDR, and it didn't sound like it was a disaster-filled event. They got by. So'll we."

The four of us gathered in front of one of the empty patient rooms, our stomachs jumping over the absence of a PDR.

"Well, there's only one thing to do here," I offered.

"Just figure it out," Rose finished for me. "Between the four of us, we should be able to come up with a list of drugs and doses that cover most circumstances . . ."

"If we pool what we know," Rose offered, "we can pull this off."

"OK. What specialties do we have here?" I started the new discussion by adding, "I was in general practice."

"I'm in infectology," Nitda offered, giving the modern name for infectious diseases.

"I was in orthopedics. Been retired for ten years," Lance offered. He was the oldest among us. I guessed that he was in his early seventies. "I still know my way around bones, but am clueless about AIDS."

"I can cover that," Nitda replied. "The question is—will the meds be available?"

"I just finished a psych residency," a new voice offered. We all turned.

"What's your name?" Rose asked.

"Hilda Peterson," the young psychiatrist answered.

"Well, if we need psych medicines, we're going to rely on you," Rose declared.

"For treating the patients, or treating us," Lance interjected, getting us all to laugh.

"If all we have is our memories, then our memories will have to do." Nitda offered. "Well," I added, "let's figure out what we know."

Nurses began to fill the rooms with patients as the five of us took stock of our talents.

Hilda said. "It's been ten years since I've seen a back injury."

"I can cover you on that," I answered. "I used to see them all the time. But I haven't treated anaerobic infections for years."

"I'll let you know what antibiotics to consider," Nitda offered. "Also, every patient we see will need a tetanus booster by definition."

We agreed. The combination of partially healed lacerations exposed to fetid water and soil made each survivor a prime target for tetanus.

"What about foreign bodies," Rose asked.

"I'll deal with those." I added, "under the skin as well as in the eyes. I'll need help with cancer regimens though."

"I've done some oncology," Rose responded, "so feel free to ask."

And so around and around we went, starting to reacquaint ourselves with medications and treatment protocols some of which each of us knew completely, while the rest of us didn't know much about them at all. It was a fifteen minute crash course in ambulatory and emergency medicine. Minutes earlier, we were complete strangers. Now, we were sharing our best treatment strategies with each other, each of us busily scribbling notes.

"By the way, I asked, "what instruments do we have?"

We all "threw down." Five stethoscopes. One blood pressure cuff in addition to the ones the nurses had. Only one otoscope/opthalmoscope to examine eyes and ears. Two penlights. One reflex hammer.

"That's pitiful," Nitda said. We all nodded.

"Yeah," Lance replied, "Looks like 'pitiful' is going to have to do for the next few hours."

"Hope the battery's charged on the ophthalmoscope," Nitda said, looking it over. "It's going to have to last."

"We can plug it into the wall to recharge it when we're not using it." I offered.

"I think we need to agree on something," Rose stated. "We probably just can't see the patients who fall into our own specialty."

"Why not?" Nitda, the infectious disease specialist asked.

"There'll be too many patients," Rose responded. "If they all have diabetes and hypertension, but no one has an infection or psych problem, then some of us will be worn out quickly, while others aren't seeing anyone at all."

"That's how it's done in the real world," Nitda offered.

"That's right," I agreed, "but this isn't the real world, at least not for a few more days. I'm with Rose on this."

So we decided. At least for this first day, we would put any specialties we had aside. Each of us would see the next patient, regardless of what problem they had. We would all be generalists, calling on each other for whatever specialty training the other one had. We would share instruments, knowledge, insight, training, and experience. In short, everything we had. And we would trust each other. A commodity that is normally available only after months or years of joint experience would have to be in ample supply *today*.

We took up station, each of us standing before one of the currently vacant patient rooms. We had arranged things the best that we knew how, and were ready to start. Seventy-two-year-old Lance, ten years into his retirement from orthopedics, leaned over to me, saying, "I can't do what you young people can, but I can do something. So, here I am."

It was a heady moment. We'd all seen and heard of the Katrina survivors' mistreatment. The pre-storm promises of support that in the end were just talk. The promises of supplies during the storm that were just talk. The promises of timely rescue that were just talk. *We were tired of talk that came to nothing.* Now it was *our* turn to contribute, *our* turn to be measured, *our* turn to "ante up and kick in."

"Anybody know if we have a crash cart?"

We all gaped at each other for a moment. None of us had a clue. Glancing helplessly at each other, the same thought went through our minds, *We will just have to make do.*

A minute later, we were all seeing patients.

———————————

The flow of patients was steady and relentless. We each went at our own speed, sharing medical information as the survivors' conditions challenged us to "think outside of the box." Affected as I was by my earlier experiences with the evacuees, I tended to see fewer patients, spending more time with each one. Some patients easily unburdened themselves, while others remained quiet and reticent, waiting until they were sure I was genuinely interested before volunteering any information.

Later in the day, I noticed a new physician among us. He appeared about thirty years old, thin, and soft spoken. Capable and efficient, he saw patients at a fairly rapid clip, and much faster than I did. Later, I introduced myself to this effective young doctor whose name was Mitch Skylar, a medical resident at one of the hospitals in Houston. He had not been scheduled to work at his hospital today, yet he had chosen to volunteer some of his precious time away from the hospital to work at the Katrina Clinic.

"You know, Lem," Mitch began, lifting his head up from the prescription he'd been writing, "I'm surprised we're not seeing patients with worse infections so far."

"So am I," I agreed. With all of the concern about the dirty contaminated water, fears were rampant about a cholera epidemic spreading.

"Well, maybe it's too early to tell," he said, looking around for his next patient.

"You've seen quite a few patients today, haven't you?" I asked.

"Yes," he said. "So far, the patients that I've seen require some medical care, but what they really need is some counseling."

"You're not the one to do that?" I asked.

"Ah. I'd rather not," he replied. "I'd like to stay focused on the medical problems. Besides," he added, "they've just set up a counseling unit over there," he said, pointing off to the left, "I'd just as soon stick to the medical problems, and leave the counseling to them."

Well, I thought, *to each his own.* I'd spend more time with these patients, he'd spend less.

"Besides, I get to practice some real medicine here," he continued, beginning to turn his head in search of his next patient.

"What do you mean?" I asked, confused. "You practice medicine in the hospital all the time don't you? You see heart attacks, gastrointestinal illnesses, kidney diseases, cancer. It seems to me you practice medicine every day over there." I finished.

"Oh sure," Mitch replied. "But it's different there. At the hospital there are so many layers of care and supervision. Everyone has someone watching over his shoulder. The staff physicians watch the residents who oversee the interns who see the patients while keeping an eye on the medical students. Don't get me wrong," he protested, fearing my reaction, "Inexperienced doctors need supervision. I understand that clearly. It's just that . . ."

"What?" I asked.

"We all have some responsibility for the patient, but it's so split up that no one has total responsibility," Mitch finished.

I saw where he was going, Taking his arm, I steered us to the side of the corridor that was bustling with nurses. "It's different here, isn't it?" I said.

"That's right! Here I'm responsible. No other doctor sees the patient but me. No one has to review the progress notes I make. If I miss a diagnosis, then the diagnosis is missed, and the fault is mine. Period. Nobody checks behind me."

"Really," I said, fascinated with this young doctor's take on the unique situation he was in. It was like being in practice on your own for the first time.

"It's a little overwhelming at first," he continued. "But, this is how I think of it. Here, I am my patients' doctor, no one else but me. So I have to find everything that's wrong with them. If I can't, I try to find someone here who knows more about the problem than I do."

"And what do you think of it?" I asked.

"I love it!" Mitch replied, his eyes filling with fierce determination.

"I'll tell you something else," Jay Posner, another medical resident said, joining us. "Where I'm training, the treatment regimens are fixed. If the patient has heart failure, then you follow the heart failure protocol. If the patient has asthma, you follow the asthma protocol. It's all pretty rigid. We just follow the rules."

"What's wrong with that?" I asked. "You always want to use the best treatment plans, don't you?"

"There's no room for flexibility," Jay replied, "or originality, or ingenuity. This morning, I had to come up with my own strategies for patient management. I had to improvise."

Just then, I received a call from a fellow physician and friend, Barry Davis, who was seeing patients at the George R. Brown Convention Center, just four miles away. After a brief conversation, we shared our mutual dilemma.

"Several of the patients that I've seen don't know the name of the medication that they've been taking for their chronic condition, e.g., diabetes," Barry stated. "All that they have is a pill that they brought with them. They show me the pill, and expect me to recognize it. But there're hundreds of medications, and I don't recognize the pills by their appearance. Since the evacuee can't give me the name of the pill, I'm stuck."

"We're stuck without a PDR here as well," I admitted. "I try to see if the pharmacy workers here can recognize it," I offered. "Trouble is, it takes too long."

"That's right," Barry agreed. "The pharmacy is way behind. As of now, it takes them 24 hours to fill a prescription. They try to help, but those folks can't always stop what they're doing to try to recognize a pill or a caplet."

"So, what do you all do there?" I asked, raising my voice to help drown out the ever present background noise?"

"I just call Harris County Poison Control," Barry deadpanned.

"What?" I laughed, "I didn't think of that!"

"Those folks are used to medical emergencies," Barry continued, "so they respond quickly. And a lot of what they do is to listen to descriptions of medications people may have overdosed on at home. They're in the identification business. I've called them four times today, and they've been able to help me for each pill."

"What's that they do?" Nitda asked, walking over.

I explained Barry's novel approach to her.

"Pretty clever," she agreed.

"It's not Poison Control's intended use," Barry continued over the phone, "but improvisation is the key now."

"Yeah," I offered. "We'll call this the new 'Davis SOP' for drug identification." Laughing, we both hung up. That's what we liked about practicing medicine on this day. Hospital standard operating procedures couldn't work, so we had to come up with something else.

"Sometimes, you feel stymied at hospitals." Nidta intimated. Caution is choking off desire to provide good care."

"I understand that," I responded. "But the key is having good docs. Good doctors will improvise, but they'll do it carefully. They know to look out for trouble down the road, and quickly intervene if their idea fails. In the hands of good practitioners, initiative is good. However, with careless doctors, originality can be lethal."

"Yes," Nitda agreed. "So the system protects us from the bad docs, but the good ones are prohibited from applying the best of themselves to their patients. That's why it's so refreshing to be here. We get to be original."

The nurses broke our conversation up with the call to see additional patients.

"We have a situation," the charge nurse rushed up to me a few minutes later.

"What's that?" I asked, looking up from writing in a patient's chart.

"Both a child and her mother need to be seen by doctors, but the mother won't leave the child!" the nurse said.

"Not even if they both need separate docs?" I asked with surprise, pushing the chart away as I stood.

"It doesn't matter," the nurse replied at once. "Mom insists that she be near her child all of the time!"

The pediatrician, Jennifer Redmon, came up to me. "Looks like we have a dilemma," she said pleasantly. "We've been trying to see pediatric patients separately from adults, giving each patient their own room."

"The mother needs her own doctor in her own room," the nurse observed. "Maybe we can . . ."

Jennifer and I instantly glanced at each other with the same thought. "Let's just put them both in the same room," she offered. Turning to me, she asked, "Would you mind taking care of the mother if I'm in the same room seeing the child?" she asked.

"Of course not. Let's go," I answered. A few moments later, we were both bent over our respective patients, working in the callow illumination produced by fluorescent light reflected off the yellow sheets that served as walls in the tiny exam room. The child, an eight-year-old girl with a terrible cough, sat in a small chair. Her mother lay in the cot right next to her. Severely dehydrated, with a gaping laceration on her neck that was badly infected, this weakened woman kept her eyes riveted on her daughter. Only after Jen and I both promised the mother that the child would not be removed from her would the mother agree to let us treat them both.

Twenty minutes later, we were done. The mother, her cut treated and dressed, sat in the waiting area in a wheelchair, the IV in her arm providing the fluids and antibiotics she desperately needed. Her other arm was lightly draped over her daughter who sat quietly next to her. A volunteer had gone to put in the prescription order for them both. However, we had some medicines available in the clinic area that we could give them each immediately.

"Thank goodness we finally got some samples," Jennifer explained to me.

"I thought they'd never get here," I agreed. "The drug companies really stepped up to the plate on this one."

We were all thankful to "Big Pharma" on *this* day. The pharmaceutical companies offered thousands of dollars of samples for us to dispense as we saw fit: antibiotics, mild pain medicine, steroid creams and ointments, anti-asthmatic pills, and medicine for stomach cramps. They plugged a huge hole in our acute care delivery.

"These samples make our job so much easier," Jen responded, stretching her tired arms well above her head. "The clinic pharmacy's overwhelmed. It now takes them twenty-four hours to fill a prescription. With the samples, I could start that child's therapy right away."

"It makes a big difference with the parents, too" I added.

"You have adult samples as well?" Jen asked.

"Yes," I answered, sitting down in a nearby folding chair. "But that's not what I mean. It's a relief for the parents to know that their children don't have to wait for their medicine. The evacuees have been told for days that they have to wait for everything. Water, food, clothes. Even rescue. At least when it comes to medicine, they receive their care at once. No need for parents to have to wait an entire day for their children to receive the medicine they need."

"For the first time, I can actually see some relief enter the tired faces of these parents," Jen replied, rapidly scanning the area with her trained eye for another child who might need her help.

"You know," Jennifer said, changing the topic, "some of these children have never seen a pediatrician before. Back in New Orleans, some families never had access to a pediatrician. There was only the local doc who was in general practice. And, if the doctor gets old and dies, the child's care just falls through the cracks. I shudder to think what the immunization status of these children is," she finished, closing her eyes.

"Can't the parents help?" I asked, taking a moment to lean my head back against the wall to close my eyes.

"Yes. They remember when their children got shots, but just don't know what the shots were for. Actually," Jen confessed, "that's no different than the more well-to-do mothers in *my* practice. It's hard for parents to remember the details. The difference," she continued, "is that families in my practice keep records of immunizations. My office keeps them too. Of course," Jen said, looking at another child being brought into the clinic, "those records are nonexistent for these children I'm seeing today."

I opened my eyes at once, shocked by the implications of these observations. "You know what you're saying?" I asked.

"Without shots, these children are at risk for mumps, diphtheria, rubella, maybe even polio down the line. I don't know," Jen said quietly. "They'll need to be followed closely. But, just whose job is that?" she asked.

"I don't know. One thing's sure, though," I replied, "many families will fall right through the cracks."

"You know, it's easier to get guns than health care these days," Jennifer said, shaking her head.

"Where do you work?" I asked, changing the subject.

"I'm in private practice on the north side of town," Jennifer replied, finally sitting down. "It's a solo practice, and I see about twenty patients a day."

"Up north? You had a long drive getting here," I replied.

"Yep," she said, nodding in agreement, "but I'm going to be coming here to work one day a week. I'll be here next Wednesday, and every Wednesday after that until we're all done. I'll tell you something else," she added, setting her jaw just a little. "I've also contacted several other pediatricians near my practice. We're going to make sure pediatrics is covered here for the duration."

"There's another mother-daughter pair in Room 8," a young nurse called to us. "Can you 'tag-team' again?"

Answering with our feet, we got back to work.

Our first real break that night occurred about 6:00 P.M. when the number of incoming evacuees needing care slowed to a trickle. Having been a perpetual healthcare motion machine all day with only a short break for lunch, we took the chance to rest. Some found chairs, while others found the floor. All of us were relieved to be off our feet.

"Well what'd you learn today, doc?" Rose asked with a smile, sitting down next to me.

"Tons." I responded. "Lesson #1—leave the cowboy boots home tomorrow!"

We both laughed. Only sneakers made sense for spending all day on concrete floors.

Two new doctors arrived, Becky Perez and Samantha (Sam) Holdman, both psychiatrists. We all introduced ourselves.

"Where are you from?" I asked.

"Maryland, by way of Italy," Becky replied.

"Oh yeah? That's a long way off!" Jen added.

"Not if she means, Italy, Texas!" someone joined in from behind us. We all laughed.

"No," Sam offered. "That's the real deal. The two of us were on vacation in Italy when we heard about the after-effects of Katrina. We cut the European tour short to get here, hoping you had some room for us."

"We'll, we can really use your help!" Jen replied. "It's impossible to overstate the shock in the eyes of these patients. Much of what they've experienced hasn't even registered on them yet." The tired pediatrician grimaced as she reflected on her experiences that day. We nodded.

"I don't know how to measure the emotional toll on these survivors," Nitda said. "I wasn't prepared for what they told me." Then, Nitda exposed what had been etched into all of our hearts that first day. "I came to practice medicine, but the medicine was the easy part. It's only the beginning."

"I can't see how they held up," Rose added. "We look back at it now and see that, after all, the worst of it lasted only four days. But when they were going through it, the survivors didn't know how long it would last. Some I spoke to believed that they'd be stuck in New Orleans for weeks. Weeks! But, in the face of that fear, they didn't give up. You know," she said, quietly gazing at each of us, carefully searching her own emotions, "I don't know how long I could have stayed in the conditions these people put up with and not lost it."

"Maybe that's a lesson here," Jay responded. "Nobody can really say what they'd be like in this crisis. Our imaginations really don't count, because the experience is far worse than our imaginations concede is possible."

"No," Rose said quietly, shaking her head. "I know my own heart. I couldn't have done it."

"What if you had children?" I asked.

"That's different," she said at once. Her entire demeanor instantly changed, as resolution filled her eyes. The transformation was immediate and almost breathtaking.

"What I don't understand," Becky added, "is why there isn't a greater response from doctors at the national level."

"What do you mean?" asked Lance who had quietly joined our group again.

"National organizations should be responding! Doctors' organizations should recommend that doctors come down here. They overwhelm me with junk brochures and pamphlets, begging me to join. Why aren't they here now?! When they can count for something that everyone will understand . . ."

"I don't know," Lance wondered, rubbing his thinning gray hair. "Doctors can't just ignore their practices to stampede down here."

"Fair enough," Becky responded. "I understand that. But they can organize. They could cover each other's practices. One doctor could cover the practice of another for a week or so, freeing up a physician to get down here. This is a wake up call for this country, and yet, once again, we've been caught flat-footed and unprepared."

"What do you mean by that?" Lance asked, turning away from his paperwork.

"I mean that we were warned about this happening. Yet national response has been fragmented, terribly disorganized and . . ."

"Ham-handed," I offered.

"Sure, that too," Becky continued. "But private organizations with a national reach haven't reacted effectively. I don't mean the Red Cross, but other groups. How about national church groups? Once again, the local response is right on the money, but the national chapters seem to have missed the boat."

An African-American nurse caught my attention for a moment. Seeing that she had my eye, she turned away, quietly going back to work.

"Forget it," Nitda deadpanned. "That's just not going to happen. It'd either take too much imagination on their part, or they'd see it as just too risky."

"You mean they're just too damned selfish."

"I don't know," Lance responded. "It just hit too fast. There was no national plan to reorganize healthcare delivery on that big a scale."

"Well," Nitda answered, "maybe we don't need the kind of concerted administrative response we'd like to see but we know is not coming. What matters in the end is that some doctors and nurses felt compelled to do something good. To pull themselves out of their own secure lives and pitch in. "After all", she said, turning to Becky and Sam, "you just came down here right? Not just from Maryland, but from Italy. You didn't wait for permission. You just stopped what you were doing, hopped on a plane, and got down here."

Nitda finished. "Let's not wait for help we're not going to get! What ever happens for the good is what we choose to do ourselves. Not what someone else tells us we need to do."

"Well, I'll tell you what," Lance, the tired, retired orthopedist interjected. "I was pretty nervous about coming down here today. I hadn't seen patients in over ten years, and then, only orthopedics patients. I didn't see a single ortho case all day, but it was the best medicine I ever practiced."

"How so, Lance?" I asked. Becky and Sam glanced at each other.

"Because I could practice unencumbered. I didn't have time-pressure to see six patients every hour. I didn't spend time filling up the patient's chart with verbiage that had nothing to do with treating the patient, but everything to do with keeping me from being sued.

"I don't know about you all," Lance said, looking around, "but medicine for me had become choked with administrative and legal minutiae. It was . . . he thought for a moment, "coming between me and my patients. It separated us. That's why I left."

"You know," he said reflectively, surprised at his own comments, "I don't think I've said that to anyone before. Not even my wife."

"Well," Sam replied, "You're not alone. However we feel about them, HMO's PPO's, provider networks, malpractice, hospital administration, even consumer activist groups have complicated all of our lives. They're not the reason we went into medicine, but we have to deal with them in the practice of medicine. Are patients better off because of them? I hope so, but I don't really know, with people complaining on the one side about cost, and on the other about deteriorating quality of medical care.

"But, one thing's for sure," Becky added. "Practicing medicine isn't enjoyable any more. There's little satisfaction in it, and no joy."

"Except for today," Lance interjected. "Today I interacted with patients the way I always thought doctors should interact. Clearly. Decisively. Compassionately. And more importantly, I know that I made a difference. The way I always thought good medical practice would make a difference. All of the administrative and legal encumbrances were stripped away.

"Most doctors I know would be happy to volunteer for that experience," Sam offered.

"Not me!" countered Lance. "I'd pay real money for the privilege to feel this way!"

"Your colleagues are right, but they're missing the boat"

It was a few minutes later, and I looked up from my chart to see the African-American nurse I had noticed before. This time she was standing above me. "It's not the national organizations who need to be down here, it's the national black organizations we need here. And we need them now."

"What do you have in mind? The National Black Caucus . . . ," I began.

She quickly waved a hand, dismissing the suggestion. "Sure, but that's not what I mean. There are many African-American organizations that could pitch in and help."

"Like who?"

"How about fraternities and sororities? They have lots of energy, and some have lots of money. Some even have some influence for fund raising. They all have a desire to help, but aren't organized to know how."

"Well . . ."

"Look. They want to help, but they're not. They're sitting on the sidelines. Watching. Enraged. But they're not doing anything because they have no plan. They can't engage their energy. They're like a car with a good engine, but a bad transmission, it revs, but it just— doesn't—go. They should wake up, and get organized.

"Same thing for Hispanic America," she continued. "If this could be allowed to happen in ghettos, it will happen in barrios as well. I understand that politicians throw these two minority groups at each other, but there comes a time when politics . . . just . . . does . . . not . . . count.

73

It's clear from what we're seeing that the national government's unreliable. The best response, from what I've seen is a large well organized local one. We'd better all wake up."

"Sounds complicated to organize," I interjected.

"Not really," she shrugged. "Say a national organization has local chapters scattered across the country. How about a simple agreement that the local chapter will be the staging area for incoming human and monetary resources? Each local chapter is responsible for knowing how to best focus its effort in a local crisis. They will be the focal point for organizing the incoming support. That simple step will help break the logjam."

"I see what you mean . . ."

"What I've seen these past few days is that local know-how can do a lot, but commonly doesn't have the resources. The resources can flow from the national church chapters to local churches, United Negro College Fund to local minority schools, and so on. The local chapters see the best way to help. They have the light, they just don't always have the juice to shine the way they should and could in times of local difficulty."

"You know," she observed, looking up to see an elderly blind African-American patient with an amputated leg being wheeled into the clinic area, "if Katrina is a wake-up call for America, then it's *a fire alarm* for Black America." Walking toward the patient, shaking her head, she finished, "this can't be allowed to happen again."

Five hours later, dead on my feet, I headed across the mammoth building and its one huge room to check-out. On the way, I came across an isolated group of workers talking quietly among themselves, huddled over a single table with papers scattered all over it. Among them I recognized Kristy Murray, an epidemiologist.

Epidemiologists detect, identify and track the occurrence of diseases, rooting out their cause. It's hard work, requiring endurance, observational powers, and deductive reasoning. Like detectives who get only the toughest cases to crack, they arrive on the scene of the disease, cataloging and identifying all of the suspect-causes. It could be water borne, a contaminant, a genetic defect—almost anything.

Then, through a process of data collection and disciplined reasoning, they narrow down the list, closing in on the actual cause.

It's painstaking work. It's also absolutely essential. And, now, here they were working at the Astroarena late at night, generating columns of numbers. Something was up.

"Kristy, what're you doing here so late?" I asked.

"Have a look for yourself," she replied, brushing her blond hair away from her face. Leaning forward into the midst of the papers, I saw a series of hand-written tables of numbers, scattered among hard copies of e-mails received from the Centers for Disease Control in Atlanta. Zooming in on the tables, I saw the columns had titles. The first was "Number of patients," while the second said "Number with disease." The third and last one was called simply "Rate."

"What are you tracking?" I asked, glancing up from the tables to her.

"We've been following the various health problems the evacuees identified when each of them checked in." She had to be dead tired, yet her thinking was direct and her voice was clear.

"We've been concerned about the possibility of TB in the clinic," I replied, thinking back to some of the patients I'd seen earlier in the day. Tuberculosis is a bacterial infection that starts in the lungs. Left untreated, it can spread throughout the body, ultimately affecting every organ system. It's contagious, deadly, and requires immediate treatment.

"So are we," Kristy responded, sitting down, not taking her eyes from the papers on the table and their calculations. "But at least we can get chest x-rays now. So far, we haven't seen a single case."

"We all have lucked out on that one," I answered, turning away, preparing to say goodnight.

"Don't be so sure" she responded. Her all-business tone stopped me in my tracks.

"What do you mean?" I asked, frozen in place, my chest tightening.

Nodding at the columns of numbers, she said, "The new problem isn't pulmonary—it's GI."

"No!" I responded, giving the table with its papers my full attention again. "You mean . . ."

"Diarrhea. 'Fraid so."

Acute diarrhea was bad news in any circumstance. But, in conditions where sanitation is poor, it can spread through a contaminated environment like wildfire. Ripping through a healthy population, it infects thousands in a matter of hours, producing diarrhea on the order of twenty or more stools a day. The resulting weakness and dehydration is lethal. Amongst the Katrina survivors, already exhausted, acutely malnourished, and without water for days, the effects would be devastating. Kristy and her epi team were looking into the abyss of a ghastly disaster.

"Is it cholera?" I asked, my heart now racing in response to the new threat.

"We don't know yet," she replied at once. "We're sending specimens to the lab for confirmation."

"Well, are the rates going up?" I quickly demanded, straining to keep the impatience out of my voice.

Nodding to the other two workers who comprised her team this night, she coolly replied, "We're trying to figure that out now. We don't know yet. But, there are a couple of things that I can tell you."

"What?" I asked, straining to see what rates they had produced so far.

"Once somebody gets diarrhea, it gets very bad, very fast. But, it's primarily affecting only some people."

"Who?" I asked, focused on Kristy again. "Which ones?"

She looked at me solemnly. "The children."

The worst news. "Children!" I repeated. "They're the most vulnerable!"

"Right." She agreed. "They don't have much reserve, so they reach the point of no return much faster than adults. And, when they're already dehydrated . . . ." Her voice trailed off, not completing a sentence whose end we both knew.

The situation was even more critical than I'd imagined. We needed to know if this problem was spreading through the evacuee population, and we needed to know *now*.

Trying to catch my intellectual breath, I looked over to the other two epidemiologists sitting at the table. They were completely absorbed in their computations, writing down numbers as they multiplied and divided, carrying out all of the intermediate calculations to find the attack rate, or the proportion of people with new symptoms in a given time period. I stood there staring, not able to believe my eyes. Finally, I blurted out in astonishment, "Kristy! Your group's doing this 'by hand'!"

"Yeah, that's right!" she agreed with calm assuredness of someone who knew her field. I did a double take. No one was using a computer, or a PDA. There wasn't even a calculator in sight. The critical computations were being carried out by tired scientists who had only paper and pencil!

"Why?" I asked. "How can you trust these critical computations to late night arithmetic and your collective memories of multiplication tables?"

"No choice," Kristy said, shrugging. "There are no laptops around for us to use. No portable calculators and not a single Palm."

"What!" I exclaimed, incredulous at this twenty-first century lapse.

"They're supposed to be some arriving tomorrow," she continued, "but . . . well we can't afford to wait. We have to know tonight. Just a sec," she apologized, walking over to one of her calculating colleagues to ask a question.

Feeling two sudden, hard taps on my shoulder, I jumped at the interruption, so involved was I in watching the computations, waiting for the results.

"What!" I demanded, turning.

"Sorry to interrupt, sir." It was an administrator. "Can we check on your schedule tomorrow? We really could use your help," he said.

As I walked away with him to sign up for more volunteer time, I turned to look over my shoulder at the epidemiologists who continued to work their numbers that would tell us how bad "bad" would be.

Twenty minutes later, I rushed back to the epi folks. Kristy and her group were huddled over what looked like a graph. The x-axis said "Hours," and the y-axis said "Incidence Rate." I looked over their shoulders and saw a penciled line traced through the points. As it moved to the right, the line climbed faster and faster. The incidence rate was increasing. The disease was spreading and spreading fast.

We had a new problem at Katrina Clinic.

The next day, I arrived early to begin a twelve hour shift. I sensed the change at once upon entering the arena, but it wasn't a new sickness. It was appearance.

Many of the evacuees had been able to shower and groom. The old decrepit, infested clothes were gone. The day before, the few clean survivors I had noticed were a small number of children, as the parents saw to the needs of their offspring *first*. Now, many adults had also showered, shaved, and wore fresh clothing. You could tell the new arrivals that day from the evacuees who entered the Astrodome the day before by the state of their grooming.

More importantly, the dire, uncertain atmosphere of Day One was no longer pervasive or omnipresent. There was a new sense of stability and predictability as the evacuees adjusted to their new, safe environment. A sense of normality had swiftly replaced the dire atmosphere of fear, dread, and desperation that arrived with the first buses of evacuees. The welcome sense of familiarity was remarkable for its rapid onset. It wasn't the last time I'd be astonished at the rapid adjustment these evacuees would make.

"Here, Doctor" a nurse said, sticking a pamphlet in my hand as I walked back to my station.

Arriving in front of my assigned room, I carefully read, then reread the one page message. Printed on hot pink paper, the leaflet warned of the occurrence of a wave of diarrhea at the Arena. Recognizing this as the handiwork of Kristy's group I scrutinized it, then I joined the other docs who were discussing the new situation.

"It looks like it's the cruise ship virus, right?" Rose asked Nitda, our infectious disease specialist.

"It's the Norwalk virus, all right" she explained, nodding her head. "Not a common cause of diarrhea, but it's received a lot of publicity in the media since those cruise ship illnesses a year or so ago," she finished.

"At least it's not cholera," Lance observed. We all nodded. Cholera could produce fatalities quickly. The Katrina Clinic had just dodged a big bullet, but the situation could still spin out of control if handled improperly.

"How lethal is Norwalk in children?" I asked Nitda.

"They can't tolerate anywhere near the level of fluid loss that adults can," Jennie our pediatrician, added, joining us.

"You're right," Nitda responded. "But, if treated properly, we should be able to avoid deaths."

"Well, I have two questions. How do we treat it?" began Rose.

"And how do we keep from getting it?" finished Lance. We all laughed at our retired orthopedist's practical approach.

He shrugged, then with a wistful look said, "When you get my age, you need to get to the heart of the matter fast." We laughed again.

"The best way to treat these children is to treat the diarrhea, that is to say, the fluid loss," Nitda responded, smiling with the rest of us. "The patients'll need lots of salt and water to replace the fluid that they've lost. If they can replace their fluids just by drinking more, that's fine. If they're too sick to drink, they'll have to have an IV put in."

"It seems like it's not only infants infected," Rose added, tiredly rubbing her eyes with both hands, "but older children as well. Six, seven, and older. They should be able to drink," she replied more vigorously, snapping herself awake.

"Well, if their parents tell them to drink, they'll drink," I said. "Have you noticed how much control they exert on their children?"

"Sure did," Rose responded as we all nodded. Many of us were parents, and all of us had treated children before. Our personal experiences led us to expect the perpetual tug-of-war that typified child-parent interactions. Once again, the evacuees had surprised us.

"These parents don't have to say anything twice," Jennie responded. "Commonly they don't have to say anything at all. The children just stay with them, and know what to do . . ."

"And what not to do," I added.

" . . . before their parents say anything," Jennie finished.

"I love my great-grandkids to death," Lance commented, "but they're nowhere near as well behaved as these children," he finished, shaking his head.

"I'm no child doc," Samantha said, "But here's my read on what's happened." We turned to her, interested in what one of our psychiatrists had to say about it.

"Before the storm, these families were as functional or dysfunctional as anyplace else in America. Some kids were well behaved, for reasons we don't understand, and others were not for reasons we know even less about. The same thing was true of the parents. Before the storm some were good while others weren't so good. But this week changed everyone."

"How so?" Rose asked.

"Together, they saw life at its most terrible. They lost their homes suddenly. Life turned upside down, and it did it at once, with no warning. Their lives were in absolute turmoil and they had to make decisions, tough decisions about what was most important for them. That was easy for some parents. The children were always important. But other parents who weren't so good at parenting got to choose all over again. They had a 'Road to Damascus' experience early this week. In fact, it's still continuing. These parents have a new surge of protectiveness for their children."

"Katrina taught them a good lesson," Nitda offered

"Yes. And they are fortified with it now," Sam responded.

"It's their new 'reason for being'." I added.

"Yes," Sam agreed. "They gave up food and water for their children. I heard this over and over from mothers and fathers this morning. Their children are their entire focus now.

"But also," Sam continued, "children saw their parents differently. That had an affect too. Children commonly hear how much their parents love them. This time, they got to see that love on the line. What it really meant. What it can do. They saw their parents give up meals for them then find a clean spot for them to defecate. They even saw their parents physically fight off strangers. Children saw their parents hurt for them. Get maimed for them. Even die. Make no mistake. These kids have seen some rough stuff.

"Maybe for the first time, these children appreciate how harsh and brutal the world is and that they have no coping skills for it. They need protection from it, and help in dealing with it. They needed the protectiveness of their parents, and that's exactly what parents were primed to provide. For the time being, they're inseparable."

"I assume it's not good to stop the diarrhea."

"What?" We all looked over at Lance, who had posed the unexpected question.

"We were talking about this Norwalk thing," Lance continued. "I need for us to get back there. I've never treated it before." We all nodded, and turned to Nidta to finish her primer for us.

"That's right. Stopping the diarrhea just keeps the virus inside the child's system. In some sense, their diarrhea is a defense, a way to shed the virus from their system. Also, the best way for us to avoid it ourselves is to minimize our exposure. Any one of us who sees a child with diarrhea needs to 'gown up.' Scrub garments, as well as masks and gloves."

"I think I saw them setting up an isolation unit," I offered.

"What kind," Nitda replied.

"It looked like a diagnostic center to me," I continued, describing the new mobile home type structure that had entered the warehouse that morning.

"Also, they're planning to isolate the children as well."

"Outstanding, Nitda replied, breaking into a smile. "We'll get good accurate diagnoses. Any child with the infection will get good treatment while being separated from the main population of evacuees. The infection will be contained."

She was absolutely right. It started with ninety children; then it grew to affect nine hundred evacuees. However, the prompt, aggressive work of vigilant epidemiologists, kept it from spreading into the thousands. There would be no epidemic.

We went on about the business of caring for Katrina's survivors. Our status as care givers gave us front row seats to observe the true depth of the human heart.

CHAPTER 5

Beyond Anguish

The survivors demonstrated stunning courage in the face of Hurricane Katrina, but they themselves were damaged in the process. Their bodies pushed beyond endurance, their minds and hearts sometimes broke under the shattering pressure. Although they had left the physical misery behind them in New Orleans, they had no choice but to bring the emotional scars with them. Listening to these stories of unbearable anguish, always relayed in subdued tones, was like someone turning the tight corkscrew of fear into your spine. You wanted to twist away to stop the pain, but you didn't dare. You knew that while hearing it was bad, living it had been so much worse, and talking about it made it at least a little better.

"Ayyyyyy's gone!"

"There, you see?" The nurse said, almost whispering to me as I entered the small room to join her and the patient lying on the low cot before us. "He keeps repeating that."

I bent over closer to my new patient. A young adult man, covered in filth, he lay quietly on the thin yellow fabric, while his head turned regularly from side to side. I thought, for a moment, that he looked right at me. Then I realized that he was instead looking right through me. His brain was disconnected from his eyes, but not from his voice, as he said, very softly, "Ayyyyyy's gone. Ayyyyyy's gone now."

"What does that mean, Doctor," the nurse asked, genuinely concerned.

"I'm unsure," I lied. For I thought I knew exactly what this African-American man was saying, and I was too embarrassed to admit it. "Ayyyyy's gone" was the old slang-talk used to stigmatize and slander African-American speech and culture for generations. I was unwilling to confess what I feared, that this patient actually talked that way, using that discarded dialect.

Leaning forward, I tried to get the attention of his wandering eyes. "Yes," I affirmed. "You've left New Orleans. You're in Houston now. Safe. Can you hear me?"

Nothing. The same wild look and blank stare. Then, a moment later, "Ayyyyyy's gone, hon!"

We started an IV for the intensely dehydrated man, and I walked outside the room to begin writing my notes.

"How's Tim?"

I looked up suddenly, seeing another dirty man, this one with a young child clinging closely to him. "I'm not sure," I confessed. "Do you know him?"

"Tim's my best friend," he said, straining to get a glimpse of him through the closed curtain.

"I don't really understand what he is trying to tell me," I responded hopefully. Do you know what he's talking about? You can walk in to hear if you'd like."

The friend went in to see him. I could see him bend over this patient, listening for a moment. Then, leaning closer, he whispered something into the patient's ear. Standing back up straight, this friend slowly turned and exited the room, carefully closing the "tent-flaps" behind him.

"You know," I began, anxious to continue my brief conversation with him, "it sounds like he is trying to say 'I'm gone,' like he's left New Orleans."

My patient's friend stayed quiet for a moment, his perfectly dressed and groomed little girl hugging him around his waist to comfort him. Looking up, she asked, "Dad? Will Uncle Tim be OK?"

"No, sweetheart." The man stared hard at me for a long second then began to explain. When he was done, I was a different man.

"Tim and I are best friends," he began. "So are our daughters, Joy and Sherri." This is Sherri," he said, putting his arm around the child who clung to his waist.

"When it started to rain, we tried to make our way to the Superdome. The water wasn't deep, but there was all kinds of garbage and debris in it. That's what slowed our walk down," he added.

"Joy was walking ahead," the friend continued, as Sherri clung more closely to her dad, beginning to cry.

"Suddenly, Joy slipped and fell forward. Her head just disappeared under that . . . that brown water . . ."

Sherri began to cry louder now, drawing the attention of some of the nurses. Her father leaned down, whispering into her ear as he gently ran his hand through her hair, calming the frightened child.

"Joy didn't get up out of the water," he continued, standing again. "Tim reached over at once, desperately feeling around under the water for her. That's when we saw it. Blood. It started to well up around where her body was. Tim was desperate, frantically trying to feel around for her. 'Got'cha', he said after a moment, gripping on to the back of one of her arms, and then the other. Grabbing them, he tried to pull her up, but she wouldn't move. What moved was Tim. It was like ground under him was shifting."

"What do you mean?" I asked.

"He was standing on something that she was attached to. He cried out to me to help. I got on one side of her while he was on the other.

"'Ok!' he called to me. 'Pull . . . now!'"

"We lifted her out, but . . . she was stuck to something."

I was dead silent.

"We didn't just pull her up, but also a huge brown-yellow square. It was, I guess four foot by four foot. A piece of wood. Attached to her face."

"Attached to . . . ?"

"By a nail. When she fell, a long nail jutting out from the wood went into her face." Falling silent, he raised his left hand, and while looking at me, put his index finger up to his left eye. I said nothing.

"Tim stiffened for an instant," the young father continued. "He didn't know what to do. Neither one of us did! Blood was everywhere. Joy was shaking, like she was having a fit. He didn't know what to do! Should he pull her loose, or try to move with that huge piece of wood attached to her. We had nothing to cut its size down. We . . . .we just didn't know . . .

"What he did do was put his face right up to hers, rubbing it against hers as he tried to soothe her. He'd say, over and over, while we waited for help that never came, "Joy, it's OK. It's just your eye." We waited about an hour. Maybe longer, I don't know. Somewhere in there, she died. That's when he started.

"So what he's, he's saying is . . ." I stammered.

"Yeah . . . 'Eye's gone' . . ."

After checking in the next day with the shift coordinators who now kept the schedules of all working physicians on huge sheets of paper that covered a portion of one of the giant arena walls, I walked in to the clinic, running into a doctor who was headed the other way.

"How'd it go last night?" I asked, judging by the pace of the nurses that things were picking up.

"The night was just fine, I guess," the doctor responded, rubbing his eyes to keep himself awake. "Started out busy, but, as you'd expect, things quieted down after midnight. The only real problem I had was . . ." He abruptly stopped in mid-sentence, as a young African-American woman passed in front of us both.

"Except for her," he began again after she moved out of earshot.

"What are you talking about?" I asked, watching her sit down across the way. She looked older than many of the young mothers I had seen in the clinic. Clean and well groomed, I guessed she was about thirty years old.

"Her child had multiple insect bites," this pediatrician explained to me.

"Do you think the child's in any real distress," I asked, as I stared at the untreated child.

"No, but my guess is a serious infection is taking root," he replied, carefully studying the floor. "She's going to need antibiotics to beat it back."

"And a tetanus shot." I added. "Why wasn't the patient seen?"

"I got nowhere with the mother," he replied flatly. "Listen, can you see her for me? Maybe you can get through to her."

"Why should I do any better?" I asked.

"You'll see," he said, as he turned heading out of the clinic for the day.

I walked over, introducing myself to the mother, Ms. Vicky Woodson, and her seven year old, Jashanda. I asked how long she had been in the clinic area. The 5'5" woman with clear, dark skin, high cheekbones, and short hair responded at once.

"I hate white people!" she hissed angrily, shooting arrows at me with her eyes.

I pulled back for a second, then looked quietly at her. I wasn't surprised by the words. I just hadn't heard them at the clinic so far.

"Why did you tell me that now? I asked, pulling a cheap folding chair up to sit in front of her.

"Well, I just do," she spat. "I hate 'em all!"

"Let's try to help your daughter first," I tried. "So far our conversation has done nothing for her."

"White people don't help anybody!" she complained, sitting up straight, pulling away from me.

"Well, neither does that kind of talk," I persisted. "And one thing's for sure. It's definitely not helping your daughter." I wouldn't typically speak to a patient so bluntly, but I felt pressed to take care of this child. One doctor had already been rejected by this mother, to her child's detriment.

Eyes narrowing, she focused on me. "Just whose side are you on?" she responded truculently, her eyes full of anger.

"Right now," I replied, "I'm on your daughter's side. That's who I'm here to help, and at least you and I should agree that she's the one who needs the most attention right now. Listen," I offered, "Let's make a contract. For the next ten minutes, you and I'll focus only on your daughter. Anything you tell me will be about her. I promise that anything I say to you or to her will only be in her best interest. When the time is up, you and I can have any conversation that you'd like to. How about it?" I finished, holding my breath.

Silence. Then, "Never done this before," she said.

"Neither have I," I responded, shrugging. "This week, the whole world is different. Can we get to work?"

"OK."

"Can I look at your daughter for a few moments? You can stay right next to her, and you can say anything you need to about her to me, but I really need to look at her bites."

"They're not bites. They're stings. Wasp stings."

Ms. Woodson was right. There were about six stings on the child's left arm, and ten on the other. Both arms were hot and swollen. There was no doubt that they were infected, but as far as I could assess, the infection hadn't spread to other parts of her body or into her blood.

"When did she get these?" I asked.

"Two days ago," Ms. Woodson replied, keeping her end of the bargain up. "There was a pile of wood that was blocking the way of the boat we got in to get us off of our street. She grabbed on to a piece of it to move it. The wasps must've been on the bottom of the wood, because they swarmed over it to get at her in the boat."

"What'd you do," I asked, quickly inspecting Ms. Woodson's arms and legs for stings as well.

"Don't worry about me," she replied testily. "I'm OK. One caught me on my back. "There's only one thing you can do when wasps attack your boat," she finished, answering my question.

"Yeah," I said, nodding, "Get in the water. Fast."

"You been through that?" she asked.

"Yep," I replied. "A North Carolina pier. It wasn't a pretty sight."

She nodded. "I didn't see more than two or three wasps on either of her arms. I don't understand how she got so many stings."

I nodded. "A wasp has a straight stinger. It's not like the stinger of a bee that rips apart after one sting. A wasp can jab its stinger in and out multiple times. Just one of them can do a lot of damage.

"You know Ms. Woodson," I continued, "Jashanda's very lucky. Many times, stings from the wasp can cause a lot of damage to the entire body. She could have gotten very sick, and maybe much worse."

"Well, what happens now?" the mother asked, now completely focused on her daughter.

"We can do a good job cleaning those wounds up," I responded, turning to get a nurse's attention. "If she takes the antibiotic I give her, and also gets a tetanus booster, she'll be fine. Also," I finished, "you'll need a tetanus shot as well."

I left briefly to complete some paperwork, allowing the nurse to clean Jashanda's wounds, administer the tetanus toxoid to mother and daughter, and make sure the child ingested one of the sample antibiotic pills. When the nurse was done, and left the patient room, I sat down again with Ms. Woodson.

"Well," I said, "our ten minutes are up. "Now, what's your complaint with white people?" The two of us were alone with her daughter, who had been quiet through the entire visit.

Instantly, the anger was back. "They're nothing but problems for us," she complained.

"What are you blaming them for?" I asked. "What'd they do this week? Cause the storm?"

"That's stupid," she retorted.

"What then?"

Ms. Woodson said nothing. Her eyes narrowed.

"I can't know what you've been through in your life," I continued, "but, whatever it is, it's really hurt your eyes," I continued.

"What are you talking about?" she snapped.

"The people who checked you in were white. That nurse who just helped your daughter was white. The doctor that you wouldn't let see your baby was white also. What'd they do to you that was so bad?"

"They were white!" she retorted.

"You said that. But tell me, how, specifically, did these people I just described hurt you or Jashanda?" I persisted.

Nothing.

"They're not here to hurt you at all. But you couldn't see that. The only reason they're here today is to help you, but I'm afraid that you can't see that either. Most of them aren't even getting paid for this. Almost everyone is working long hours—for you. But, like I said, you can't see straight. If what you have was a disease, it would be called something like 'toxic vision.' Your vision's so bad," I insisted, "it even let Jashanda hurt longer than she needed to."

"What do you mean?" she asked, opening her eyes a little wider.

"You've been here at the arena for a couple of days," I answered.

"Yet you only came to the clinic today. And, when you finally did bring Jashanda in to be seen, you wouldn't let the doctor examine her, right?

"That's right," she said, not quite as angry.

"So, Jashanda waited for two days to get seen because of your problem with all of the white people in the world. Yet, not one white person hurt her, or even threatened to hurt her here. Tell me the truth, which is the stronger of the two: your love for Jashanda or your hatred of white people?"

"Well, I brought her over here finally, didn't I," she retorted angrily.

"Ms. Woodson," I said as gently as I could, "you have some growing up to do."

She looked sharply at me. "Who do you think you're . . ."

"So do I," I continued. "No adult stops growing just because they become a parent. But, I'm afraid that, in your case, you have to do your share of growing fast. I don't know what happened to you that caused you to react to white people this way, but you have to begin to learn the right lesson right now."

"What's that?"

"That even in this demented, slaughterhouse of a world, compassion still makes sense. That's why they're here. They could use some compassion from you."

After a moment, I continued. "People here have tried to show you that, but you refuse to see. But I tell you, if you don't fix your vision problem, you won't recognize the good people you've waited your entire life to meet."

"I didn't see it that way," Ms. Woodson said.

"We get hurt trusting people we shouldn't sometimes," I went on. "But we're also hurt by not trusting some who are here and want to help. We both have to choose wisely, but we shouldn't choose blindly, right?"

On that point we agreed, parted, and went our separate ways. What made these days unique was not that we were all learning. Learning is something everyone, child and adult alike, does everyday. What made this time of our lives so special was that we could be so open with strangers about what we did not know, and grow from the sharing.

However, this transforming experience that I had shared with Ms. Woodson did not prepare me for the shock of the Jenkins sisters.

I met them later that morning, Their chart simply stated that there were two women who required prescription refills. That's all it said: Rx refills.

Walking in, I saw a pair of women who should have been identical twins. Same height and build, same faces, same brown hair and dark eyes. Nevertheless these two women, so identical in features, were completely opposite in appearance. The lady standing up, facing me, her right arm draped over the shoulders of her seated sister, was well groomed, wearing skillfully applied makeup. She wore a fresh set of clean clothes.

"Hello doctor," she clearly and courteously began. "I'm Theresa Jenkins. This is Tomasina, who needs your help." Then, very clearly she said, "We're sisters."

"Ms. Jenkins, how are you?" I asked, introducing myself to Tomasina.

"Can you say hello to the doctor, Tomasina?" Theresa gently coaxed.

Tomasina Jenkins looked terrible. Her hair was dirty and unclean, hanging down around her face. I could see where the dirt had been wiped away in uneven swipes. Her dress was in tatters, and she was barefoot. Her left foot and lower leg were covered by the filthiest plaster cast I'd ever seen. Her face, with its empty eyes and slack jaw, did not reflect a mind concerned about the terrible shape of her body; instead it reflected a spirit stunned by an unknown horror.

Leaning over to bring my face close to Tomasina's, I asked gently, softly, "Ms. Jenkins, Won't you speak to me? I'd like to help you, but I don't know how unless you speak . . ."

"LEAVE!" she shouted at me, spit flying from her mouth. "Get out OF HERE NOW!" she yelled, arms waving wildly. Her eyes suddenly blazing with anger, she cried, "MAMA!"

Her instant anger jolted me like an electric shock. I reflexively jerked away.

"Tomasina! Calm down now! Please!" Theresa said, reaching over to try to control her sister's spastic arm movements. Turning to me, Theresa said, "She's here to get her prescriptions refilled."

Needing a moment to recover, I didn't re-approach the disturbed Tomasina, but instead asked, "Why'd she react that way?"

"Those are the only words my sister has said for three days, to anybody."

"And the anger?" I asked.

Theresa Jenkins shrugged. "That's not anger, Doctor. That's hatred! And," she finished, shaking her head, "the worst is yet to come."

"Three days ago," Theresa began, "before the storm, we lived with Mom and Buddy in Mom's little house. Been there for fifteen years since Daddy died. We sure knew the storm was coming, but none of us worried too much. We grew up in that neighborhood and had put up with lots of rainstorms.

"We were all sitting in the house, waiting out that terrible rain on Monday. The TV and radio had long since lost power so the three of us just tried to talk our way through the storm. While I was talking to Mom, I felt Tomasina looking at me.

"Felt her . . . ?" I asked, perplexed.

"Yeah. You know, we could do that sometimes. I could be talking to somebody and just feel her, kind of . . . tapping on my mind. I looked over at her. She said 'Something bad's just happened?'"

"Like what?" I asked, drawn deeper into this conversation.

"'There's a lot more water coming,' was all she said. Turns out she was right."

"Well, your sister was able to talk then...," I asked, looking over to the silent, dirty Tomasina.

"Talk? Please!" Theresa responded with a smile. "She was talking like crazy. We all were! Anyway we had learned to trust these pushes that Tomasina would get. Warnings that she could sense and then tell us about. We had to think of something to do about the new threat, this . . . water on the way."

"Pushes?" I asked, puzzled.

"Yeah. You know, Doctor," she responded quizzically. "When reality pushes it on you. Gives you an idea what's coming. That's what we call it. 'A push' ."

"A push . . . ." I repeated quietly, as the hairs on my neck, almost imperceptibly, started rising.

"Anyway," she continued, "we all started talking at once. Even Buddy was making a fuss. Tomasina was struggling to get around on the ankle she broke last week. It hurt too much for her to walk on, and she couldn't get the hang of using those crutches the doctor gave her.

"We were trying to find the best thing to do. We'd never had to leave home before in a storm. But, the water was rising fast. I wanted to find someone who would help us get out of the neighborhood, but Tomasina thought we should wait for a boat to come along."

Pausing, Theresa leaned over to her, rubbing her sister's back. "You were wrong about that, girl, but don't blame yourself now." After kissing her sister's dirty hair, she returned her attention to me.

"SHOO! GET OUT OF HERE," Tomasina shouted, batting her hands at some imaginary threat. "Mama!"

"Soon the water got so high we couldn't leave the house," her sister continued. We just stayed inside all night. Next morning, a boat came by and we called to those people. They said they had room for us, but not for Buddy! Tomasina was furious. Used language I don't hear from her much anymore. There was no way Tomasina would leave without him, so we stayed behind."

"Who's Buddy?" I asked.

"He's our pooch," Theresa Jenkins responded. "Really though, he's Tomasina's dog. Had him for eleven years now. He's a nothing, scruff of a little thing, but boy, can he make you laugh," Theresa Jenkins said, smiling a little. "When she would come home from work, he'd start barking excitedly, that tail waggin' like crazy before she ever got in the house. By her footsteps, he knew it was her. That tail on that little dog would get to wagging so hard, I'm surprised he never broke it off against the furniture he banged it into! He loved us all, but Tomasina was Buddy's favorite. And my sister loved him right back. We all did."

"Well, we did what Tomasina said. We waited. Waited around for most of Tuesday. The water was over three feet deep in the street. It was too deep for Mama, but Tomasina and I could walk in it. Tomasina says to me 'You need to go ahead and get us some help.' That's just how she said it. 'You need to go ahead and go, Theresa. Get Joseph.'"

"And Joseph was . . . ?" I asked.

"Joseph is a friend who lives six blocks away and has his own boat. He always said we should call him if we needed to get out in a hurry with Mom."

"Well, how did you know that he would take your dog?"

Theresa Jenkins' look told me she suddenly questioned my sanity. "Why, because HE had one! You have to understand. Our pets were like family to us. There is just no way you can leave them behind. No way. Old Joe knew that."

"Anyway," she continued, "Tomasina convinced me to go. I thought it was wrong, but, I couldn't think of anything else to do. But that Buddy was sure upset when I got up to leave. I'd never seen him that way before! He was always so happy, that tail just wagging away. Now, the tail was tight against his back legs. And he was crying. Just whimpering and carrying on! He would cry, sitting down for a second. Then jumping up, like the floor just burned his behind, he would walk round and round between Tomasina over on the couch and me just a foot or two away, crying up a storm. It was like he was frustrated because . . . well, because," She shrugged her shoulders, "maybe he knew. "Maybe dogs get pushes too."

Looking at me, she asked "Is that possible?"

I looked at the wall for a long second. Then, quietly, I shook my head a couple of times, finally saying softly, "I don't know."

"Well, anyway, I left," she continued. "It took me six hours to make my way from our house to Old Joe's."

"Why so long?" I asked.

"It was getting dark fast," she answered, "and I couldn't see very well. Plus the usual landmarks I could always rely on were gone. Signs were torn down. Cars weren't in the streets like they usually were, but instead, were all over the street, floating and twisting in all directions. Some were overturned. I lost my way a couple of times.

Plus, I just couldn't find the right speed to walk in that water. If you walked too fast, you would stumble along the junk at the bottom. If you walked too slow, the water would slam into you. The water seemed, well, hard. A swell would rise up in it, slamming against my back. Once, it knocked me down, banging my head hard against the bottom.

"That happens to you once, you start paying attention to how fast your walking," Theresa said, pointing a long finger at me. I thought the temperature in the room had just dropped ten degrees.

"When I finally got to Old Joe's house," she continued, "I was crying, I felt so relieved. Of course all of the lights were out, but that didn't mean anything since the lights were off in the whole neighborhood. I knocked once. Nothing. Knocking again, I called out 'Joe. Joe!' Nothing."

"'What do you want?' the voice said behind me. I jumped right out of my skin, falling away from the stranger."

"It was just Junior, Joe's son! Did he ever give me a fright!" Theresa smiled for a moment, leaning her head back against the wall of the room, her hand gently rubbing her sister's shoulder. "Then, when I told him what happened, he said that his dad left town before the storm, leaving Junior with the house and boat.

"Ten minutes later, we were making our way back to Mama's house. I asked him what time it was, and he said, 'One in the morning.' It had been seven hours! Forty minutes later, we were back.

"Shoo! Get out of here now! Mama, MAMA!" Tomasina Jenkins said again sadly, this time softer. Her refrain snapped me back to the reality of the clinic.

"I tell you," Theresa said, "the forty minutes in that boat were the longest forty minutes of my life! I was caught up in a fear that had a deep root in me. I couldn't think it out of my head; couldn't shake it loose. Something had happened to my world, and I couldn't see what it was. I just knew that it was bad.

"When we turned the last corner and were on my Mom's street, it was all I could do not to jump out of the boat and rush through the water to her house. But, my head still hurt bad from my earlier fall, so I made myself stay in that row boat. Sitting there on the narrow seat in that boat, I stretched both arms out to grip each side of that boat, just trying to *will* that boat to go faster. All the time, Junior just paddled us silently through the water.

"When we finally got back to Mama's, I didn't even wait until we got to where the front gate was. I jumped out of the boat into the water. Wading through it, I called, 'Tomasina! Mama!' I didn't hear anything. At the front door, I pushed hard, but couldn't open it.

"'Must be jammed,' Junior said. We went around the side, and broke a living room window. I climbed in, falling into dirty water. At once, I heard some scurrying. I vomited instantly," Theresa Jenkins confessed, shaking her head. "I hadn't even seen anything, and I threw up!

"I had no light," she continued, "but luckily, Junior had put a huge flashlight in the boat and had it with him now. 'Something on the sofa,' he said, shining a light on it.

"His light found Buddy. The little movement remaining in Buddy's chest told us he was alive, but didn't even have the strength to whimper. His body was splotched all over. Leaning forward, I saw in the light that they weren't splotches, but jagged gashes and holes. They were all over him. His tail had been chewed into two pieces. Part of his nose was gone. Maybe an eye too. I couldn't tell."

Theresa shivered for a moment, then finished. "I heard more scurrying. Nasty, sickening tapping of small feet in water. Junior shined a light in their direction, but I didn't need no light to know what they were. Rats!" Theresa Jenkins, closed her eyes tightly, bringing her hand, drawn into a tight fist, up to her mouth. "Rats were there!"

"I was shaking and I thought my heart would pound itself right out of my chest! I took the light from Junior, and shined it back across the room. There, about ten feet from the sofa and Buddy, sitting in a chair, was Tomasina. Tomasina was rocking back and forth in the chair cradling our mama in her lap. They were both so . . . so dirty!"

"That was the first time I heard her say 'Shoo! Get out of here now. Mama!' She hasn't said anything else since."

I rubbed my hands hard over my forehead and eyes, unsure whether I wanted to understand the scene the story compelled me to see. Ms. Jenkins made up my mind for me.

"The way I see it," she said, her eyes tightly closed, forcing herself to get the words out, "Mom must have gotten sick. Tomasina couldn't walk, but managed to get to Mom and hold her until help could come. Then the rats came in from below the house. Tomasina couldn't look after both Mom and Buddy. So, she sat there, holding Mom, keeping those rats off of both of them, trying to scare them out of the room with her shouts. But, those rats don't listen, especially when they know there's . . . there's food around. Buddy was just too small, and there were too many of them. They caught him on the couch. It was dark, so Tomasina didn't see it, but she heard it. She shooed and yelled at them, trying to scare them off. Didn't work, though."

A woman sitting quietly, taking care of her ill mother, forced to listen as her pet was torn apart. Lost in this thought, I had involuntarily backed up one or two steps before I caught myself.

Coming forward then kneeling down, I looked into Tomasina's eyes, desperate to say something to this woman who was still reliving those terrifying hours. I found no words for her. I simply put my hand on her shoulder for a moment then I quickly wrote the prescriptions.

"Nurse," I called, turning to leave the room "can you please get some transportation for . . ."

"Oh!" Theresa Jenkins said, "Don't bother about that. We can manage, right, Hon?" she said looking at her sister. At Theresa's urging, Tomasina got up and, leaning against her sister, limped out of the small room.

We got Tomasina comfortable in a chair outside the cubicle for a moment. Then, touching Theresa's shoulder, I motioned her to take a walk with me. Once we were out of her sister's earshot, I turned to face her, saying, "Ms. Jenkins, when you get a moment, and Tomasina recovers from this, you must tell her how brave she was. She saved your mother. I know the loss of Buddy deeply hurts her, but she saved your mom."

"I can't do that, Doctor," Ms. Jenkins replied evenly, looking right back at me. "When Junior and I found them, Mom was dead. Stiffening up, right in Tomasina's arms. Our mother had been dead for hours. Must have died right after I left them both to go to Old Joe's. Tomasina didn't know that then. She doesn't know it now. She still misses Buddy too much."

Theresa Jenkins rolled her sister in her wheelchair away. I never saw the Jenkins sisters again. Months later, my hair still rises whenever I think of them and their experience.

The nurse put the chart in my hand. After listing the patient's vital signs, it said simply, "headache." Taking the chart, I entered the room to see a teenager, Ronnie Carson, who appeared to be thirteen but whom the chart declared was seventeen years old. Ms. Carson was lying on the cot on her back. Both legs were bent at the knees. Her right hand was down by her side, the left up covering her forehead. She was dirty beyond belief, her eyelids almost glowing red with the profound fatigue that filled them.

"Hello," I began. "Are you here alone? Where are your parents?"

"Dead!"

I was shocked into silence, desperately working to collect my thoughts. This patient was a mere child. Her simple statement was but the thin cover over a sea of tumultuous emotion.

"I didn't know that." I began quietly. "When did it happen?"

"Last week. My dad died in the flood, I think. My mom died after that." Her words were delivered in a monotone, conveyed by a fatigue-laden and emotionless voice.

"Are you here with anyone?" I continued.

After a moment of silence, she uttered two words, "Just me."

It took only a few moments to complete her exam. I concluded that her headache was cause by her profound dehydration.

"When was your last meal?" I asked, giving the BP cuff to the nurse who would rush it over to where it was needed in another patient's room.

"I don't know," Ms. Carson said, lying back down on the cot.

'Well, today's Friday. Was it yesterday?" I persisted.

"No."

"How about Wednesday?"

"No."

"Tuesday?"

"No."

Anytime since the storm came?" I finally offered.

"I don't think so." Five days. She hadn't eaten for almost a week.

"How about your last drink of water?" I asked.

"I'm not thirsty at all."

"Ms. Carson, we need to get some good food and water in you if you're to get better."

"I just don't want anything," she said, barely audible, turning her head from me.

If there was any time to apply what I thought I had learned earlier that day, this was it. "I'd like to listen to you. Just tell me what happened," I asked.

"It was all of that water!" she began. For the first time, her voice filled with emotion, yet I had to strain to hear her over both the noise of the clinic construction and the conversations of the patients, doctors and nurses just on the other side of the curtain separating the small room from the outside world. I scooted closer to her.

"It rose so fast," she continued. "Before we knew it, the water was up to our necks. My parents are about my height," the 4'11" patient explained, "and we struggled to keep our heads above it. It was a filthy mess, so cloudy that we just couldn't see where we were walking. Plus, waves moved through the water. It pushed and pulled us, sometimes trying to turn us around in it. We tried to hold hands, but the pushing and pulling of that water wouldn't let us do even that." She paused for a moment.

Then she said, "my Dad was there, one minute, gone the next."

"You mean he just disappeared?" I asked, incredulous. "What do you mean? Did he get swept away? What . . ." I asked, totally confused.

"He had been teasing Mom, saying, 'I hope you don't think all this mess means I'm going to buy you some new . . . .' But he didn't finish. It was like he was just . . . just sucked down. Dragged under. Pulled under." She shivered at the sinister, unknown force that had taken her dad.

"At first Mom was angry. You know, she thought he was just playing around like he always does. She called and called to him. Then she got scared. She couldn't see him anywhere. She thought he had slipped and was under the water, so she and I tried to look for him."

"How did you do that?" I asked, my stomach tightening as I viscerally reacted to the image of people deliberating exposing their faces, even their eyes, to the toxic liquid.

"We would hold our breath, and then put our heads under the water, trying to see him, feeling around for him," she said. She was breathing a little more rapidly now, making a face as she relived the horrible moments.

I couldn't help but shudder. The water was filthy. Holding your face under it exposed you to infection. I couldn't imagine keeping your eyes open.

"We did it again and again," she continued after a minute. I threw up once. But we never did find him. We didn't know what else to do. The water kept rising, and we just couldn't stay there. Finally, a boat came by. They picked us up, but we kept looking around for him. We never saw my dad again."

She stopped speaking, perhaps to catch up with her emotions that threatened to break their leashes and stampede freely inside her. There we were; she lying on the couch and me sitting next to her, the only noise coming from outside the "room."

"Mom and I got on the bus two days later. We hadn't showered for four days. I guess we should have been hungry or thirsty, but we didn't feel like anything. My head was already hurting. It was like I had a hammer inside of me, pounding away, trying to break me open from the inside out. We tried to talk to each other, but just couldn't find words worth saying to each other. Then, about half way over here, Mom got quiet." Ms. Carson's eyes closed as the emotional storms in her heart pushed hard to get out.

Resisting for a few moments longer, she said. "When we finally got here, I went to wake her up but she didn't move. Finally, one of the helpers came on the bus to help me get her off. They had to carry her in, and she still wouldn't . . . move . . . on . . . her . . . own. A nurse came over to look at my mom, then . . . went . . . to . . . find . . ." She could barely finish the sentences.

"The . . . doctor . . . looked . . . at . . . her," her voice, thick with grief, caught on itself, "and . . . spoke . . . to . . . the . . . nurse . . ."

Suddenly, Ms. Carson abruptly sat up. "They said my mom was dead. SHE WAS DEAD! MY MOMMIE WAS GONE!" She repeated at long last breaking into sobs.

The pain at her losses that bitter day completely enveloped her as she sat on the thin cot with her arms pressed tightly against her stomach and her head down, rocking herself back and forth in grief. Each of this child's parents had been sucked from her life in front of her eyes.

I sat with Ms. Carson, as she cried, her face pressed hard against my shoulder. Through it all, her eyes remained red-rimmed and dry since her body, desperate for water, spared none for the emotional extravagance of tears. Five minutes later she stopped and lay down again, struggling in vain to kill the headache that painfully proclaimed how extreme her dehydration was.

"What do I do now?" she asked.

I was silent for a moment, pondering this question which I had known would come. Then, in whispered voice, I replied, "You have to decide if you want to live."

Moving her hand from her eyes, she turned to look at me.

"If you continue like this," I continued, "You'll die. It's that simple. And I don't mean in a year or in a month. I mean in a few days. Maybe in a few hours. The fact that you're not eating or drinking will kill you. The fact that you don't care anymore will kill you. So, you have to decide, pretty soon now, whether you want to live."

Putting my hand on her arm, I finished. "Your mom and dad were innocent, and the storm killed them. Is that what you want to happen to you too? Will that be the fate of the Carson family? All of you killed by that beast?"

"What do I do without them?" she asked.

"Just take it a small step at a time," I replied. "But for now, Ronnie Carson, decide that you want to live today. Just make that decision. *Leave tomorrow's problems for tomorrow's strength*. Choose to stay alive today. That's the only decision that you have to make. Will you do that?"

She just nodded her head.

"With your help, we'll get you better." I turned, calling "Nurse!" as I rose and left the room.

Within fifteen minutes, Ms. Carson was on a stretcher with an IV in her arm, the desperately needed nutrient salt-water pouring into her dry body.

"Are we going to send her to the hospital?" the nurse asked. The nurse's question was legitimate, yet I hesitated. It would take a long time to get her there, plus it was just one more disorienting trip for her. I wanted her to begin to get settled, to have part of her life be predictable again. Also, I knew that food, water, and companionship were plentiful here. These were the three things she needed.

"Let's keep the IV fluid going here," I responded. "I'll keep an eye on her. If it looks like she's getting worse, we can send her on to the hospital. But, I think she'll be OK here."

"All right," the nurse acquiesced. "I'll watch her, too."

Fortunately, we guessed right. The IV fluids we were giving her began to reverse the dehydration at once. As I saw other patients later that day, I noticed that Ms. Carson didn't need to lay down anymore, a clear sign that together we had beaten back the dehydration threatening to kill her. She was talking to some of the nurses, and also with one or two of the other evacuees. True to her word, Ms. Carson had decided to live that day.

Yet, we couldn't let her just go back to a cot in the open area alone. Correctly or not, I feared leaving her alone with her emotions would do more damage than good. Calling one of the nurses aside, I said, "We need to arrange some companionship for her," I don't think a volunteer can do that, what are we going to . . ."

"I can stay with her!" a familiar voice called out.

Startled, both the nurse and I looked up to see a woman with a dirty white handkerchief tied around her neck.

"Ms. Bonet," I said remembering my conversation with her during my slow walk to the clinic area earlier. "Looks like you're a volunteer after all!" We shook hands.

"I told you I was ready," she replied.

"Well," I confessed. "I could really use your help now."

"Happy to do what I can," her voice broadcasting that she was determined to do just that.

I took a few moments to explain the situation to her.

"Sure, I can help," Ms. Bonet said. "Ronnie and I can sit together here for awhile, and when it's time, we'll find cots together. She can stay with me and my sister."

"I don't know how to thank you," I responded, genuinely thankful for this evacuee's intervention.

"You can't. I'll need to thank her, when she's ready, Ms. Bonet said looking over at Ms. Carson. "You see, I lost my parents to Katrina too."

"I had no idea . . ."

"Of course not!" she replied quietly. "How could you? Go on now and do your job. Ms. Carson, my sister, and I have some grieving to do, and some healing."

A nurse called to me that my next patient was ready. When I emerged from seeing them, the two ladies were gone. I never saw them again.

These evacuee recollections uncover the ghastly side of the Katrina catastrophe. People with no coping skills and little education were suddenly confronted with the destruction of their families and loved ones—the dismemberment of their lives. Hundreds of survivors had stories like these. Many had worse. The emotional damage will remain for years. All they have is the fellowship of friends and families.

Facing emotionally crushing decisions in solitude can shred the human spirit. These people needed the support of community, support of their city, and support of their nation. Their pain was not the disease; merely the symptom of the disease. The disease is the rejection of these gentle hearted people by the institutions they relied on but were AWOL.

CHAPTER 6

Young Mothers

The Katrina clinic wasn't just an area for medical treatment. It was *a flashpoint for feelings* as both evacuees and responders reacted to the suffering, deprivation, pain, and dislocations produced by the storm. Like Katrina herself, these reactions appeared and moved in unpredictable ways, churning up the spiritual soil with expressive emotional conflict, ripping new furrows with agitating passion.

The strongest of these emotional forces were undoubtedly generated by the mothers.

While many survivors were pushed to their limits, young mothers were hurled beyond theirs. The Katrina catastrophe threw many of these woman beyond what they could tolerate, bending and twisting them beyond recognition. They were stretched to supernatural limits, and survived due to supernatural strength.

Strong men could not bear what these diminutive women, some no older than fifteen, were forced to endure for the sake of their children. Attacked by acute stress, physical punishment, and serious illness, these women repeatedly and exquisitely balanced pain, sleeplessness and gnawing fear with the right touch of endurance and discipline, all held together by the tight, binding love for their children. They were by and large uneducated, but what they demonstrated could be found in no textbook. Their ability to withstand punishing fatigue and intense physical pain was incomparable. By just watching and listening to them, they compelled you to pay homage to the human spirit.

Two hours into my first shift at the Katrina clinic, I had my first young mother as a patient. I may have made a difference for her. To be honest, I don't think I did until the very end of our visit—I'm not really sure. However, if we had been operating a regular clinic where you paid for what you received, then *I* would be the one writing the check.

The nurse saw her first, carefully charting her vital signs, and writing a brief note that the woman had a sore throat and swollen glands. Walking into the room, I was surprised to see not one woman with her children, but four children of various ages. The youngest looked to be about three; the oldest was a young teenager. While three of them were sitting on the low cot to my left, the oldest was on the bed to my right. This oldest child was the fifteen-year-old mother, Donita Phillips.

The contrast between Ms. Phillips and the other three children astonished me. Ms. Phillips was the detritus of life. Dust completely encased her soft, dark face and scalp, and her full head of tangled hair hadn't been combed for days. Small abrasions in various stages of healing covered her face, neck and arms, and her feet were terribly contused and swollen.

Watching this short, broken young girl, the thought that *this was the most tired person I'd ever met!* shocked me like a physical blow. The fatigue didn't just pull at her red-rimmed eyes—it drew her cheeks, mouth, and jaws downward, as if the skin was being pulled off her face. Covered by weariness, the condition consumed her, hollowing her out. I couldn't begin to guess how long this young woman had gone without sleep—she looked as though she'd never slept.

Yet, the three younger children appeared fine. Between two and four years old, all were clean, hair combed and in place, each dressed in a new set of clean clothes. And they were awake and refreshed—the full force of life coursing through them. They reminded me of sisters sitting in church. They wanted to talk but, knowing that they shouldn't, followed their training and not their impulses. The contrast between these spotless, attentive children on the one hand, and Ms. Phillips on the other hand, was astonishing. It was like every drop of the essence of life had been painfully wrung out of Ms. Phillips and poured, renewed and refreshed, into each of her children.

106

Ms. Phillips had opened one eye as I approached her. She was not attentive to my introduction, to my questions, or, for that matter to my exam. Finally, I just put the chart down, sat with her so our faces were level, and asked "How can I help you, Ms. Phillips?" The thought *Antibiotics and twenty-four hours of sleep would be the best for this desperately tired woman* forced its way through my stunned mind.

I was way off.

She looked at me, and said, simply "I've lost my baby." Her head was up now, new tears following the dirty tracks of those that had flowed down her face before.

Instantly agitated, I asked, "You mean here, or in New Orleans?"

"She's gone!" Ms. Phillips replied, in as agitated a voice as her cloak of fatigue would allow. "I think she got pulled away!"

Emergency! my mind shouted at me. If the child was missing at the Reliant Arena, I would need help, and help fast. A search must commence at once! "I would like to try to help you," I stated, failing to keep the alarm out of my voice. "Please, can you tell me about this?"

Her head aching with the lack of sleep, Ms. Phillips began to speak in soft, slurred, but understandable words. Her children and I listened alertly, her phrases swaying heavily in a deep, southern accent.

"The five of us were in our home. When the water started to run along the streets, I knew we had to get out of there. I never moved as fast as I did those few minutes, getting my four girls ready. I got us over to Mom's house, which was on higher ground."

"Go on, please, Ms. Phillips," I urged. "I need to know about your missing child!"

"But I left so fast, I forgot to pick up some things we needed. So, I went back to get them. When I came outside, the water was already up to my waist." Ms. Phillips was less than five feet tall.

She then made the one statement that began for me one of the most horrifying conversations I'll ever have.

"You know," she continued, allowing her eyes to meet mine for the first time, "the worst thing about wading through that water was a manhole cover."

"Manhole cover?" I repeated, completely confused. "What do you mean?" *What are you doing listening to this?* my mind raged. *You have to find out where that child was lost!*

"Many times," she said, in a dry monotone, "the rush of all of that water pushed the manhole covers off, making a hole in the street."

"Yes . . ." I said, still not clued in.

"It makes a hole that you can get caught in as you try to walk through the dirty water."

"A hole you couldn't see, right?" I asked, my concern for the missing baby pushed aside by a new, thick revulsion to what I feared was coming.

"Yeah. You would be walking along, and suddenly, you would fall down into one of those holes. If you fell all the way down you could drown. I think some people died that way. Most times you would have a big swallow of that water as you got pulled under. Parents were all afraid of them. That's why we didn't want our children walking in the water if you couldn't see the bottom. If your baby fell into one of those holes, she would be . . . be gone. OH!!" she cried out suddenly.

My stomach turned over and my mind reeled with this new horror. Anybody walking through this water in the streets was in danger of serious disease, even death from the fetid water. Full of dirt, sewage, dead bodies and petroleum waste, this mixture was toxic to the skin. We were already seeing thick running sores full of blood and pus that required immediate antibiotic therapy. The effect of a mouthful of this poison was particularly ghastly. And, when you fell into one, you didn't just get a mouthful. You got a stomach-full. And that's if you were lucky. An unlucky little girl would actually breathe the fluid in. Her lungs, already working overtime for air, would receive a ghastly mix of liquid waste and gasoline that could hardly be considered water anymore.

"NO. NO!" she cried.

And, worse than that, a young child, only three-feet-high would fall right through the open manhole. Right to the bottom. She would disappear suddenly, falling rapidly through tens of feet. Instantly, the toxic slush would slide into her, filling her mouth, nose, and eyes with the poison. Frightened, she would inhale it into her lungs, where it would kill her in two to three minutes. In the dark, and alone.

"MY BABY'S GONE!"

Over a period of twenty-five years, I had seen some ghastly injuries. Dog bites, machine accidents, traumatic amputations, even a decapitation. Yet, until this moment in my career, I never wanted to bolt from a patient's room as I did right now. I didn't think I could bear what I feared I would hear. But, there was no way I could leave her alone, as she explained to me what happened to her child.

"Ms. Phillips, pl . . . please finish . . . ," I pleaded, my stuttering betraying my own nervousness.

"When I got back to where my girls were, there were only the three waiting for me. Their grandmother took the baby, and told the others that I would be back for them. The three were waiting for me when I got there. But I don't know what happened to my mom and my baby?"

"But . . ."

"My three remaining children and I just had to walk," Ms. Phillips said. "I got out in front of them, and they followed, each holding the hand of the one in front and one behind. We walked connected that way in the dark afternoon through the water. I tried so hard to remember where the manholes were, but I couldn't. I was just too scared. Shisha," she said, pointing to the biggest child, "fell in one. My heart stopped! I reached back to get her, and missed her hand. I turned around and reached out to her with both hands and caught her hair. I pulled her up by her hair!" Ms. Phillips was crying again now, her three small children holding on to each other, watching their mother. "If I hadn't done that, she'd have been pulled away. I wanted to stop right there. I wanted to go home! But, I had my three babies so we had to keep going, going, going through the water. I tried to feel my way through to avoid the manholes, but couldn't. I stumbled into three more of them."

"Is that where you got your bruises?" I asked.

"Most of them, I guess," she said, wincing some. "Two on my thigh where I fell against the side of the hole. This one on my lip was from the third," she answered. "But, my other baby . . ."

I looked over to her children. Not a scratch on them. Perfectly healthy. They had been protected for the entire time by this mother, a child herself. "Their grand mom and your baby didn't come to Houston?" I fearfully asked.

"I don't see how? My mom's not strong. She couldn't have held Tamika if Tamika fell, and children were falling everywhere in that water. I think . . . I think."

"But you don't know that Tamika got pulled away, right?" I interrupted. I was as desperate to convince myself as well as Ms. Phillips that her fear, now our fear, didn't come to pass, while fighting to control my own raw emotions at the specter of this mother losing her youngest child, and perhaps her mom, down one of the septic holes in the city's squalid streets.

"I don't know," she repeated. I haven't seen her or her grand mom since I went back to my house to get the things."

"Ms. Phillips . . . ," I began and then paused, searching for words, "you are the bravest person I have ever met." I along with everyone I know believes that their mother would do what I had just heard described. Ms. Phillips had actually done it.

She looked at me through tired eyes.

"I've given you some medication to help your infection," I said, struggling to get back on track with my young patient's care. "It's good medicine, and you will start getting better from your throat infection tonight. But," I continued, "you have other problems. You haven't had nearly enough water to drink. And I am concerned for what that dirty water did to you." Concerned wasn't half of it. I was frightened for this brave woman. *How big a price must she pay for her children?* I wondered.

"Yes, but my babies are drinking enough," Ms. Phillips replied. She was right. The three children across from me were well hydrated. The contrast between the appearance of these well nourished, well groomed children and their shattered mother couldn't have been more striking.

I persisted. "You have to take care of yourself. When was your last good meal?"

"Three, maybe four days ago."

"I don't want to ask you how long it has been since you have gotten some sleep."

"I haven't slept since we left home on Monday." This was now Friday.

I tried something else. "You want to be a good mom for your children, but how good a mom can you be now, when you are so run down like this? You're worn out, and sick. Your mind is shredded by fatigue. You haven't gotten sleep in sixty hours. You may have to make some important decisions for your children and yourself in the next few days. You can't make the best choices when you are run down like this. "You know," I finished, "sometimes, not all of the time, but sometimes, the best way to take care of a loved one is to first take care of yourself. I think you have to do that now."

"My baby's gone. She's been pulled away! I HAVE TO KNOW!" she responded, crying again.

The skin on my forehead began to tighten and my stomach convulsed with a new spasm of despair. I needed, yet was failing, to convince this young mother that she would age five years worth in five days if she didn't start to take her own healthcare seriously. Yet the missing child's status was an acute emergency as well. She, so completely broken down, couldn't support the search for her child, but I didn't want to alienate her.

Not knowing what else to do, I changed the topic. Pointing to a black, dirty trash bag that she brought into the small room with her, I asked, "What do you have there?"

"Everything I brought with me."

"Oh. These are some of your belongings? Can you show some of them to me?"

She nodded, slowly sliding off the cot to the floor.

The bag was full. She reached in and pulled out three dolls. Each of the children reacted at once.

"Mom! You brought my doll!"

"Mom, you remembered!"

"Mommie! Mommie!"

The first smile I had seen emerged from this broken mother's face as she handed the dolls gently to each of them, one at a time. The motion was soft and complex as she wouldn't just hand each figure over, but paused in the midst of the giving over each of them, gently stroking their hand, or hair, or face. For a moment, I glimpsed a loving though incomplete family at home.

Looking into the bag, I saw clothes. Ms. Phillips was a small woman, but as I looked at the size of these clothes I knew they couldn't be hers. I made the connection instantly.

"For the children?" I asked.

"Yeah," she replied tiredly. "It's what they needed."

111

"Well," I asked, already knowing the answer to the question that I would ask, "where are your things?"

"Didn't bring any. No time."

I slumped back against the wall, overcome with emotion. This gentle child-woman, after bringing her children to the safety of their grandmother's house, returned to her own home, returning with only her children's things! Ignoring her own possessions. No money. No papers. No personal items. She carried what the children needed to be happy. And she made herself sick, almost drowning in poisoned water in the process.

I knew then, that I had absolutely no chance of convincing this mother that she needed to begin to care for herself until she found out what had happened to her child. I looked at her from a mind emptied of useful ideas.

Then, a miracle.

"What's that in your pocket?" she asked pointing at my white jacket.

My cell phone was exposed in my lab coat. I took it out to show to her, "Just a phone," I replied. *Had she not seen one of these before? I wondered.*

"Can I make some calls please to find my family?"

"Ms. Phillips," I responded placing the small instrument in her hand, "make all of the calls you need." Maybe a phone call to a relative would get her the answer she both dreaded and needed.

"Well, I'm going to be using some of your minutes. Is that OK?"

Incredible! She was afraid I'd get mad if she used my phone too long! After all she had been through, she was actually sitting here worrying about my cell phone bill! She didn't know that I'd have given the phone to her. *No, I thought. I'd pay her to take it!*

Use it . . . use it as long as you need to," I answered softly, leaving the room to her, her children, and her desperate phone calls.

I returned in fifteen minutes. She was still on the phone, but in animated conversation. I walked out again and caught up on some charting, praying that she was hearing good, or at least promising, news about her missing child.

Ms. Phillips came out in a minute.

"My mom's already here in Houston!" she exclaimed. "They're at another shelter."

"And your baby," I asked, not daring to breathe.

"Fine! She's OK!"

Sweet relief washed over us both. She gave me the name of the shelter, and I called for a volunteer at once. A young woman rushed over, taking down all of the information about the location of the grandmother and grandchild as it spilled from the thankful Ms. Phillips' parched lips.

The transformation was immediate. Her face was one of peace. Not childlike, but just not eaten away by the blunt buzz saw of anguish. Ms. Phillips was a woman healing the right way—from the inside out. This mother's emotional conflict had come to an end. She knew where her family was and would soon be reunited with them. I discharged the Phillips family from the clinic and had to leave the clinic for a few minutes, trying and failing to wrap my mind around what I had just seen and heard.

The uncommon strength Ms. Phillips had demonstrated was the common reaction of these young girls who had become mothers. They fought with everything they had for their sons and daughters. With absolutely no mental preparation and with minimal warning, their lives were thrown into upheaval and their families devastated and separated. And they fought. No older than children themselves, with little recognizable education, poor diction, grievous healthcare, sometimes already obese and suffering from diseases that, left unchecked, would kill them. Hypertension and diabetes were already putting nails in the coffins of these young mothers. All they knew how to do was to be the best mothers they could be. Ground to nothing, mere shadows of their former selves, these women continued to risk their own lives with energy they should no longer have had, searching for their children, and struggling to put their families back together.

The week of August 29th, didn't just threaten these young mothers with deceased children, but also with deceased husbands.

Walking into the clinic, a young woman labored to breathe, clearly in respiratory distress. Her chest heaved outward as she unsuccessfully tried to force open the narrow living tubes that move air into her lungs. Muscles in her neck, desperately trying to keep her from asphyxiating, contracted wildly, trying to help as well. She was drenched in sweat from the process, her wide eyes betraying her shock and fear at no longer being able to get fresh air into her lungs. Ripping the stethoscope out of my pocket, I quickly listened to her lungs through her clothes.

Ms. Sally Thompson's bronchial tree, under chronic attack from the stress, the filthy water that she had inhaled, and her inability to take any medicine for her asthma, was losing its integrity, and the thousands of living airways in her lungs that she relied upon to stay open to deliver clean, moist air were breaking down. Her lungs, starved for oxygen demanded that she breathe and she valiantly complied, struggling for breath, using every muscle, from her navel to her jaw, to try to move air. But the narrowed airways guaranteed that her efforts would be in vain.

Recognizing the emergency, Lisa, the nurse, and I rushed to save this seriously ill patient who was losing the fight to get air into her lungs. Her children watched in silent shock, their minds unable to translate the horror of their mother's distress into vocal concern. They were simply too frightened to cry.

Do we have any epi around?" I asked. It could cause other problems, but right now, a little epinephrine under the skin would begin to reverse the airway closure that was not letting the air she breathed into her lungs.

"Nothing like that," Lisa responded, "but we have some ventilin."

"Let's go with that," I said, helping Ms. Thompson into the exam room, her children following behind.

Once in room number eight, Lisa and I fumbled to put the antiquated ventilator together. We knew that if we could get Ms. Thompson to begin to inhale some medicated air, she would improve at once. But the delivery system was old, with several pieces of plastic that had to be fitted together on top of an oxygen tank, so that the fresh oxygen would flow from the tank into some fluid that dissolved the medicine and then turn into a mist that she could breathe in. Her three children were on the cot, watching the nurse and me fumble as we tried to help their mom.

We were so close to finishing the assembly, but Ms. Thompson's distress signaled that we were running out of time.

"I think that piece goes right here!" I declared, trying and failing to get it to fit on the tank.

I glanced at the children, who sat, faces fixed on their mother. When their mom sweated, so did they. One brought her own little hands to her chest as she watched her mother struggle for air.

"No, wrong way! Reverse it!" Lisa responded, herself sweating from the haste of our work.

"There!" I said. Finally, the air was coming out of the mask.

We instantly applied it to Ms. Thompson's anguished, sweat-drenched face. We both felt as well as heard the fresh cool medicated air flow out of the mask and into her nose and mouth.

It would take several minutes to see if the medication would work. If it failed, she would have to go to the hospital. I groaned inwardly at the idea of putting this family through yet one more dislocation in their jarred and shaken lives. But if the approach we were trying didn't produce an improvement in a couple of minutes, and I didn't send her to the hospital, she would die. There was nothing to do now but wait and count down the long seconds.

"This is good medicine, girls" I said, crouching down to talk to them face to face. "I think she'll be OK." I don't know if they listened to me, but I know that they had eyes only for their mom.

It would have been unforgivable, even cruel for me to ever have allowed children to see this scene in ordinary circumstances. But, given what I had learned about these survivors and the angst that separation between mother and child could cause, I was loath to disconnect them. So I talked to the mother and the children for the next couple of minutes. Finally the medicine began to work. As Ms. Thompson's breath came more easily, she stopped sweating and was able to relax some. With that, her three children began to relax. I relaxed some along with everyone else. That didn't last long.

The mother was breathing better, but the asthma medication had not been able to drive the sadness from her eyes. I had to ask: "I think this medicine has helped you. But you look like something is troubling you. Do you have all of your children here, Ms. Thompson?"

"Yes. These are all of my children. It's their Dad"

"Where is he?"

"He passed." I was struck by her attitude. She did not break down. She wasn't hysterical. She was—plain. Matter of fact.

"Oh. When"

"Just this week"

Ms. Thompson, I will listen if you would like to talk about any of this."

"Not much to say about it really," she replied. "He asked us to wait for him at our house. He said he would be about ten minutes. Then, a neighbor came to tell me they saw my husband in the water. Floating. Twisting around. They tried to help him but it was too late. He was dead. He may have hit his head on something in that dirty water. The water was full of pieces of rock, chunks of metal, that kind of thing."

"Oh! I'm so sorry," I uttered.

"It wasn't like walking across a stream. It was like walking in a rushing river," she replied.

Not just a rushing river, I thought, *but a rushing river full of fast moving and dangerous debris.*

By this time at the clinic, we had counselors and even at times had one or two psychiatrists. I offered her the chance to see them. But she just sat there. Her head began to hang. This time, the problem wasn't her asthma. It wasn't her breath that she was losing. It was her spirit, gored out by the past five days.

"Mommy!" It was a chorus ·the three children cried at once. Startling me, startling the nurse who was walking just outside the small tent-room. The young mother, herself no older than seventeen, looked up, like a dead woman infused with life. She looked at her children with a trace of a smile on her face, saying simply, in a thin, reedy voice, "Babies!"

They came to her, holding on tight to each other. I was in the way now.

Stepping out, I wrote a few prescriptions. So moved was I by the powerful scene I was part of, that I fumbled writing the scripts for Ms. Thompson's allergy refill. This woman was a danger to no one. She threatened no one. She wasn't even asking for her "fair share of the American pie." Sally Thompson would have been content, even

thankful if the world had left her alone in her poverty. She never wanted a house like the rich, in fact, she wouldn't have known what to do
with it. She simply ached to keep her family together. *What has she
done,* I wondered, *that so many belittle her for her station in life.*

I finished writing her prescriptions. Walking back in the room, everybody was wiping the tears from their eyes, trying to be presentable.

"Ms. Thompson, I am not a psychiatrist or a specialist. I'm just a
doctor. I will be working here the next few days. I would be happy if
you would come back to see me here at the clinic. If you would like,
I would like to hear more from you. I will advise you if you think that
will help. I can give some guidance if you like. But I will always listen
to you."

Holding one of her children in her arms, she said, "Thank you.
Everybody here has been so helpful for us. Some other people said
that they would help me as well. I'm almost ready to talk some more.
Not yet, but soon. I don't know why we had to leave our homes, our
city, to get this help."

"Well, you have a new home here, if you like."

"Yes," she replied with new fatigue filling her voice. "New Orleans
is dead now. We won't go back."

I left the room thinking: *Why does America choose to listen to the terrible things that were said about women like her, and not take the time
to hear her story?"*

On the way out of the exam room one of Ms. Thompson's children pulled on my coat. She said. "You were nice to help my mom."

I leaned over again, "You think I did a lot to help your mom?"

She simply nodded.

"Your mom is the most important person in the world. When she
needs help, we all have to stop what we're doing to take care of her."

It wasn't false modesty. Any one of several hundred doctors and
nurses could have assisted this woman. There were lots of people to
help her. Doctors and nurses were readily available. But there was only
one mom for these children.

After the Thompsons had left, I got to take a break for a few minutes. The number of adult patients had declined, the slack being taken

up by pediatric cases. In room after room there were children. Some were sick and quiet, an especially worrisome set of circumstances. A child who didn't come to a doctor crying was a danger sign. Others were there for relatively minor problems. A terrible new rash from walking through the polluted New Orleans street waters. A flare-up of their asthma. They have run out of their seizure medicine. A foreign body in an eye. And in every case, the mother was right there. Another doctor and I fell into a brief conversation.

"I'm not seeing what I thought I would here," I began. "I knew I had an imagination, but it did not prepare me for the experiences of these women."

"Yeah, the problems are primarily small ones now," he replied. Most of the patients that I see just need their medication refilled."

"That's not what I meant," I answered. I've seen a lot of Moms today. I have to say I am just amazed at the extent to which they go to look after their children."

"Yeah. I don't see how they put up with so much and kept it together," he observed.

"They don't leave their children alone," I continued. "These young women sacrifice everything of themselves just to stay with their children. Mothers who themselves need to be seen, are too busy protecting their kids. Most parents believe they would take a bullet for their children. These mothers take bullets every day for them."

"Yeah, they're pretty watchful of their children," he sighed. "Guess you can't blame them for that."

"Well,' I continued, "it just isn't the image I've been catching from TV"

"The mothers we're seeing don't represent the average mom, right?" he asked. "I heard a commentator say that we may be seeing the best of them, since the other moms just stayed in New Orleans, and, well, didn't care to leave. So the women we see here don't represent what they as a group were really like."

The next comment was out of my mouth before I knew I even thought it.

"Well, that's always possible, but you know, it could also be true that the very best of the mothers *died* with their children trying to get out. So, we never got to observe those truly exquisite mothers. I guess the commentator said nothing about that possibility, did they?"

"Uh . . . No." Pointing over to the triage center, he said, "Well, it looks like more patients on the way."

In all of the hours I spent treating patients at this clinic, I saw only one outburst of anger. It was a mother who felt that her child was not being seen quickly enough. She was loud, she was angry. No. She was *furious*!

"My child needs to be seen. Right now! Why won't anybody see my baby?!" she protested.

Not to be reasoned with or consoled, this mother would not cease her tirade until she got what she demanded. As the pediatrician and then the nurse came rushing over to assure her that they were caring for her child, I thought I noticed something else, another feeling that moved across this mother's face. After a half hour had passed, and she and her child were walking out, I was washing my hands at one of the many sinks in the warehouse that was now filled with equipment.

I introduced myself to Ms. J.J. Summers and her four year old, Letty, then asked her to sit down with me. I really didn't want this conversation to spin out of control, and I certainly did not want to reignite her frustration, so I started slowly.

"I'm a doctor here, and I want to first make sure that you are comfortable with how Letty is doing," I began. "One of the mistakes we doctors commonly make is using very large words for very small facts. That's our fault, not yours, and even though we may believe your child is doing well, we have to say it in a way that makes sense to you. I just want to make sure that you are OK and that all of your questions have been answered."

"I feel better now," she started. Anyone could see from her watchful eyes that her guard was way up.

"If you don't understand how your Letty is doing, that's our fault as well. If you like, I would be happy to answer any questions that I can about your daughter." I was stepping on another doctor's turf here, I suppose. But, I needed to be sure that she was satisfied before I proceeded.

She sat very still, saying nothing.

"There is a lot to be angry about these last few days. But you know, when I looked at you about a half hour ago, you didn't seem angry to me."

"No?"

"No. You seemed to me to be hurt."

"Well, I was!" she instantly responded. "Even though you all are working hard to be good to us, it only takes a small thing to make me feel like I'm right back in New Orleans. I don't really understand it myself," she confessed.

"Where were you in New Orleans when you got out?" I asked.

"The Convention Center," she responded at once. "That's where they told us to go. We thought we would be safe there. What a lie! It soon became a miserable place. When no one showed up to clean the bathrooms, we tried to get some groups together to start to clean them up ourselves. But there were just too many people. Some people were, you know, using the bathroom on the open floors there."

"Sounds horrible," I said, feeling my stomach convulse.

"Nobody was organized," this articulate woman continued. "What are people supposed to do? We tried to organize ourselves. Every time we did, there was more information coming in to us telling us help was on the way. We would wait, the help wouldn't come, and things would get worse. We would try to organize, and the same thing would happen. Are people supposed to not use the bathroom for five days? We tried to keep things together there, but there were too many tired people and too little good information."

"And that hurts . . ."

"It hurts to feel that you don't count. It hurts to feel that the love of your life doesn't count. It hurts to learn you are being lied to by people who you thought, who told you that you'd be helped. And, you know, it's going to be a long time for that pain to go away."

She stopped and squinted some. "I get these headaches now. They're new, and they're from what we just went through. But," she said, now stroking her child's back, "that's OK because I know it will be better in a few days. But the feelings that come from being treated like we were worthless, like we were forgotten. Like we were trash to be left there, to be picked up whenever they felt like it. That won't go away. You know, I don't know if time is going to fix that."

For this wary mother, New Orleans and the system had betrayed her, and her acute reaction was to be wary and to test the offers of assurance by others. This mother was deeply hurt in parts of her that the flood waters never touched.

"Well, let me ask you," I said. "What do you need from me and the others here?" pointing to the scurrying doctors, nurses, volunteers, and administrators. "How can we help with this now? You just tell us. What do we need to know?"

"Give us a chance to show you the kind of people we are. Look. We're like you. No different. Maybe poorer, maybe not enough school. But we're people! Just like you. We want what you give each other, but don't give us. This is not about money. It's just about being human. The only difference between you and my daughter is who your parents were.

"Now that we're in Houston," she continued, "we get to watch television. They have the huge screens on in where we stay during the day, and we get to see what happened. But what they show is not how it was. I mean, they got the facts right, but it's not how it really was," she said.

"What was different?"

"That wasn't how *we* were."

I thought I knew what she was saying, so I tried. "TV showed the what. It didn't show the why," I offered.

"No. It didn't even get the 'what' right. TV concentrates on all that happened at the Convention Center. We didn't all get there to protest. We were there because the people we trusted told us to go there. What would they have thought of us if we hadn't gone to the Convention Center? That we were not following their plans? When we did what they said, they didn't do what they said they would do. And the promises were worse.

"The promises of water—water that never came. The promises of food that never came. How about the promises to bury the dead? There were children playing within a few feet of dead people! They told us when to expect help, but what we were told didn't count. And we tried to do for ourselves. But more people kept arriving! Most were good, but some were angry. Angry and out of control. They weren't angry at each other. They were angry at the situation. They were angry that we were being disrespected. They thought that we were being laughed at by the people who were supposed to help us. That is a painful, new wound, and they began to lash out. They were wrong to do that. It made it tough for us all. A situation that was unhealthy was now becoming violent and unsafe. But they weren't the only ones who made bad choices. The people we relied on let us down. We just weren't prepared for that."

"What do you think that you'll do now?"

"What I'm not doing is going back," she replied at once, raising her voice some. "I'm not going back to New Orleans. I may get back to Louisiana, but I am not ever going back to New Orleans. It's not because of the hurricane. We could get through a hurricane. It's because of how I was treated. By people who should have known better."

She rocked her child back and forth in her arms. "No, sir. No New Orleans."

I walked back to the clinic—and right into a conflict. A young, obese woman with shoulder length, straight hair was standing right between the adult and pediatric sections of the clinic straining to push through several nurses, shouting repeatedly "No, No, NO!!" Three nurses had gathered around her, working to both restrain and to soothe her. But this tough woman wouldn't stop. She wasn't trying to hurt the nurses, but she struggled and shoved, to push through them. "No!" she cried again as the nurses struggled to force the five-foot-tall woman, dressed in dirty red sweat pants and a gray T-shirt, into a chair. But the defiant woman—sick, scruffy, tired, and young—wouldn't stop.

A quick look to the right revealed the problem. One of the nurses was carrying a child into a pediatric room. The child, dirty and dehydrated, resting her small head quietly on the nurse's shoulder, resembled the struggling mother with the same long black hair and large dark eyes. The mother, eyes blazing, kept her intense gaze focused on the child as she was pulled away. After spending three days at the

Katrina clinic both the nurses and I understood what was going on and tried to explain.

"Ms. Ramirez, you also need to see the doctors." Pointing off to the left, the nurses said, "This is where they will treat you. Your daughter will be close by." But, the angry, defiant Ms. Ramirez wanted none of it. She wanted, insisted, demanded that she be right with her child, Nina.

I hadn't yet been assigned to her, but felt compelled to start working with this determined woman. After introducing myself, I explained, raising my voice to be heard, "Ms. Ramirez. Ms. Ramirez! Look at me. Please! Your daughter is going in that room over there," pointing in front of her. "I would like to see and take care of you in this room," now pointing to the right. "These rooms are only fifty feet apart. I promise you, I promise you, Ms. Ramirez, that, if they are finished treating your daughter first, then they will bring her over to see you." The nurse holding the quiet child nodded in agreement, looking right at the agitated young mother.

"On the other hand, if you and I finish first, then I will bring you over to see your daughter. Is that OK? Can we please take care of both of you at the same time. We only want to help you both get better." Lowering my voice some, I finished, "That's all we want to do, I promise."

Ms. Ramirez was acutely ill. Hot to the touch, she had suddenly stopped resisting, and was starting to retch. A volunteer quickly snatched an emesis basin from a nearby table, and Ms. Ramirez vomited into it. Finishing, she collapsed back toward a chair, but, missing it completely, fell sprawling to the floor. Helping her back to her seat, two nurses and I coaxed her to Exam Room Eight in the adult section, where she lay down on the cot. Finally, the combination of the nurses and me and her illness convinced her to stop fighting us all.

I was wrong again.

The nurses left and I tried to talk to her. However, Ms. Ramirez, profusely sweating, wanted nothing to do with my conversation. She jumped right up at me, grasping my coat, trying to pull my face down to where we would be face to face.

"Where is my baby?" she demanded, her disheveled hair falling across her face.

I was so startled I almost pitched forward, knocking us both to the ground. "Ms. Ramirez," I began, trying to recover my balance. "She is right where you saw her go, right where I said she would go. A doctor is seeing her right now."

"I have to see," she demanded, not letting go.

I would not fight this woman. "Of course you can. Anytime you like. Let's go."

She let go, I opened the curtain and we walked the few feet over to the pediatric area together, with me holding her arm to steady her. Clearly ill, struggling to breathe, she was beginning to shiver. Breaking free of my grip, she hurried over to her daughter's room, where we both saw her child being cared for by a pediatrician and two nurses. The young girl opened her eyes. Already looking better from the fluids and the gentle treatment by the pediatrician and the nurses, she smiled at her mom. That smile from this recovering daughter to her mom transmitted more than anything I might say. But, I tried anyway.

"See," I said, looking at Ms. Ramirez as she gazed at her daughter, "She's getting good care. Won't you please come back now?"

Again we walked back to Room Eight. Again, her agitation increased the further we got from the room. Once in Number Eight, this fatigued, ill mother demanded.

"Where is my child? Is my child OK?"

Two additional times I abruptly interrupted my exam of this sick, unyielding young woman. Then, I finally got the message.

"Ms. Ramirez," I said, while putting my stethoscope away for good, "not only can you see your child, you can wait with her." We walked down to her child's room again, and I spoke to the pediatrician for a moment. The pediatrician, having worked the clinic for several hours, already knew my question and the answer. Ms. Ramirez collapsed into a chair, took hold of her daughter's hand, and did not let go for the duration of the child's treatment. In other conditions, I might have been more insistent on the separation of a clearly sick mother from her weakened child. But the rules were different at the Katrina Clinic.

One half hour later, Ms. Ramirez was back in the adult area with her child. Of course, I gave the child the best seat in the room which happened to be a cot. It was just across the room from the table where her mother sat, only a few feet away. Looking better, she was more energetic, engaging herself in some solitary game. After I examined and treated Ms. Ramirez for her viral infection and her dehydration, Ms. Ramirez was herself feeling better, and started a conversation with an apology and a smile.

"I'm sorry, doctor, but you have to understand, you do not leave your child alone."

"Well," I said, smiling back, "I understand now. You were pretty insistent, and I realized I was wrong to get in your way. You didn't know that she was safe with us?"

"That's not good enough," Ms. Ramirez responded at once. "'Knowing' is not *knowing*. Seeing and touching is the only way to know."

"You know, I hadn't heard that before."

"You learn that at the Superdome."

By now, everyone had heard the stories about the Superdome. It was all over the media. Beatings. Rapes. Torture. It took years to build, but, in the space of four days, Katrina, the levees, government indifference or worse and the media had together reduced the Superdome from a great sports center to a symbol of gutter depravity.

"Tell me what happened if you would like, but only if you want to," I offered.

"Well, we got there on Sunday because we had no way to get out of the city," she started. "Nina," looking over at her daughter, "and I had never been there before, and we were kind of looking forward to it. And, actually, it started out pretty nicely. People were calm. We met and spoke to other families there. Nina made some new friends. We were all relieved that we were being protected from the storm. It was kind of like a Sunday outing without much food."

"Why didn't you take any food?"

"Well, it wasn't like a church picnic you know," she replied with a smile to soften her response to my naiveté. "We had to get out of the house quickly. The rain was coming down hard, and I didn't have a lot of time to prepare to leave our home. All I had time to do was grab a change of clothes for Nina. Some people got food, but we didn't.

There was water, but it wasn't enough for everyone, and it didn't last long."

"I saw that the roof of the dome ripped," I said.

"That was early during our stay, and it was a real problem. All Monday morning when the winds got bad, it sounded like somebody was pounding away on the roof, tearing at it. Finally part of it ripped away. But, you know, it wasn't getting wet that was so bad."

"What was it?" I inquired.

"It was the sense that things weren't going the way they were supposed to. Nobody thought the roof would come apart. It was a real shock when it happened. When it did, we all began to feel that things were starting to spin out of control." She stopped for a second, sweeping her long hair back out of her face. Getting up, she went over to hug Nina. Delighted with the attention, the child hugged back. Ms. Ramirez brought her back over on the exam table with her. With her child in her arms, she began talking again.

"That was when people started being afraid. When the roof came off, we didn't know what to expect. But even then, we still thought we would leave the next day, on Tuesday.

"The bathrooms were already getting bad late on Monday. Nobody was cleaning them. We did the best we could with it all. People were still trying to be friendly. Most of us were getting along, and we still expected to leave the next day. I told Nina 'We'll leave soon. Don't worry. We get to go home tomorrow.' That didn't happen."

"Tuesday morning, we learned that we weren't going anywhere. We couldn't go home, even if we wanted. There was a little drinking water left, but it was hard to find. Food was gone. Up to this point, we were ready to leave but knew that we would have to wait the storm out. Nobody really expected to leave before Tuesday. Now, nobody could leave. *We volunteered to come. Now, we were forced to stay.*"

"Then the rumors started. 'We could leave later on Tuesday', we heard. That was a lie. Then, we heard that we could leave Tuesday night. That was a lie also. We couldn't believe anything anymore. After the rain stopped on Tuesday, it got hot. Very hot. There was no cool place anywhere, and no breeze. The heat made the stinking bathrooms much, much worse. There was so much . . . mess on the bathroom floors. Many of us had only slippers or just bare feet.

You couldn't even walk to the toilets. You couldn't use them. It was against everything I had taught Nina to use a place like that. But you had to. No mother wanted her child in there. But kids and adults had to use them." She made a terrible face and shivered, reliving the experience.

"We all knew now that things were out of control," she said simply.

What had been a collection of thankful evacuees, gladly accepting brief protection from a terrible storm, was now a huddled, unprotected mass, sealed off from the world they knew. Families, wanting only refuge from the storm, were now trapped. They were penned in without food, without water, in conditions worse than animals. No one could leave and no one knew when it would end. These people, these families, were now caged and abandoned.

"People began getting sick and throwing up," Ms. Ramirez continued. "Anywhere. Everywhere. Many tried to make it to the bathrooms, but it was too difficult. The floor where people tried to sleep became sticky with trash, water, urine, throw-up and much, much worse. You tried not to lay in it, but you couldn't keep standing all the time. And it was crowded. The air stank with all of the mess, with all of the garbage, with all of the people." Then, more quietly, she said, "with all of us."

"But you survived it all," I responded, trying and failing to inject a tone of optimism into this dark conversation.

"Not all of us. People were getting sick, but there was no place to take them. Both the dead and the living lay still. Then, just when we thought it couldn't get worse, the violence started.

"Some people had gotten into the dome with knives. Others had gotten in with guns. We . . . "

"Wasn't there security available?" I blurted out. Even the smallest airports have security, and having attended stadium events recently, I knew all customers had to pass through metal detectors and have bags searched.

Ms. Ramirez simply shrugged "Some got through with weapons. Suddenly, one night, we heard 'BOOM!' followed by shrieks, and people running in all directions. I thought it was thunder, but a man next to me, sick like we all were, smelling bad like we all did, said, 'I think that was a gunshot.'

"'Maybe the police shot somebody?' I remember asking," Ms. Ramirez continued.

"Getting up quickly, he turned to look at me 'The police? I haven't seen police here and it's been three days. Have you?' He got up quickly and moved. I never saw him again."

To me, it didn't sound like Ms. Ramirez was describing a refuge. She was describing a jail-like environment where violent convicts were taking control.

"First they started with robberies," she continued. "But then things began to get physical."

With her daughter there, I was suddenly uncomfortable where this conversation might go, but, as usual, I was no match for these mothers. She knew how far to go.

"You know. There wasn't a lot of shooting. It wasn't like there were raging gun battles. But there was enough. 'BLAMM!' followed by the screams and the running. Enough to keep us all frightened. It was the fear of violence, never-ending violence, that was the worst. The terrible feeling that you could not be safe was with you every single second. It wouldn't let you sleep. Regardless of where you were, you thought you would be next. That, through no fault of your own, you would be singled out. That you would have to decide whether you would be shot or held at knifepoint while a wife, sister, or child was... hurt.

"When you hear the screams and the agony of the violent attack, rising above the groans of the sick and dying in that hot, stinking air, the fear drills down your back like a giant corkscrew, twisting you up inside. Your hair stands on end and your mouth fills with a terrible taste, like sour milk and turpentine."

Looking over at her daughter, who was asleep, Ms. Ramirez said to me, "You know, I knew that I would die, and that made it all right."

I had followed this ghastly horror story so far, but now I was lost. "What do you mean?" I was talking as quietly as she was.

"Because I decided to die for my baby. They would have to kill me to get to her. You know. I thought I would always give everything up for her. Buy her what she needs, not what I need, look after her health before mine. That kind of thing. But it wasn't until that night that I realized that I might have to die for her. Really lose my life for her."

The nurse was going by my room, giving me a signal that she had another patient ready for me to see, but I wasn't willing to end our conversation just yet.

"I knew the answer before I even finished asking the question," Ms. Ramirez continued. "If someone came at her, I would die. I mean, I would fight, and yell, kick and scream, bite and punch and scratch until they had to kill me. Putting a knife to my throat wouldn't stop me. Pointing a gun at my face wouldn't keep me from fighting back. That night, in all that stink, I had the cleanest thought of my life. 'Tonight, I will die for my Nina.' It was all right after that."

"You weren't still scared?"

"Oh sure I was scared," she said, her eyes half closing, fatigue closing in. "All of us with families were. Now, though, I was scared *and ready*. That was a big difference for me. I would talk about this with other women who had children there when it was light. We didn't deserve this hell. But, we were where we were. Nothing could change that. We had to be strong for our children. That meant being willing to die for them."

"You got out of there, though, without being harmed."

"Yes," she said, nodding her head. "Most all of us did. But I never let her out of my sight during the whole time we were there. We were always holding hands. When she slept, I held her and watched over her. When we had to use 'those things'," she said, referring to the bathrooms and making a face and holding her hand up, "we went together. To let my baby out of my sight was to lose her. I made up my mind. I would fight and hold on to her. Three more nights or three hundred more nights. Whatever it took. If we were there forever, I would fight forever. There were no more decisions to make. No more thinking to do. It was settled. Each night, I prepared to die for my Nina."

"Ms. Ramirez, it's lucky for us all that you didn't have to die. The more mothers like you on this planet, the better and safer we all are. Thanks for talking with me."

She got herself off the cot, clearly sore, plainly bone-tired. When she leaned over to wake her Nina up, the child, now feeling better, now safe, reached up for her. Her mom's tired eyes lit up, and they hugged each other. Now rising to a standing position, this young mother gave me a look of both kindness and fierce determination, and then took her child back to where they were staying in the Arena.

Ms. Ramirez was not the only mother who learned that lesson of the Superdome. Mothers throughout the Arena would not allow themselves to sleep. Many were up for days before they left New Orleans. But when finally seated on the buses, they still refused to sleep. Upon arriving in Houston, in a safe, vigilant, and well-protected environment, they still would not sleep. They would continue to stay awake in the darkened arena. No doubt the shadows and the occasional moan reminded them of the horrors of the Superdome, and they would not go to sleep. They had been part of a new and deadly environment where the message was "sleep is vulnerability." They willed themselves to stay awake, some for over six days.

I was not alone. Other volunteers recognized this reactive, protective, and continued alertness in these mothers, far beyond the point of caring for themselves. It got so bad that finally the volunteers, always in the best of spirits, helped to set up a child care center at the Arena. It didn't take long to find enough gentle hearts to agree to watch over the Katrina clinic children as their parents slept. Word about the childcare facility spread, and we all began to relax, thinking that these tired women, sleepwalking through the days, would finally get their well earned rest.

The first night, not one single mother signed up. Even though they were safe, they would trust no one, no one, no one with their children. They were mothers.

CHAPTER 7

Husbands, Fathers, and Sons

Modern America has declared war on African-American men. Characterizing us as rootless, senseless, and moral-less, she mocks us, segregates us, incarcerates us. Ultimately, she does not understand and therefore fears us.

These sensations, impressions and reactions were propagated and reinforced by the media during the Katrina debacle as television repeatedly showed video loops of gun-toting African-American males stealing and taking advantage of the desperate New Orleans situation. While despicable acts were conducted by men and women of all races, they were not common. In general, African-American men loved, supported, protected, and stood by their families to the bitter end, and in some cases, even beyond.

The entire time that I spent talking to each of the evacuees in the small group that I saw in my first few minutes at Katrina Clinic, I continually noticed a young man in the arms of an older man. Sometimes the young man cried openly, other times he whimpered, the gentle sound serving as a mournful backdrop to my conversations with each of the survivors. Finally, it was time for me to speak with this pair of men.

I approached the two, getting down on one knee to be at eye level with them. As with each of the others, their clothes were ruined beyond recognition. The older man looked about forty, with dark complexion, against which the gray stubble on his unshaved face made a remarkable contrast. He wore a hat that had completely lost its brim; it looked like a dirty, black, lipless bowl sitting upside down on top of his head.

He held the younger man, who appeared to be a teenager, just a child really, in his arms. Both were dressed in foul jeans and filthy T-shirts. I looked carefully, and saw the young man was shivering quietly as he whimpered. It was impossible to tell the reason for his tears.

I introduced myself, and spoke quietly to the older man, who kept his arm around the other one, and looked right at me.

"I am James. James McGill," he began. "This is my son-in-law, Lester," he finished, gesturing down toward the young man in his arms.

"Is there anything that I can do for you, Mr. McGill, or your . . ." I began.

"Nothing for me. But Les needs some help," he finished, nodding for me to look at his legs.

I shifted my position to inspect Les McGill's feet. The young man paid no attention to me, continuing to cry. I saw that, while dirty, his calves and thighs had no obvious defects, lacerations, or swelling. However, his ankles were remarkably swollen. In fact, each was almost twice its normal size. They appeared to be red as well, although I struggled to make out the color in the relatively dim light and through the dirt that covered every inch of his skin. *Infection*, I thought. Looking further down, I quickly found the reason.

His feet were grossly thickened and discolored. Across their swollen tops ran deep, jagged gashes, some as long as four inches. Other parts of his feet were covered in blisters of various sizes. Looking more carefully, I saw some of the blisters had broken, leaking their pus onto the surrounding, inflamed skin. Open ulcers and running sores took up most of the rest of the skin on these dying feet.

Examining his toes, I saw that two of the smaller toes on his left foot were gone, completely missing. Four toes remained on his right foot, black from the grime, but the small one was hanging by just a small thin strand of dead tissue. The skin on his left foot where his toes used to be was swollen and discolored. I struggled to make out the colors, but failed in the poor light. Taking a chance, I gently sniffed, then withdrew my head at once from the foul, hallmark stench of gangrene.

"How long have they been this way, Mr. McGill?" I asked, genuinely alarmed. Only rapid action would save his feet.

"What day is today?" he asked.

"It's Friday. How many days have his feet been this bad?" I persisted, thinking, *it may already be too late.*

"The toes just turned black today, I think the burns occurred on Monday," Mr. McGill replied.

I looked at his feet again. Les McGill was going to lose them. And that's if he was lucky. *The pain had to be incredible,* I thought. Most people would be out of their mind from the sharp throbbing these kinds of injuries caused. And it would just get worse if they weren't treated promptly. *No wonder he's crying,* I thought.

Excusing myself, I left at once to find a nurse. Within a minute, I identified one who was herself in the middle of directing a number of volunteers to carry out several urgent tasks. Working to get her full and immediate attention, I just jumped in, exclaiming "We have a medical emergency!"

The young nurse was clearly overwhelmed, but it's the good fortune of patients and their doctors that most nurses keep a solid, almost unshakable sense of balance and perspective. Stopping at once, she looked at me with clear eyes, asking "What's the emergency, doctor?"

I explained the situation, giving her the name and location of the patient.

"We're transporting patients to the hospital now," she responded without hesitation. "I'll be sure that he goes on the next ambulance."

Thanking her, I replied, "Your quick response will help to save this young man's life."

Returning, I explained to Mr. McGill the seriousness of his son-in-law's condition.

"When will he get to go to the hospital?" he asked me.

"In just a few minutes," I responded. *I hope* I thought, finishing the sentence in my mind. "How did this happen to his feet?" I inquired.

"They were burned," Les's father-in-law responded.

"No wonder he's crying," I said softly, hoping that the young man couldn't hear. "The pain from this kind of burn is intense."

"Yes," Mr. McGill responded, "but that's not why he's crying."

"Les was eighteen years old when he married my daughter," Mr. McGill explained. "They were wed last year. She was sixteen. I didn't think much of the idea, but my wife reminded me how old we were when we got married, something I guess I'd forgotten."

"Where is your daughter now?" I inquired.

Mr. McGill looked at me strangely for a long moment. Then he simply said, "Back home in New Orleans. Anyway," he continued, scratching his forehead with his right arm, while continuing to hold his son-in-law in his left, "Les worked at the chemical processing plant just a block away from home. It was a messy place, with barrels of foul smelling liquid all around. It was so strong I bet it'd burn your nose off if you put your face down in one of those vats that the owner sometimes kept in the open.

"Les wanted to be an engineer, but didn't have enough school for that, so he got a job as a janitor, cleaning up the mess every day. He had thick boots he needed to wear to protect his feet, and it seemed he needed a new pair every month, so strong was the waste that would slosh on the ground over there.

"Ronnie worked four blocks away from home at an office. She'd just gotten a raise that allowed her to park in the new underground garage. Made a big difference on those hot days. Her car had vinyl seats."

"I know what you mean," I responded. Vinyl seats heated up fast in the summer. Sitting on vinyl seats in a car that had been out in the summer New Orleans sun all day would feel like napalm.

"We were all together Monday morning when the rains hit the hardest. The three of us were at home," Mr. McGill continued.

"They lived with you?" I asked.

"Yeah," Mr. McGill responded. Les had gotten quiet again. "After my wife died last year from the diabetes, I had more room than people in my house. Les and Ronnie were struggling to make ends meet, so I invited them to live with us, I mean me."

"Monday morning, the rain was fierce," he continued. "It came down so hard that it hurt when it hit you. But it started to slack off some later in the day. We had one TV that was working, and the weathermen forecasted that the storm was moving on up north, away from the city. We actually felt we were lucky.

"That was when the phone call came in," Mr. McGill continued. "One of Ronnie's coworkers said she was going in to check on things at work. She wanted to know if Ronnie wanted to come in as well.

"I thought it was a bad idea," Mr. McGill said, trying to keep his voice down. "The storm wasn't even over yet! But Ronnie complained that they had a busy week ahead of them as it was, and missing part of Monday just made it worse. And she could be so bull-headed when she made up her mind about something!" Mr. McGill said, letting his voice rise.

"Les said he thought it would be OK, and agreed to go with her," Mr. McGill continued, rocking his son-in-law in his arms. "It was just a few blocks from the house. He and Ronnie just drove over there. Even though it was a four block walk, they felt safer in the car.

"They parked in the indoor garage and took the elevator on up to Ronnie's floor. They stayed there for about four hours, I guess. I'm not really sure. But it was too long to stay," he said. "None of us realized that, although the rain had ended, the real flooding had yet to start."

"Yes," I responded. "The levees."

"My two kids went in to the office just before the levees gave way," he replied, nodding his head. "Even though the rain slacked off some, and there was no real street flooding when they left the house, the situation changed that evening. I think it was about 6:00 P.M. that night when they were done. Ronnie's friend had left much earlier, so it was just Les and Ronnie by themselves. Alone.

"Apparently, they got in the elevator to go down to the garage to get the car. The elevator worked just fine. But halfway down, Les remembered that he left his jacket upstairs. He stopped the elevator before they got to the garage levels. He told Ronnie to go ahead and go to the car. He would join her shortly. So she went on ahead of him.

"When he got his coat, then tried to catch an elevator back down to the parking level, it seemed forever before the elevator came for him. When it finally arrived, it was a different elevator, and it just wouldn't work right. It would stop for a few moments between floors. Then go up for a floor and stop. Then come back down again. He said it took about ten minutes for the elevator to finally go down the way it ought to. Then, it finally stopped on L1, one floor above where Ronnie was with the car. The doors started to open, but then stopped. Les was able to force them apart wide enough for him to get out.

"He found his way to the steps and went down one level. When he got to Ronnie's level, Les struggled with getting the door that led from the stairwell to the cars open. When he finally did, water poured in! It was a wall of water, knocking him back. That's when he lost his shoes. He got up and turned to get up the steps, out of the way of the water that was flowing into the stairwell and swirling down the steps when he saw her. He reached his hand out and grabbed Ronnie as she was carried along in the flow. He picked her up and pulled his way up the steps with her."

"I'm not sure I understand this," I asked. "She was walking to her car when the floor flooded?"

"Near as I can figure." Mr. McGill paused for a second to collect himself. "The parking floor was already flooded before Ronnie and Les left her office floor together. Neither Ronnie nor Les knew that when they got on the elevator. They stopped the car at a higher level, to let Les off for him to get his jacket. Ronnie went down to L2. The elevator still had power and made it down to her floor where the car was. It opened out onto a completely flooded floor. That water must have come rushing into the elevator when the doors opened.

"I guess I thought elevators were protected against that," I said quietly, working to picture this catastrophe in my own mind.

"It's happened before," Mr. McGill replied. "Actually, here in Houston when you all flooded out before." We were both silent for a moment.

"Anyway," this father-in-law continued," he picked Ronnie up and carried her to the ground level. The underground floors were badly flooded, but you could still walk through the streets. He carried her home, talking to her the whole time, asking her to hold on. He walked through the water with my baby." Mr. McGill began to cry now.

I was quiet for a few moments. Several of the evacuees reached out, putting a gentle hand on his knee or his shoulder, doing their best to console an inconsolable grief.

"He just walked back home with her body," Mr. McGill continued, strengthening his grip on his son-in-law. "Les thought she was still alive, and couldn't think of anything else to do but to bring her back home. The water on the street smelled bad. The whole neighborhood stunk. It was the smell of those barrels at the chemical plant. They had opened and spilled into the water. But Les had to walk by on his way home, and I guess, he gave no thought to what must be in the water. He just walked his way through it. His feet were already in bad shape from the broken glass, twisted metal, and junk that sat on the streets under the water. A lot of those chemicals didn't have a hard time working their way into his feet."

"I heard him screaming and calling for me before he got on our property," Mr. McGill remembered. "He still thought she was alive when he brought her in, but it wasn't no use," he continued, shaking his head sadly. "She had to have been under that water in the garage for about five or ten minutes. Plus, you could see the way her head was hanging that her neck was broken. My baby was dead! We both cried so hard that night, me for my young daughter, Les for his wife. There was nothing else he could have done that I can think of. Ronnie was stubborn. When she wanted to do something, there was no stopping her.

"He's my only family now," Mr. McGill said, dropping his head, crying with his son-in-law.

"When it was time for us to leave," Mr. McGill continued, "we just left her in her bed. We couldn't bury her because there was no ground to bury her in. The water was everywhere."

"How'd you finally get out?" I asked quietly.

"Caught a boat out. By that time his feet were red and swollen with blisters. But, you know," Mr. McGill said as he looked down at his son-in-law's feet, "I don't think he can feel much of that yet. Other parts of him hurt more right now."

The paramedics had arrived with a stretcher. Mr. McGill and I helped Les onto it, making sure that his tender feet didn't strike any part of the bed as we lifted him up and onto it.

"Can I go with him?" Mr. McGill asked the closest paramedic.

"I'm afraid not, sir. However, you could follow behind us," the paramedic kindly offered.

"Don't have a car," Mr. McGill replied, shaking his head.

I left for a minute to find a volunteer. I had to speak to several, but finally found a young woman who knew exactly what offer to make after I explained the situation. The two of us walked back to the grieving father and his young son-in-law.

"I'm Linda Pomosa," she said, introducing herself to Mr. McGill. "If you come with me to my car, we can follow the ambulance to the hospital. That way you can stay with your son-in-law there."

"Why, thank-you. Thank-you young lady," he said, lifting the remnants of his cap from his head in gratitude.

As the paramedics were putting Les in the ambulance, and the volunteer left to bring her car around to the entrance of the Arena, Mr. McGill and I found ourselves with a few moments alone. Turning to me, he asked, "You know, I need your advice about something."

"What's that?" I responded with one eye on the survivors with whom I had started the interview process. I was anxious to get back to them, but also wanted to finish my conversation with this remarkable father-in-law.

He felt around his dirty, hanging jeans for something then stopped. Putting his hand into his right pocket, he pulled out a grey mound that he held in the palm of his right hand, offering it to me. At, first, I thought it was a hornets' small, pulpy nest. Then, I looked closer to see it was really a rough, gray mound of paper. It had been folded many times over, and was still damp from the water that immersed him back in New Orleans.

"She told me about this the night before the storm," he replied. He wiped his hands on his clothes after giving it to me, as if he was relieved to be free of it. Whatever it was, it was my responsibility now.

I tried to delicately unfold it, but pieces of it came apart in my hands. I could make out only the letters "BORAT."

"What's this?" I asked, while failing to disentangle its pieces.

"These are some results on my daughter," he said, pointing to the paper. "You know," he explained, "lab tests."

"Well, you're going to need to tell me more than that," I responded. "I can't make anything else out that's on it."

"Actually, I couldn't make anything out on it either when she gave it to me. It was in much better shape then," he said, smiling. "But, I really couldn't understand the words."

"Well, what did she tell you it said?" I asked, looking up at him.

"That Ronnie was pregnant," he replied evenly.

Pregnant! At a loss for words, I gaped at him for a moment. "I don't understand. What do you need from me?" I finally asked, not knowing what else to say.

"Should I tell him?"

"Les?"

"Yeah," he responded.

"He didn't know?" I was backpedaling, stalling for time as I struggled to absorb this new piece of information.

"She wanted to tell him when the storm was over. I asked her to do it earlier, but she refused. She said that she wanted to wait until the bad weather had passed, when they could have a moment with no distractions. 'A perfect moment for us' is how she put it."

"A moment that never came," I said.

"Right," Mr. McGill agreed. "But, now, what should I do? Should I tell him Ronnie was pregnant?"

A counselor would probably have a good answer for this, but there was none around. Just this father-in-law and a doctor. And he wasn't asking a counselor. He was asking me.

Lifting my head up from the decrepit piece of paper I held in my hand, I said. "Tell him, Mr. McGill. When he has stopped his crying and can hear you with a clear head, you be sure to tell him what you just told me."

"You really think so?" he asked, looking directly at me.

"Les needs to know that he was a father that last night with Ronnie, and that when he was trying to rescue his wife, he was also rescuing his baby."

"I'll try that," Mr. McGill said.

His ride pulled up, he got in the car, and he was gone.

The next day at clinic, a nurse walked a tall quiet man right by me and into the examination room for me to see. Young and African-American, you couldn't help but notice that his jeans as well as his shirt were about three sizes too large and grimy.

When the nurse came out, she gave me his chart, saying, "You'd better be careful, doctor. I think . . ."

The patient charged out of the room at once. He was excited, with eyes wide and arms outstretched.

"Is someone going to see me?" he demanded.

Startled, both the nurse and I jumped up and turned to face him. His sudden, surprising appearance threatened violence, yet his voice was subdued.

"Yes. Yes sir, I am," I answered, hoping I hadn't let my surprise at his sudden appearance slip into my voice. Holding my right hand out, I showed him the way back into the room, following right behind him.

"Hey, how are you?" the patient, Mr. Franklin, asked as we both entered. At 6'4", thin and muscular, he sat tall and straight on the bed facing me. However, with his restless eyes moving rapidly from me over to the yellow curtains that served as "walls", then in the direction of the noise outside the room, and then back to me, he was clearly nervous. Noticing again how large his clothes were for his slender frame, I too wondered if he was hiding anything in them—like a weapon.

Could he rob us? I thought. We didn't have any narcotics in the clinic area. The pharmacy might have some but he should be there, not here. But of course he might not know where the drugs are and assume we would have them near the patient rooms. There was no way to know . . .

I glanced at his chart, "I'm not sure what your problem is," I began. "How can I help?"

"Well, here it is," he replied, jumping off the bed at once, immediately pulling his shirt up and over his head, exposing a scarred chest and abdomen. My hair stood on end as my pulse rate jumped to well above a hundred within a second of his sudden motion.

"I was shot at a club a few years ago," he continued, holding his

Catastrophe and Chaos
in the Crescent City

ONE DAY AFTER Katrina strikes, water pours into the stunned city from towering Lake Pontchartrain.

Photograph by US Air Force. Courtesy of the Department of Defense.

DAYS AFTER THE hurricane has departed, downtown New Orleans remains flooded.

U.S. Navy Photo. Courtesy of the Department of Defense.

Catastrophe and Chaos in the Crescent City

THE WATER FILLED streets, overwhelmed with debris, waste, and the dead, were particularly hazardous for victims, already weakened by injuries, malnourishment, and dehydration.
Photo by Tech. Sgt. Mike Buytas/ U.S. Air Force.

AN EVACUEE, SURROUNDED by water, grimly considers the next move for himself and his baby on August 31, 2005.
Photo by Airman Jeremy L. Grisham/U.S. Navy.

Catastrophe and Chaos in the Crescent City

SURVIVORS SCRAMBLED ONTO evacuation craft of all shapes
and sizes as they struggled to leave the stricken city.

Photo by Jocelyn Augustino/FEMA.

Catastrophe and Chaos in the Crescent City

EVACUEES AWAIT ARRIVAL of aircraft for passage to
safety. Some stood in lines, exposed to sweltering heat, for
more than four days.
Photo by Michael Rieger/FEMA.

WHEN FINALLY INITIATED, evacuation efforts
struggled daily into the wee hours of the morning.
Photo by Win Henderson/FEMA.

Exhausted But Determined Survivors
Arrive in Houston

THOUSANDS OF WEARY evacuees are bussed into Houston.

Photo by Ester Fant, University of Texas Medical School at Houston.

QUIET SURVIVORS, STUNNED by their experience, line up to be checked in at a Houston evacuation site.

Photo by Ester Fant, University of Texas Medical School at Houston.

Exhausted But Determined Survivors
Arrive in Houston

EVACUEES DISEMBARK IN the Reliant Center-Astrodome.

Photo by Ester Fant, University of Texas Medical School at Houston.

COLLAPSING WITH FATIGUE, a young mother holds tightly to her baby upon arriving in Houston.

Photo by Ester Fant, University of Texas Medical School at Houston.

Exhausted But Determined Survivors
Arrive in Houston

A FACE, TRAGICALLY grim, for a young child

Photo by Ester Fant, University of Texas Medical School at Houston.

GAUNT DESPAIR AND quiet dignity reside in the heart of this aged survivor.

Photo by Ester Fant, University of Texas Medical School at Houston.

ACUTELY WEAKENED BY the ordeal, an evacuee finally receives the attention he needs in Houston.

Photo by Ester Fant, University of Texas Medical School at Houston.

Houston Pitches In

MAYOR BILL WHITE briefs members of the press about Houston's plans to care for the desperate hurricane survivors.
Photo by Ester Fant, University of Texas Medical School at Houston.

DR. MCKINNEY OF the University of Texas receives an update on Houston's response.
Photo by Ester Fant, University of Texas Medical School at Houston.

Houston Pitches In

COMFORT AND AID rendered by a Red Cross worker help to make loneliness a little more bearable.

Photo by Ester Fant, University of Texas Medical School at Houston.

A HEALTH CARE provider and evacuees share a humorous moment together.

Photo by Ester Fant, University of Texas Medical School at Houston.

Houston Pitches In

A SURVIVOR SHARES his experience with an attentive physician.

Photo by Ester Fant, University of Texas Medical School at Houston.

A DOCTOR FOCUSES on the needs of her new patient.

Photo by Ester Fant, University of Texas Medical School at Houston.

FIRST RESPONDERS (clockwise from back to front) Doctors Lem Moyé (the author), Kristy Murray, George Delclos and Barry Davis of the University of Texas School of Public Health.

Photo by Michelle Mocco, University of Texas School of Public Health.

Houston Pitches In

A MOTHER WITH her watchful child enjoys a light moment with a nurse.

Photo by Ester Fant, University of Texas Medical School at Houston.

A TIRED VOLUNTEER and survivor share a quiet moment of support.

Photo by Ester Fant, University of Texas Medical School at Houston.

A NEEDY FAMILY receives support from a member of a faith-based organization.

Photo by Ester Fant, University of Texas Medical School at Houston.

Rehabilitation and Recovery

EVACUEES SELECT CLOTHING for their families as they prepare to
move forward with their lives.

Photo by Ester Fant, University of Texas Medical School at Houston.

FEMALE
SURVIVORS
PREPARING
for the new
challenges
ahead.

*Photo by Ester Fant,
University of Texas
Medical School at
Houston.*

Rehabilitation and Recovery

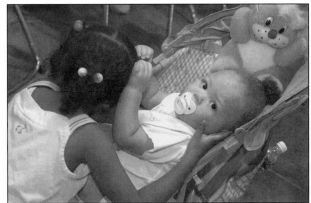

THE BOND BETWEEN two sisters is a source of strength.

Photo by Ester Fant, University of Texas Medical School at Houston.

A FATHER GIVES encouragement to his child.

Photo by Ester Fant, University of Texas Medical School at Houston.

A SURVIVOR SEARCHES the thousands of post-it notes for information about her family members' whereabouts.

Photo by Ester Fant, University of Texas Medical School at Houston.

Rehabilitation and Recovery

A BROTHER AND sister are cheered by each other's company.

Photo by Ester Fant, University of Texas Medical School at Houston.

EXHAUSTED BUT NOT yet ready to rest, two survivors bond while absorbed in a book.

Photo by Ester Fant, University of Texas Medical School at Houston.

Rehabilitation and Recovery

YOUNG MOTHERS ANTICIPATE the delight of their children
who will receive the donated dolls they hold.

Photo by Ester Fant, University of Texas Medical School at Houston.

YOUNG WOMEN AND workers enjoy each other's company
while engaging in an old, familiar activity.

Photo by Ester Fant, University of Texas Medical School at Houston.

Rehabilitation and Recovery

A MOTHER, GRATEFUL for the survival of her children, basks in their love and looks to the future.

Photo by Ester Fant, University of Texas Medical School at Houston.

RENEWED AND RESTORED, a family poses for a final photograph before moving on together in their new lives.

Photo by Ester Fant, University of Texas Medical School at Houston.

shirt in his hand. "See? The bullet entered here," he continued, pointing to a huge raised, badly sutured but well healed scar about nine inches long. The healed rip in his skin started just below his right nipple, and traced a long crooked S-like pattern down across his body, moving first left, then right, then left again as it traced its way below to his abdomen, ending just above his umbilicus.

"I think this may be infected," he said, running his hand over his own scar, pushing and poking at it for himself, testing its integrity.

"Infected by what?" I asked.

"Being in that water, all that mess," he answered instantly.

"Well, you'd better let me take a look at that for you," I said, beginning to relax. Examining it, I thought it was a little tender to the touch but that was all. "It's a little sore," I observed, "but there's no evidence of active infection," I finished, as I completed my exam and stepped back. "You're pretty lucky," I replied, sounding more nonchalant than I felt.

"Well, that water was pretty bad," he said, almost pleasantly.

"How long were you in it?" I asked, recognizing at last that this young fidgety, but gentle man was not planning to hurt anyone.

"Two days," he answered in his rapid fire style.

"A whole two days?" I said, surprised at his comment. "How could you be walking around in it for that long?"

He answered only with silence.

"Mr. Franklin," I persisted. "Why would you stay in the water for that long? As you just told me, it was pretty nasty. Full of germs. The fact that you're here concerned about the possibility of infection, shows that you had to be worried about that. Why didn't you get out of it sooner? Couldn't you find something, anything to climb out on?"

Nodding, he said simply, "There was nothing else I could do. When the rain started, my brother and I went by my parents' house. Both of them are pretty sick, and really can't take care of each other very well anymore. My mother had a heart attack a year ago and she's never been the same. My daddy, well, he has cancer. He's supposed to go for treatments, but doesn't always make it. He had a real rough summer with it, and doesn't have any energy anymore.

"My brother and I got to their house when the rain started coming

141

down hard on Monday. We didn't think going to the Superdome was a good idea, so we decided to stay with them to make sure they got through the storm in good shape.

"Right after we got there, my mom began complaining about not feeling good. She said her chest was hurting, like a big hand was pressing hard against her, making it tough for her to breathe," Mr. Franklin said, holding his own right hand on his chest to illustrate. "She also didn't look good. My brother Arthur agreed to take her to Charity hospital, and I decided to stay home with Dad.

"I helped Arthur get her to his car, and they started off. It was raining steadily, but I didn't think too much of it. I stayed outside for a couple of minutes to bring the lawn chairs out of the yard and up onto the porch. Just when I finished, it seemed like the sky opened and the rain really started coming down. Hard."

"It was raining hard before, right?" I asked.

"Not like this," he responded his eyes widening. "The water wasn't just falling now. It was like the rain was being thrown down. Driven down. Slammed down. I don't know," he said, struggling for words. "It was like there was so much rain it was taking the space of the air. There wasn't much air to breathe, there was so much rain."

"I understand," I responded. It was an apt description of drowning's early stages.

"I heard a loud noise behind me. A hashing, slashing noise. I turned, and saw something I had never seen before."

"What was that?" I asked, settling into the plastic chair across the small room from him.

"There, from one side of the street to the other was a huge wave of water, rushing right down our street toward me! It was about five feet high, with foam on the top. It was a real wave, like a beach wave! It crashed right into me, knocking me off my feet, picking up all of that lawn furniture I had moved right along with it and slamming it into our neighbor's house. I got back up and saw another wave. And behind that another one. And another."

He looked right at me, for a moment lost in the fright and wonder of that earlier moment. "We actually had waves breaking against our house! It was like our home had been picked up and moved to the beach. No. Like it had been moved out into the gulf!"

"Another wave knocked me down. That wave hit me so hard I wanted to scream. It was like getting punched in the side with a one hundred pound fist.

"I scrambled up onto my feet and tried to get up the front steps to the porch. One more wave hit me from behind, throwing me forward onto the porch steps. I got up and staggered to the house, just as the third wave smashed into the living room right behind me.

"'Dad!' I called out, as I turned around to close the front door. A wave pushed against the door, making the old wood creak. The wood on the door was swollen, and I couldn't get it to close tight enough to throw the deadbolt. The only way to keep it closed was to lean my back against it and push back. I felt like I was trying to keep the world's biggest and worst burglar out of the house."

"How long did you do that?" I asked, leaning forward some. He was describing an invasion of his house, by water.

"Not long at all. I heard a crash, and, looking to my right, I saw a wave break through one of the living room windows. Water was now flowing over the top of the window sill into the room. But it wasn't just water. It was already dirty," Mr. Franklin continued, dropping his voice a little while wrinkling his nose, "with what looked like small clumps of broken up sausage. I didn't think anything could smell that terrible! And the mess kept sliding in through the window. Like someone was throwing buckets of sewage into your house every few seconds.

"I didn't know what to do. All this junk was rushing into my folks' house, and there was no way I could keep it out. And the floor was so slippery I couldn't keep my footing to keep the door open. The water pressed harder and harder from the outside, trying to force its way in. I got over to Dad, who just sat there across the room, the grimy water starting to inch up his wheelchair. I knew I had to do something. He couldn't move on his own, and I couldn't let him stay there. But, if I went to get him, all of that filth would come crashing through the front door.

"I made up my mind. Leaving the door, I rushed over to him, slipping all over the floor, trying to keep my balance. The grimy water poured into the living room, forcing the front door open, and crashing onto the floor. When I got to his wheelchair, I picked him up out of it and carried him upstairs. He didn't say anything, but that wasn't anything special. He would be quiet all day sometimes when the cancer pain got too bad. The moving around must have hurt him terribly.

"I tried to hurry, but only made it up the first two stairs to the small landing before I had to stop to catch my breath. I don't know why I did this, but I turned around, and with my dad in my arms, looked at the living room.

"The water was already two to three feet high in the living room! Swirling around the legs of the dining room table my parents loved so much, it left thick brown deposits on the wood. As I watched, a piece of junk in the water entered the house with another wave and slammed against that table, breaking one of the legs.

"You know," Mr. Franklin said, looking up at me sighing deeply, "my Dad had finished that table himself. He must have put ten coats of varnish on it, working to make sure each coat was perfect. Then, seeing that it wasn't, gently wiping it smooth after it dried, he would apply another coat. My brother and I used to make fun of him while he did that." He shook his head, either trying to hold onto, or dispatch the memory.

"What happened next?" I asked quietly.

"The slop was everywhere," he continued. "It was all over the sofa and the two sitting chairs in the living room. It covered the screen of the TV. Clumps of it got thrown up high on the walls by the splashing water, where it stayed for a moment before slipping down into the stink below, leaving a sickening stain where it had been. I climbed the rest of the steps with my dad in my arms, stumbled to their bedroom, and placed my dad down on their double bed. Right then, I knew we were in trouble; there was nothing to drink. Water was the only thing I thought at the time that we needed. I guess I couldn't bear to think about food after the sickening sight on the first floor.

"I asked Dad was there some water in the refrigerator, and he nodded yes. Kissing him, I told him I would just be a minute and left, heading toward the steps again. Part of me knew this was a mistake, but I had to try. I had no idea how long we'd have to stay upstairs.

"Halfway down the steps, I sunk down into the sludge until it was stomach deep. Trying not to splash any of it up in my face, I cursed myself for wondering what those small soft things that I felt against my hands and brushing against my wet pant legs were. I got down into the living room. The filth was now chest level. I stopped, overwhelmed by the stench, my stomach suddenly turning into a knot. I suddenly leaned forward, vomiting into the filthy water that was just six inches below my mouth.

"But, I just couldn't stop there. Slowly, I made my way through the water into the kitchen, and then over towards the refrigerator. The water was already up to my neck. I threw up once more struggling to make it over to the refrigerator. I wanted to move faster but the water slowed everything down. The stench was overpowering. Every step was a slow, disgusting, drawn-out movement. It was like . . . .like living the worst moments of your life in slow motion.

"Finally I got within reach of the refrigerator door. I felt my way under the water for its brass handle, shivering as my hand touched the soft submerged stool in the water. I finally found the handle. With a grunt of triumph I gripped it and pulled hard.

"Nothing. The door wouldn't budge. Must have been the weight of all of that water surrounding the refrigerator. It just wouldn't move. I grabbed it with two hands, took a deep breath, and jerked hard. The old handle broke off in my hand, I lost my balance on the slippery floor, and fell backward into the water.

"I wanted to scream, but didn't. I twisted violently first one way and then the other in the water, getting confused which way was up. I jerked around like I was being electrocuted, so disgusting was the sensation. I tried and tried, but couldn't find the floor with my feet. Finally, flailing my feet around, I found something level that they could rest on. Without thinking, I bent my knees and pushed up hard.

"Bang! My head slammed against something hard. I couldn't help but open my mouth in astonishment and some of the greasy mess slid into my mouth. I closed it at once, desperately trying not to breathe or swallow. I moved my head again in the same direction. Again I smacked into a hard surface. Why couldn't I stand? I was desperate. I started to shift my feet, moving them along the slippery surface on which they were trying to find traction. My chest was burning and I wanted to try to breathe so badly but I knew I couldn't. I tried moving my submerged head up again, hitting the hard object again, but this time, only the left side of my head made contact. Moving a little to the right, my head emerged out into the air. I spit at once, and retched three times. Hard. The stink was overpowering, and it was all I could do not to pass out.

"Opening my eyes, I saw that I had hit my head against the underside of the kitchen table that was floating in the sludge. I guess that when I slipped, my body drifted under the table. That's what I kept hitting as I was trying to stand.

"Suddenly, I heard a crash upstairs. I had to get back up to where Dad was! I walked slowly though this debris-filled mess, making my way out of the kitchen and over to the stairs in the living room."

He paused for a second. Looking at me, he asked, "Have you ever tried to walk up steps that were under water?"

I shook my head no, not able to say anything. My stomach was tightly twisted, but I shoved those feeling aside. Nothing I had ever been through, or for that matter, ever heard of, prepared me for this story. *No wonder he was concerned about infection*, I thought.

"Walking up stairs that are under water is just impossible," he continued. "The steps were too slippery and I kept losing my footing. The banister was slick and disgusting. Plus the water is moving rapidly around you, and it's full of junk—desk drawers, phones still attached to the wall by cords, pictures in big frames that have been yanked off the walls and swirl around collecting the slop on them.

"I made it upstairs, my eyes on fire from the filth that filled them. I could barely keep them open! The crash I had heard was the upstairs windows breaking. Water was now pouring through the broken upstairs windows. This was the second floor! Where was all of this coming from! The water had to be twenty feet deep outside! And it was still rising! I looked over at my dad. He was lying still on the bed, the filth sloshing around its sides. I retched hard again. I thought only one thing."

"What was that?" I managed to ask.

"My dad will not drown in this!" he said, his eyes filled with resolve. "He might die, but I wouldn't let him drown in this muck!

"I splashed my way over to a chair, falling and banging my chest against the back of one of its heavy arms. I dragged the chair over to the bed. Lifting it, I put it on top of the bed. Then I got on the bed and pulled my dad up and into the chair. After pushing and pulling him, I got him sitting in the chair. I told him to hold onto the arms of the chair with his hands, and then I got down. Splashing into the thick brown water that was already waist deep. But, you know, then, it didn't bother me so much anymore."

"Why was that?" I asked. "It's still the same mess that was downstairs, right?"

"Yeah," he agreed. "But now I was in it to save my dad's life. That made it different. I could stand it for him.

"That first night I stayed with him. I tried to throw up, but just heaved up nothing. The sludge didn't get any higher than my waist; it covered the bed where my dad had been laying, but no higher. Outside, the rain had stopped but the water wasn't going anywhere. I looked outside the broken window, but could only see that the water was above the window sill. And, the mosquitoes were back, as miserable as ever! Shoot! They probably loved the situation. Taking revenge on us. I actually think I dozed off for a few minutes. At first light, I think..."

"You were able to fall asleep?" I asked incredulously.

"I guess I must have. I was standing facing my dad, with my arms on the chair to keep it steady. I must have dozed off. Anyway, at first light there he was and there I was. And I was in agony from a toothache."

The observation about his tooth brought me back to the reality of the clinic. "Let me take a look," I said. Shining a light into the mouth he opened wide for me, I peered into his mouth. There, around some badly swollen gums, was a molar in the back left with a huge, ragged hole it. The hole went as far into the tooth as I could shine the light.

"You've got quite a cavity there." What an understatement! An angry infection was unavoidable, given the filth that had filled his mouth three days earlier.

"Well it's pretty sore," he agreed. "It's hurt for a few days now. That's one of the things I wanted to talk to you about today."

"Well, I'll get you in to see a dentist this morning. That tooth looks pretty angry," I replied, making a mental note to handle the referral. "How did you and your dad do on that second day?"

"Well, we couldn't go anywhere. We would try to talk some during the day. Most of the time, we wondered about my mom and Arthur. We also talked about the storm. How bad it was. He was really weak. Actually, we both were. But," Mr. Franklin smiled, "you know that he still had a sense of humor? One time, he woke me up. I heard him call 'Son . . . son.' I said 'What Dad? Are you OK?' Do you know what he said to me?"

Absolutely clueless, I responded, "No. What?"

"He said, 'You know, it really stinks around here!' We both laughed. The first laugh I had with him in two days since the storm started. And the last."

"We stopped talking after a while. I knew he was in bad shape. No water and no food for a day. He got quiet for awhile, and started mumbling some things. I didn't understand all of it. I actually thought he was talking to Mom, thinking she was there. Then, he got quiet for what seemed like a long time. I called up to him and he wouldn't say anything. I tried shaking the chair, but he didn't respond. I stopped, too tired to keep trying. Then, out of the blue, he said to me, clearly, "Gotta go now, son." That was it. I looked up at him and he was absolutely still, looking quietly at me with eyes that didn't see me. My Dad had just died. That night was tough because I was just there with him. Nobody to really talk . . ."

"Wait, wait." I said. "You stayed with him on that second night? You didn't try to leave?" I persisted, incredulously.

"Where could I go? The water was still high. I couldn't take him anywhere."

I sat down, looking at him silently.

"I thought a boat would come by to pick us up, but none ever came by that day. What else could I do?" Mr. Franklin asked.

"It was a tough night," he continued. "The burning in my eyes spread all over my skin. I was pretty scared that night. I didn't know how long we would have to be there. I heard noises in the night that worried me. But, it was better when I talked to my dad. Telling him I loved him. I knew he was dead, but, you know, I just wasn't ready to stop talking to him. Telling him that I missed him already. Apologizing for the things I had done wrong. All the times I let him down. Maybe part of him was still in the room. Maybe not, but I think the important part of him heard me.

"The next morning, I noticed the water had gone down. At least the second floor was dry. Disgusting, but dry. I heard a motor outside. Sure enough, it was a boat.

"I called to them from the window, asking if they could take me and my dad. They said they could only take me. 'Can't take any bodies,' the boatman said.

"I knew it was time for me to go, but I hated it. I didn't want to leave my Dad. I thought I was deserting him there. But, it was just time. I was beyond thirsty. My jaw was killing me. Now that the water was down, I could smell the air outside. It was fresher, and it smelled so bad inside! I . . . I just couldn't stay. I said goodbye to the house, and then to my dad. Then, I went downstairs, swam through that filthy sludge one more time to the outside door, then down the steps, and swam over to the boat."

"Is your mom alive?" I asked quietly.

"Uh, no. She died on the way to the hospital. After I got here, I called my brother, who made it to Lafayette. He told me." Mr. Franklin was shaking some now. I placed my hand on his shoulder to steady this courageous and devoted son.

I had been in with him for fifteen minutes. I turned, leaving him alone in the cubicle as I wrote some prescriptions. After I emerged, I turned, surprised to see him right behind me.

"Mr. Franklin, I need for you to wait inside where you were," I said, placing a hand on his shoulder. "I'll be back in a moment with the information we need to get you to see the dentist." I escorted him into the patient room where he had been, then exited.

After exiting again, I sat down to write the information for the dental referral. Looking up, I was surprised to see Mr. Franklin emerge and come over to me.

Pulling up his shirt, he asked, "Do I have an infection? Am I going to be OK?"

Why can't I get through to him, I wondered, stunned at his continued appearances. Explaining again what I was doing for him, and that I would see that a dentist looked after his tooth, I escorted him back to the cubicle.

Mr. Franklin and I replayed this scene two additional times. Finally, I agreed that he and I would sit together while I wrote the dental referral. Visibly relieved, he sat down with me and I completed writing in his chart. Finished, I found a nurse, and she walked with him the thirty feet to the dental clinic. With puzzlement, I watched this tall, tough-looking young man being quietly led away then I turned to see my next patient.

Later that night, at home in bed, I awoke with a start, realizing why Mr. Franklin kept bolting from the examination room. *He was afraid to be by himself!* This strong, caring son had spent all of his courage for his father, and, for the time being, had none left. He couldn't stand to be alone.

"Doctor, quickly! We need you here at once!"

I looked up to see the nurses excitedly wave me into the exam room. I dropped the patient's chart I was working on, and rushed into the room to observe a man in intense agony, laying flat on his back. He couldn't keep his legs still, his knees first bending, then flexing, as he tried in vain to find a comfortable position. Nurses gathered around him, working furiously in a futile attempt to make him comfortable. Behind the nurses, on a small cot, sat a little girl. No more than six or seven years old, she sat quietly, tears rolling down her face.

Suddenly, he cried out, arching his back off the table, stretching his arms out wide in a last ditch attempt to avoid a new wave of intense pain.

"Mr. Giletson, Mr. Giletson!" one nurse said to him. "We know you hurt. We only want to try to get your blood pressure! We'll . . . be . . . done . . . in a moment," she finished, struggling to help control him. His only response was to twist his body hard to the right as another spasm of pain wracked his body.

There were no lacerations, no obvious external bleeding. Leaning over the nurse who was desperately trying to get his vital signs, I peered into the man's face. No horrendous facial injuries such as the traumatic loss of an eye or obvious open head injury. Trying to look even more closely, I noticed something emerging from his right eye, and run down his face to fall on the pillow and disappear. A tear.

I pulled back at once. Classically, there are three types of pain that will make a grown man cry. Acute pancreatis, in which the pancreas essentially ruptures, spewing its caustic contents on to the surface of the internal organs such as the stomach, liver and small intestines. These acidic, biting chemicals, designed to be released inside the long tube through which our food travels, are instead released on top of it. Essentially the patient digests himself from the inside out.

The second possible cause of this intense pain is a dissecting aortic aneurysm, where the largest artery in the abdomen tears on the inside. The acceleration of the blood flow in this huge artery is so great that it drives blood into the wall of the great artery itself, forcing the wall's tear to get larger. Eventually, the aorta will rip itself apart.

The third is a kidney stone. The small living tube leading from the kidney to the bladder, designed to carry fluid, fills with a huge jagged stone. This narrow conduit, now violently jammed wide open by the rough intruder, causes intense agony.

I needed to quickly learn if Mr. Giletson suffered from any of these conditions.

"Mr. Giletson," I began, literally in his face. "I would like to help you. Can you tell be about your pain? When did it start?"

Turning his head to look in my direction, he said, "Can you breathe? Can you breathe!"

I had no idea what my patient was talking about.

A few minutes later he calmed down, responding to the small quantity of pain medicine that we had given him. However, in twenty minutes, his twisting motions on the bed indicated that it was wearing off. The nurse leaned over to give him his medication.

"This will make your pain a little better, sir," she replied as she prepared to give him his medication.

"Can you breathe now?" was his same cryptic response.

In a half hour, we had our answer. The problem wasn't Mr. Giletson's pancreas, aorta, or kidney. He had ripped several of the huge muscles in his lower back. Attaching to the spinal column, these muscles sweep out and around the sides, attaching to the ribcage, spinal column, and pelvis. The weight and stresses that these muscles must bear daily is enormous, and it's due to their strength that we are able to stand upright. Mr. Giletson had torn his. Not large tears that would require surgery. Mr. Giletson's tears were microscopic in size, deep in the muscle tissue itself. These were small tears, but there were hundreds, maybe thousands of them, scattered throughout the strong muscles. I tried to explain this to him.

"The muscles, sensing the damage, clamp down. They go into spasm, and it's the spasm that produces your stiffness and your pain," I finished.

"Can you breathe?" he answered.

Ignoring his statement, I continued. "Now that we understand what has happened, we can start the right treatment. You'll feel much better in a few minutes."

"Breathe baby! Please BREATHE!"

I left the room giving the nurses the orders to begin his treatment, wondering, *What's he talking about?*

The nurse gave his medication. Within fifteen minutes he had stopped his painful movements. Fifteen minutes after that, he was asleep. The nurses, checking in on him from time to time, saw his daughter, standing by his side, holding his hand. Every now and then, she would bring it to her lips, rubbing it gently across her face, kissing it.

I came back to check on Mr. Giletson in an hour. He was awake, his daughter by his side.

"Hello," he began tentatively.

I was relieved to see that he wasn't going to ask about my breathing. After introducing myself, I asked, "Mr. Giletson, how do you feel?"

"My back and sides still bother me, but not like before."

"Once we figured out what was bothering you, we were able to give you the muscle relaxant you needed." Explaining again what the nature of his injury was, I noticed he was alert, showing no signs of the disorientation he exhibited when I had first seen him. "Do you know where you are, sir?"

"Yes, I'm in Houston, We just got here today."

"Is your family here?"

"No sir. It's just me and Carla for now."

I had to ask him. "You know, Mr. Giletson, when I met you a little while ago you didn't seem like you knew where you were?"

"Why do you say that?" he responded, his eyes focused on me and reflecting genuine concern.

"You kept asking about whether the nurses and I could breathe," I replied.

"No. Not you all! I was asking Carla."

"Carla?"

"Yes, Doctor. Carla. My daughter."

Hurriedly looking over to his daughter, thinking *Did I miss something?* I carefully observed her. In my haste to treat the father, had I made a critical mistake by ignoring his daughter?

She looked at me. Embarrassed, she giggled. Then, all smiles, she looked back over to her dad.

"Mr. Giletson," I began, somewhat confused. "Your daughter appears fine. I don't understand . . ."

"This is how it happened," he explained to me. "My wife had been in Alexandria the last few days of the week before the storm. Carla, my daughter," he said pointing to the child who now was very playful once she saw her dad was OK, "and I were supposed to catch a bus to join her there on Tuesday. Of course, the storm killed that idea."

"Is your wife . . . ?" I began, wanting to ask if she was OK.

"Don't worry. She's fine. We're going to see her as soon as we can, aren't we, sweetheart?" Carla's energetic nod showed that she agreed.

"Carla and I headed for the Superdome late on Sunday. It was Carla's first time there. Tell you the truth, we were looking forward to it. We just didn't know what would happen.

"It was already pretty crowded by the time we got there, but that was OK. The rain started falling that night. We could barely hear it, but we didn't care one way or the other. We just expected to stay there a day or so. We planned to be home on Tuesday, and heading to Alexandria that night.

"We walked around for awhile. I didn't see anybody I knew, but everyone was friendly enough. It got crowded fast though, and even though the A/C was going, it was getting warm. Carla started to wheeze a little, and I gave her some breathing medicine."

"Medicine . . . ?" I asked.

"Yeah. She has asthma," her father responded. "She has to take medicine every day. It makes a big difference for her."

"OK . . . ," I answered, trying to put this story together.

"There was no room to lie down, so we slept sitting up that first night," Mr. Giletson continued. "Next day, Monday, food was getting a little scarce. We were talking about when we might go home when we heard it."

"Heard what?"

"The banging. Horrible banging. It was the terrible sound of the wind when it's up to something bad. It sounded like a . . ." he paused to look over at his daughter. Seeing she had gone to sleep, he finished by whispering, "a monster. Like a monster banging on the roof, trying to get in."

"Finally part of the roof ripped off," Mr. Giletson continued. Just a small part, I think, followed by another, bigger piece. Things were instantly worse as the bad wind blew all of the rain down on us. It was really getting pretty sloppy in there. It really frightened a lot of people, but I didn't worry about it too much."

"Why not?" I asked.

"We didn't think we would be there much longer. Carla and I were planning to be home in a day, and then with her mother the day after that. We didn't have problems with the rain; it was when the air conditioning stopped that we began to worry. The combination of no A/C, thousands of people, and the ruined roof pushed the humidity up. Way, way up. My baby started to wheeze again.

"She took the last dose of medicine I had for her that evening. That was a mistake, I think, but I thought we would be home the next day. I wasn't going to let her suffer without it now, if there was plenty available and waiting for us at home. Why save it? At least that's what I thought.

"On Tuesday morning, I woke up at . . . .I don't know what time it was. But I heard her again. 'Wheeeeeeeeeeeeeze—cough—cough—cough. Wheeeeeeeeeeeeze—cough—cough—cough.' I knew Carla was getting in trouble. I thought I would try to get her to stand on her feet some, but she gets a little sluggish when she has trouble breathing.

"The air was really starting to stink, probably because the bathrooms weren't working anymore. I thought it would help her if she could get higher in the air. So I lifted her up, and let her sit on my shoulders. After a few moments, her breathing improved.

"I let her sit upright on my shoulders for fifteen minutes or so, then told her it was time to come down and rest for awhile. She climbed down from my shoulders, but, not five minutes later, she started wheezing again. I just shrugged, and said, "Hop on back up there." She turned her back to me, lifting her arms out from her sides. I grabbed her under her arms and lifted her up. That's when my back went bad.

"I don't think my muscles made any noise, but I sure thought I heard them. Maybe I just felt them go 'SPPRROONNGG!' as they ripped. Anyway, they tightened up fast. It was like I was being squeezed by a vise, and any movement of my back brought on white hot pain. Carla thought something was wrong as I lifted her, and asked, 'You OK Dad . . .' But then she started to wheeze."

"What did you do?" I asked.

"What could I do?" this father replied. "I told her I just stumbled, and to try again. "I'm glad she didn't see the face I made when I lifted her up. I felt the beginning of a fire building somewhere in my low back, but I thought I could get through it because we would get home that day."

"She sat on my shoulders all day. She was breathing a little easier. I moved around some, trying to find a comfortable position, but no position was comfortable for more than a few minutes. And the fire in my back was growing hotter.

"Tuesday afternoon, they told us that no one could leave the Superdome. The entire area was flooded, and it was just too unsafe to let people go. Worse than that, though, was that no one there knew when we would be able to leave. Finally, I had to let Carla down for a few moments. I couldn't take the pain much more, and the fire burning down deep in my back was now spreading around my sides. She did OK for a few minutes when she got down, but soon the wheezing started up again.

"It was getting toward the evening now. Most of the rain had stopped, but that only made it worse. The air was thick and hung heavy on the thousands of us in the dome. We were all wet from the rain and from the sweat. The humidity was awful, and the stink was terrible.

"My back felt like it had a red hot rod in it that burned any muscle it touched if I twisted one way or another. Part of me wanted to get angry with Carla as I heard her struggle for air. But, I knew it wasn't her fault. She wasn't trying to have problems breathing! In a way it hurt her to breathe, like it was hurting my back to support her on my shoulders. And, I couldn't let her hurt. Maybe one day, she'll hurt for somebody else. But I couldn't let her have trouble breathing just for me. So, we tried to get her up on my shoulders again. I was in tears from the hot poker that stabbed my back, but I finally got her up there. This time, though, her wheezing never seemed to go away. So I would ask her, "Can you breathe? Can you breathe, baby?" I just wanted her to continue breathing.

"I couldn't hold her up without some support anymore, so I tried to lean against something. I found a cement post near one of the entrances. She figured out what to do, and when I leaned with my back against the wall, so did she.

"Hour after hour we sat up there. My back was a raging inferno. The pain and tightness had spread up to my shoulders and even my neck. I bit my bottom lip to keep from making any noise.

"Finally, early Wednesday morning, I had to bring her down. I couldn't feel my legs, and it took me a couple of hours just to begin to shuffle some. But, the air was awful. I think, if you looked at it through the light that came through the torn roof, you could actually see it, like you can see brown, foul smelling smoke. That poison was all we had to breathe.

"Both Carla and I were pretty thirsty. We had to get some water, but when I put Carla down she couldn't breathe. So I just carried her. She would hug my neck, wrapping her legs around my waist. As I held her, trying to shuffle walk to find some water, I cried out a little with each step I took."

"It's amazing that you didn't cry out more than that" I exclaimed, imagining the short sharp sounds that this powerful man's muscles ripped out of him.

"Sure," Mr. Giletson replied. "I wanted to cry out holding her like that, moving slowly, slipping on the dirt and vomit and other stuff on the floor. I wanted to stop. But with her head resting like that on my shoulder, I could hear her wheeze. That sound got me through it. You see, I either walked carrying her, or she would stop breathing and die. Before my mind would let me imagine that, I would take another step, then another. That was the only choice to make. *My baby had to live!*"

"Wednesday night was the worst. We still couldn't go home. The air was wretched, and people were crying, moaning, complaining all around us. But, Carla's wheezing was getting worse. She had to get up on my shoulders again.

"I couldn't do it. My back, consumed by terrible fire-pain, wouldn't do what I told it. I wanted to get her back on my shoulders. I needed to. She needed me to! But, I couldn't. I couldn't even bend down to lift her! I tried, over and over, but it hurt too much. And her wheezing got worse and worse.

"That was the worst part. Not the pain of having her on my shoulders. It was the agony that she would die there in front of me because I didn't have the strength to help her. That wasn't back pain. That pain was here." Looking at me, he used his left hand to tap on his chest. "Heart pain for your baby is much, much worse."

"Suddenly, somebody said, 'Give her to me!'. Before I knew it, a stranger had scooped Carla up in the air, holding her face to face with him. I tried to reach out in anguish. *This man is stealing my baby! He's taking my girl, and I can't do anything!* I'll remember that shocked expression on her face for the rest of my life!

"Then, before I could do anything, he smiled, turned her around and placed her on my shoulders. When he saw how weak I was with her up there, he steadied me up against the wall. 'That's better' was all he said then he disappeared. You believe in angels, doc?" he asked.

"Yes."

"So do I, now. That's how we spent Wednesday night. Leaning up against that wall. I don't know if Carla slept any. I know I didn't. If I live a hundred years, those will be the worst hours I had on earth. I was sick to my stomach from the stench. I wouldn't let her sleep because I needed to be sure that she could still breathe. So, over and over that night I asked, 'Can you breathe?' You know, sometimes I could hear her answer, and other times not. So I kept asking.

"There wasn't a single part of my body that wasn't in agony. I felt like the hammer pounding inside my head would tear my head open from the inside out. My eyes hurt with the back pain. My feet hurt with it. Sharp as a blade knifing through me from head to foot. And all I could say was 'Can you breathe?'

"Next day, we walked outside. We were among the first to be let go, but because I had to go slowly, we didn't get out until late. But the air! That air! Nobody ever said New Orleans air tasted good, but I tell you, yesterday afternoon I breathed the sweetest air in the world! You wanted to just stand there and live in it—to devour it!

"Finally, we got on a bus for the trip here. It was the first time we both sat down on something soft in three days. I let her sit next to the window. I was hoping we could open it. But the bus we were on was air conditioned so it didn't matter."

"Those bus rides weren't the smoothest," I observed.

"No matter," Mr. Giletson said, shrugging. "She could breathe."

"We'd better make sure she gets her medicine now," I said, a little anxious.

"Oh, she got it already."

"What!" I asked, surprised. "How?"

"We went to where the kids are seen by doctors. Got her medicine first. Then, I came over here where, you know, I saw you."

I just looked at him for a second. This man quietly waited with his daughter while she was seen by a pediatrician and treated. Then they waited in line to get her medicine and she took it. Then, and only then, did he come over to the adult section where he collapsed from his back injury.

He had ruined his back for years, maybe for life. Yet he insisted on ensuring he did everything he could think of to keep her safe. He thought Wednesday night was his worst. It seemed to me that he had described his *best* night. I wondered what Carla would remember of this. Would she remember the stink, the cries, the despair?

Leaning over, I said to Carla who was now awake, "You and your dad are safe here now, Carla. Can you tell me what you remember about this week?"

"My daddy saved me!"

Standing up, I shook Mr. Giletson's hand, watching him and his daughter leave the clinic. *A father among fathers.*

Stereotypes of African-American men, deeply etched into the American psyche do grievous harm to Americans of all colors. However, the cataclysm of Katrina, so terrifying in its destructive power, brutally and unapologetically tore through these stereotypes, revealing these men for who they were. In the wake of the hurricane, fathers, husbands, and sons responded time and time again with courage, insight, and discipline, basing their actions on their loyalty to parents, allegiance to wives, and devotion to family. Not always well educated, they were often well-grounded, portraying the best traits of men—strength and honor. Katrina gave us the uncommon opportunity to view these men as they were, allowing light to dispel the stale illusions, and thereby elevate us all.

However, because the corporate-dominated media insisted on upholding its one dimensional, one-sided and false view of African-American men, a tremendous opportunity to re-educate America about the strong moral fiber of many of its poorest and strongest citizens was lost. The implications of this discarded opportunity are just too sad to think about. I hope this book helps to set the record straight.

CHAPTER 8

Katrina Survivors Look to the Future

Being at the clinic was not like sitting on a quiet lake that was calm, placid and predictable. Working at the clinic was more like riding a rushing river. There were twists, turns and unpredictable eddies as the river redefined itself. After being off for a few hours, your return placed you at a different point in the flow. The kinds of problems you saw a day or two earlier had long since flowed by, and now there were new unexpected issues and needs to address. It was unpredictable, and sometimes unnerving. But, like any rushing river, it was going somewhere and there was power behind it.

I wasn't working in the middle of a clinic anymore, but in the midst of a revolution.

My first patient of the day was Thad Cassell. Tall, thin, twenty-five years old, he appeared to be in good health. Sitting upright on the exam table, he turned to face me as I walked in. After our introductions, he explained that he needed his prescription for his asthma medicine refilled.

"Are you breathing OK now?" I asked.

"Sure. I'm doing fine. I just don't want to run out of my medicine." A quick check of his lungs revealed no breathing problems for now. But he was right. Without his meds, he could get into trouble quickly.

"What medications have you been on for your asthma?" I asked, prescription pad in hand.

"It's called theophylline. Can you do this for me?"

"Sure. Do you remember what dose you're taking?"

"No, Not really. Just the name. Theophylline," he replied.

"OK. It'll take a minute though." Theophylline had to be given in the right amount. Too little, and Mr. Cassell wouldn't receive much benefit. Too much, and he could have seizures.

"Is there going to be a problem?" he asked, leaning forward a little anxiously, real concern in his voice.

"No. I just need to know your weight first so I can give you the right dose."

"145."

"Thanks. The heavier you are, the more medicine, you need," I said, as I put the prescription pad aside, and took out my calculator, taking a few moments to enter the numbers.

"Who are you calling?" he asked, interrupting me. "You need to call somebody just to write my prescription?"

"No. Nobody," I replied. "I'm not dialing anyone. This isn't a cell phone. It's a calculator."

"You need a machine to write my prescription?" he asked with genuine wonder.

"Yes . . . no . . . yes . . . no," I stammered, thrown off by this conversation. "No. I can write it without the calculator. But I have to know how much medication to give you. In order to do that, I have to solve a small math problem."

Pointing to my PDA, he said, "That thing's going to do math for you?"

"Yes. It's only a calculator. It just does the arithmetic for me."

"You're serious," he said with real curiosity.

"Yes, sir. Here it is."

Taking a step or two toward him, I turned around. Now we were standing side by side, both facing the screen of the PDA, I tried to orient him.

"Let's do an example," I said. "If you had three prescriptions and each cost six dollars, then this can show you how much it costs." I got him to enter in '6', then the multiply button, followed by the three. The number '18' appeared at once on the display.

"See," I announced. "It calculated the total cost of all three prescriptions."

"Well yeah," he responded. "But, I mean, how do you know it's right?"

"What?"

"How do you know this answer is right? Maybe the machine is wrong."

For a moment we just looked at each other. Mr. Cassell was serious.

"For a problem like this," I tried to explain, "they don't make mistakes."

"Well," he said, equally serious. "I guess I don't trust it. Will you check it?"

"Sure," I agreed. "I know that three times six is eighteen. And, since we need to get your dose right also, I'll do the arithmetic on the calculator, and then check it 'by hand'."

"I can live with that," he replied, relief in his voice.

It took a few moments to finish the dose calculation on the PDA, and just over a minute to do it by hand.

"Here are the results," I replied. "The calculator was able to get it right."

I quickly wrote the prescription for him, and we walked out of the small room together. I stopped for a moment to talk to a nurse, losing track of my patient.

"Uh Doctor? What's this?"

I looked up, and saw Mr. Cassell, pointing to a computer display on one of the tables. The chirping screen he was interested in was announcing that it had just identified a local wireless signal and was ready to connect.

"Does this help you write prescriptions too?" he asked, still pointing,

How do I explain the internet to someone who ten minutes ago didn't know about calculators? "If you like, and you come back, we can talk about it"

I sat down with two nurses, Sydney and Rayna. They had heard Mr. Cassell's last question.

"How are you going to explain that?" Sydney asked.

"I don't know, I guess just start at the beginning, wherever that is," I responded.

"He needs a lot of education," Sydney replied

"What he needs," I answered, "is someone to spend a lot of time with him."

"Lots of luck," Rayna chimed in. "Many people are still afraid of them. Did you hear that a volunteer was raped here?"

"Do you really know that?" Sidney asked, surprised.

"I heard about it!" Rayna protested

"Well," Sydney retorted. "Fact is fact, and rumor is rumor."

"People are still fearful," Rayna added. "Did you hear the rumor about Sam's Warehouse just down the street? They had to close because of the sudden surge in shoplifting!"

"Well," Sydney retorted, waving her hand dismissively, "I know that's not true. I was just there and they were open for business. So much for rumor, Rayna. Now, let me give you a fact. The police chief of Houston just announced that crime in this area is down 1.2%."

"What?!" Rayna responded, leaning back in her chair.

"That's right. Crime is down in the neighborhoods where the evacuees are staying, walking, shopping . . ."

"Maybe," Rayna interjected, "it's because of the increased police presence."

"Well maybe it's because, in reality, these people are harmless," Sydney answered. *"They're not predators—they're prey."*

Disposition was the order of the day! I had the pleasure to meet with a young family, the LaSalles. Both the mother and the child, a five-year-old son, were ill. The young husband, Charles, was healthy, but he couldn't keep still. His wife was in one treatment room, and his son in another, right across the makeshift hallway from each other. Mr. LaSalle would dash from one room to the other, first checking on his son, then on his wife, staying with her for a moment. Then back he went to hold his son's hand, where he would start the process all over again. Someone could have explained to him that the rooms were close enough together that he could choose one position and keep an eye on both his son and his wife, but the nurses and doctors understood. Mr. LaSalle was responsible for his family, and this is how he demonstrated his love for them. We simply worked to keep out of his way, explaining as best we could the treatment we were providing to each of them.

We had just finished treating his family, when a social worker approached Mr. LaSalle. They engaged in a quiet conversation. Moments later, a man and woman approached, talking into a pair of cell phones. Ending their conversations, they shook hands with Mr. LaSalle and entered the room where the mother and son, both feeling better, were now waiting.

The social worker explained to me, "That couple that just entered are from the New Faith Gospel Church of Houston. The church is interested in sheltering the LaSalles."

When the male church member exited, I walked up to thank him for his group's commitment to getting the LaSalles back to a normal life.

"Oh!" he replied. "We're not interested in sheltering them. This is what you're doing here at Reliant Park. We have something else in mind."

"There are many groups involved in sheltering," he continued. "Our church has a house on the land we own. We would like the LaSalles to move in there. While they stay, we will look after them. We can help to find Mr. LaSalle work, and see that they are comfortable. We're trying to be careful about the families we choose."

"Families?"

"Yes. You see, we have five of these houses. We are looking for one evacuee family per house. We want to be sure that each house has a mother, father and children. Each of these evacuee families will have a guiding family from our congregation. This family will serve as advisors or mentors for one of these evacuee families. To help steward them about living in a new culture. This is important. Sometimes, it's best for a father to speak to a father, you know? For a wife to speak to a wife."

This man reflected a growing concern about these families. As the acute phase of the evacuees' care was drawing to an end, we all began to wonder what would happen next. This church had decided to do more than shelter. A shelter was a short-term solution. The church had considered some of the long-term implications of the displaced survivors, and had responded with the idea of mentorship. This church was part of the Houston faith-coalition that had come together to create long-term solutions for the evacuees.

The displaced families were anxious to make decisions for their own lives and the lives of their children. The LaSalles were a family devoted to each other. There was never any doubt about their bond. Now, they faced a challenging road. Not an impossible one. But they would need to receive new training. They needed coping skills.

What to do about the absence of coping skills was a central question. And people who only wanted to help the evacuees responded the best way they could. This church took advantage of its unique position to adopt five families, and hoped to help shepherd them into twenty-first century living.

The shift ended. Two social workers, Esther and Michael, joined me as we headed out into the September, steamy Houston evening.

"Well," Michael said, turning to Esther. "I don't know about you, but some of these families I spoke to were agitated."

"About what?" I asked.

"Maybe that's the wrong word," Michael responded, correcting himself. "They were confused. For example, there were all kinds of rumors flying today about credit cards."

"Yes. I saw a story on TV today about an evacuee going to a mall to try to buy perfume with her new card," Esther replied.

"I don't know about that," Michael scoffed. "But I can tell you, many of the folks I saw today wouldn't know what to do with a credit card."

"Come on! How can that be?" Esther responded, surprised.

"Look. I'm just telling you what I saw," Michael persisted. "They don't know how to use them."

"Don't they have TV? For heaven sakes, how can you not know how to use a credit card?" Esther said, unable to accept this proposition.

"Hold on now," I replied. "You don't learn how to use a credit card from TV. Think about it. Sure, TV will show you some things. You learn that they have something to do with money, but not how to use them. And no TV commercial I ever saw said 'Be sure to pay your bill every month, or else you'll have to pay a whopping finance charge!'"

"Ha!" Michael responded. "You got that right."

"So how could they learn?" I continued. "Their parents never had them. They didn't need them."

"Wait a minute," Esther protested. "They understand some modern things right? Like cars, TV, radio. Why is that?"

"Cars have been around for a hundred years," Michael offered. "Radio and TV have been available for generations. Parents and grandparents understand those. But what we're talking about, credit cards, debit cards, etc., are relatively new. Everything moves faster now."

"How do you teach someone about the internet who doesn't know how to use a calculator?" I mused.

"Very slowly," Michael answered.

We headed to our cars.

After several days getting through the crushing workloads of seeing patients suffering from physical and spiritual neglect, the number of new bus arrivals began to diminish, and with that, the number of new patients also began to decline. Finding myself with some leisure time, I felt compelled to speak to the evacuees. Part of this was to begin to help them with their assimilation into a new life in a new state. But that wasn't the whole story.

The media carpeted my daily arrival at the clinic with tales of spiritual desolation and depravity from New Orleans. The media had a new affection for the word "animal." The message was always the same, desperate angry survivors sacrificing others as they clung with "animal-like" tenacity for existence. The evacuees' hunger was "animal-like." They had "animal-like" sexual urges that required gratification. They developed "animal-like" survival instincts. I had been "media-prepped" to stiffen my own spine when dealing with these "aliens" who were bereft of reason and forced, despite their better nature, to care only for themselves. I had essentially been told that I would be treating not human beings, but humans reduced to animals. *The media had created an atmosphere of antipathy.* By this point in my experience with the Katrina survivors, I knew better than to breathe it.

Now, after treating these evacuees for several days, appreciating their sensitivity, watching them respond warmly to my sincere interest in them and my treatments and interventions on their behalf, the simple truth was—*I missed them.* I didn't miss treating them, and I was glad that the number of diabetes emergencies and hypertensive crises had subsided. But, I missed talking with them. *I had connected with them.*

Maybe, listening to their experiences, I had found some new fine and decent thing in myself. I didn't expect that people so harshly treated could be so encouraging in their stories. These were not criminals and malcontents to be shunned, but people to be sought out, invited to talk, engaged in conversation. So, when I had a few moments, rather than take a break with the doctors or nurses or volunteers, I would walk the floors of the arena and, finding one evacuee standing quietly alone, or a number in conversation, I would just join in.

It was one of the best things I could have done. I hope my conversation was helpful for them, because I must confess it made a difference with me. Even in their pain, they managed to uplift the up-lifters.

One of my patients the next day was Mr. Emanuel Rathbonet. He was sitting in a chair, and was in very good shape, at least from the ankles up.

His feet, crisscrossed with several huge lacerations in various stages of healing, were tender and swollen. Checking his chart, I saw that Mr. Rathbonet had been seen several times in the clinic for these injuries, and was already on antibiotics.

"It's good to see you. Why are you here today?" I began.

"The doctor I saw yesterday asked that I come back to have my feet checked," he replied.

"OK." An examination of his injuries revealed that, although angry, his lacerations were healing nicely. There was no sign that the infection was spreading, and his feet were much less tender than they had been before. I quickly noted the findings, made sure he was continuing to take his antibiotic, and asked the nurse to apply some new foot dressings. We then spent a few moments together, and he told me how he had received his injuries.

"I was in my house for several days," Mr. Rathbonet started. "I was waiting for the water to recede but it didn't, so I decided to make my way to the Center."

"The Civic Center?" I asked.

"That's the place," he replied. "That meant walking though the water. That was tough because the surface you planted your feet on below the water level wasn't clean. There was all kinds of junk on the bottom. And the water was flowing. Walking with the current was a real problem because it would rapidly sweep you along."

"You cut your feet on that debris?"

"I lived across from an auto parts shop. They always had all kinds of junk lying around, tools, old car parts, that kind of thing. The storm really smashed that shop up, and all of that metal was pushed by the water into the street. It was easy to tear your feet up on it.

"I didn't feel the cuts though. At least not at first! I was just so anxious to get to someplace that was dry. But, I guess I cut myself up pretty bad." Mr. Rathbonet paused for a moment. "They decided my feet couldn't be stitched up when I got here last week."

"Yes," I agreed. "Typically, doctors don't like to put in stitches if it's been six or more hours after the injury. The risk of trapping infection under the skin is far too great."

"Yes," he replied.

People were reporting skin rashes from just being in the corrosive liquid. This man had that poison pouring over and in each fresh laceration as he walked.

"You know, if the stuff was that bad, you'd think it would kill the germs," he chuckled.

I gawked at it him for a second and then we both laughed.

"Yeah," I responded. "Too dirty to touch, but not too dirty to kill the germs."

"How does that work?"

"Badly."

We bantered for a couple more minutes. Then I asked. "What do you think you're going to do? Head back to New Orleans, or stay here?"

"Oh, I'm not going back. I've been interested in leaving New Orleans for a long time, even anxious to leave. But, I grew up there and never really got myself worked up enough to go. Well, Katrina fixed that for me."

"You going to stay in Texas?"

"Well, actually, I'm thinking about staying right here in Houston!"

"Great, what do you do?"

He gave me his card. It said:

Mr. Emanuel J. Rathbonet

Banquet Organizer

"Well! OK. I've heard about the banquets in New Orleans. They're famous."

"World famous," Mr. Rathbonet said at once, correcting me. "World famous, and I'm one of the best. It's been my work for twenty-five years. I did it all. Picked the best hotels. Chose the chefs. Helped with menus. Even provided some advice on guest lists. It always paid to know who was in town and available to come. Sometimes, celebrities would attend my banquets."

"So, we can look forward to some good banquets in Houston."

"Better get ready. As soon as I can walk on these feet, I'm going to start lining up some interviews here. It's time I got back to work. My work."

I looked at his feet again. They were in bad shape. I guessed he wouldn't be able to walk for a few more days. I had an idea.

"Mr. Rathbonet, why wait?"

"What do you mean?"

"Just start your interview process now. Are you planning to interview at hotels?"

"Sure. I thought I'd start with those."

"Ok. Why not call them. Tell them who you are, what you do, and more importantly, where you're from."

"Why does that matter?" Mr. Rathbonet asked, his face full of genuine puzzlement.

"You know, right now, Houstonians are anxious to help out. But attention spans are sometimes not very long. You never know what's coming next in this town. The fact is, people are anxious to help now and may not be so anxious a month from now. Calling around now can set the stage for a good interview later. You know, they may come here to interview you."

Mr. Rathbonet sat up straight at that idea. "I'll start making my calls," he replied without hesitation. "Right away!"

I wheeled him out in his wheelchair.

"Thanks for the information," he said, with a big smile on his face.

The volunteer showed up to take him back to the Arena area where he was staying.

"It was my pleasure to meet you, Mr. Rathbonet. You know, I never met a banquet organizer before."

"The pleasure is mine. I love what I do, and I really love to cook. I think there's a chef in everybody. Do you like cooking?"

"Not exactly."

"Come on now, tell me about an original dish you fixed," he persisted.

"Baked beans and graham crackers," I confessed.

He wrinkled his nose in distaste. Then, "Well, nice meeting you, Doc. Don't quit your day job!"

The mood in the Arena had completely changed. Five days before it had been unmistakably bleak. That first Friday, it was like a huge emergency room after a natural disaster (which of course is exactly what it was). Now, to watch the evacuees, you'd think they were a huge church congregation that had just been released after an inspirational sermon. The attitudes were lighter. People were beginning to mingle together, talking to each other, sharing with each other. Strangers weren't threats but simply people who had common problems. Family groups were eating not just inside on their cots, but outside. And, people were hooking up.

Conversations were all about the "hook-up!" Making a connection for a job was hooking up for a job. A connection for housing was "hooking up" for housing. There were hundreds of these conversations and, walking among them, you could hear snippets of them.

"Somebody just told me that an employer was looking for fifteen families with men who were able to work in low-level construction. If the men were willing to work, then the employer would find and pay for an apartment for them and their families!" one evacuee said to another.

To the right, one survivor announced "I just spoke to a guy who owns an auto shop. He's willing to pay for auto mechanic-training for some people!"

There was a new energy in the air. I spoke to a young man, Theo Larson. "What's all the excitement about?" I asked, raising my voice to be heard above the many conversations swirling around us.

"There are new jobs, and maybe new places to live."

"But, you had those before, right?"

"Yeah. But this is different. Sure, there were jobs back home. But there were never enough of them. You had to work to find them. You had to scratch for them! Here, we get to *pick*. You know, I could pick from one of three or four different jobs right now. At home, I never had that chance!"

Shouting to be heard, Mr. Larson finished, "At home I had to settle. Today, I get to choose!" Fishing the ringing cell phone out of his pocket, he apologized for abruptly ending our conversation. "Sorry, I have to get this."

I got back to the clinic and immediately noticed a change. Gesturing to a nurse who was walking by, I asked, "Where are all the children?" Half of the clinic's population had been children in the last few days. Today there were none.

"School started for them," she said, and hurried off.

Some semblance of normality began to encompass the Katrina survivors. Bolstered by the solid foothold that intrepid volunteers and innovative faith-based organizations and local business owners provided, the Katrina victims were rising to their feet. However, we also felt there was trouble ahead if the notoriously short attention span of America contracted yet again. Consider the following conversation I had as I was leaving the Astroarena toward the end of the Katrina Clinic experience.

"We're doing all right with meeting the acute medical needs of many of these survivors," I said, eating a bite of lunch with two social workers, Rebecca and Matt. "I must tell you," I continued, "that we really need you and the other social workers to work out the disposition issues. That alone is an overwhelming task."

"It's not just the physical disposition," Rebecca replied as she considered the task of finding homes for the survivors. "We can place them. It's their well-being after they've been placed that worries me. Their spiritual and intellectual disposition will be critical if they're to have a chance to survive."

"What we're looking at," Matt said, swallowing a mouthful of food, "is something far more profound here. A huge *physical* displacement."

"It's more that that," Rebecca replied, shaking her head slowly, deep in thought. "We are witness to a massive, *cultural* displacement. Look at many of these families," she continued. "Sure they're poor. But they're not really agitated by that. They don't feel cheated because of it. It's part of their tradition. Call it their cultural inheritance. These families, including grandparents, aunts, uncles, and cousins have been poor for years. No. For generations." Matt and I both nodded in agreement.

"Same thing with education," Rebecca continued, becoming more animated. "Many of these families have no one who has graduated from high school for decades. That's not just true for them, but true for their neighbors as well. Again, they've become accustomed to that. It's just the norm for them. They make their way around that obstacle. I'm not casting aspersions, doctor," Rebecca said, concerned about my reaction to this characterization of many of the survivors. "It's just the plain fact of the matter. They have survived that way for as far back as they can remember."

"In a way," I responded, "America has passed over these people."

"How so?" Rebecca asked, looking at me curiously, confused by the sudden change in direction of the conversation.

"Well. America moved on ahead of them." I answered.

"Now wait a second," Matt started, his voice rising at once. "There've been all kinds of programs over the generations for these people. I don't think . . ."

"I don't want to start a fight about *why*, Matt," I reacted, gently patting his arm. "We both know the problem is complicated for lots of reasons. Social ones; economic ones; racial ones. Ethnicity, culture, economics and history are inextricably bound up here. But whatever the combination of reasons, these communities have been left to find their own way. Many have stayed cloistered in poverty, isolated in ignorance. It's a fact of their lives."

"And America has become comfortable with it as well," Rebecca joined in. "The well-being of these people has not been high on the country's priority list. It's been a 'live and let live' situation. People on both sides have made their peace with the status quo."

We stopped talking for a few moments, working in our own individual ways to sort this conversation out.

"So what has happened here?" I asked. "These families that have spent decades immersed in a poorly educated and impoverished culture . . ."

"Have now," added Matt, "been swept up onto center stage . . ."

"And are just as surprised at the rest of America as America is at them," Rebecca finished. "For the first time in who knows how long, these two American cultures are staring at each other. Eyeball to eyeball. And they have to deal with each other."

"You know, that may be the true legacy of Katrina," Matt replied. "In all of this chaos and despair, the storm brought two disconnected parts of America together . . ."

"You mean, slammed them together," I interjected.

" . . . in a way no one anticipated," Matt continued. "Over the years, they had become comfortable ignoring each other."

"Now, they're in each other's faces," I concluded.

"So," Matt asked, "what next?"

"Well," I started, "this can be a time of either tremendous

opportunity, or great tragedy. These families, having been passed over, or fallen behind, or however you want to say it, have a second, great chance. For the first time in generations, they have America's attention, and a chance at some of America's resources. Thousands of impoverished families are being poured into the mainstream of twenty-first century U.S. culture.

"If the U.S. handles this correctly," I continued, "we can have the benefits of their full involvement. Their insight. Their devotion to family. Their inventiveness and flexibility. Their great strength of heart. They can make a powerful contribution."

"Or," Rebecca offered. "they'll again be shoved aside. After playing with them for a few weeks, America will get impatient. And then, in a hundred U.S. cities, the new arrivals will once again sink to the underclass, and they'll be right back where they started."

"Yes. This is a social problem. It's not just about money, but about providing education about modern life and sharing some coping skills," I added.

"But only at a level that they can absorb," Matt replied. "You just don't put a high school student into graduate school. They'll have to grow into it, and that takes time."

"Did you see that some of the survivors were flown to Los Angeles in a private jet?" I asked.

"Can you imagine the shock that must have been," Matt observed. "One moment, you are in the depths of poverty, ignored in the anguish of a storm. Then, three hours later, you're deplaning from a private jet in Lala land."

"Yes. You just can't take a family that knows little of how to function in modern, electronic America and give them resources they don't know how to use. This isn't the 'Beverly Hillbillies' here," Rebecca added.

"Yet, some people will handle that kind of transition," I countered. "Sure, many can't. But, with the right encouragement and the right support system, there will be a few who will respond well to that drastic change."

"Each family should be given only what they can absorb," Matt offered. "Provide too much, and they'll give up. On the other hand, they'll all need to be challenged."

"Everybody, rich or poor, educated or unschooled can respond to a challenge," Rebecca stated. "But the challenge must be at a level that they can tolerate. I get the feeling from the evacuees that they're ready to be challenged. They are fearful, to be sure, but they're also gathering their strength for a new and different life."

"This means . . ."

"You bet. A lot of conversation has to begin, not just *about* the evacuees, but *with* them. Each family must be treated differently, given the chance to respond individually."

"You all have your work cut out for you," I observed.

Matt turned to me. "What do you mean 'you'?! You too, Doc! If I had my wishes, every contact you have with an evacuee has to be one that first lets them drain themselves of the strain and burden. Then, you have to find what they need. I don't mean to pick on you physicians. I mean, you have some standing, so people are inclined to listen to you. But this is something that every worker can do. Every volunteer—from maintenance people on up. It's now time to stop talking *about* them and start talking *with* these survivors. Find out what they need. Where they want to go, then get them the resources they need. This is not the movies where after dusting themselves off, they march forward, arms locked, into the sunset with a spirit of bold curiosity!"

"It is for some!" Rebecca declared.

"Not for all. We have to treat each family differently and attend to their needs differently. Each family to the extent that we can, with the power that we have, needs individual attention and treatment because the needs will vary widely."

The last patient I saw at the Katrina clinic had been coaxed to come to the clinic by his wife. I was due to get off at 7:00 P.M. that night; Mr. Jamond appeared about 6:45 P.M. It didn't take long to write the prescription for his antihypertensive medications. However, this nineteen-year-old father of two was clearly distracted. Like so many of the evacuees, the Jamonds had fled New Orleans with only two or three garbage bags full of clothes.

"How long have you and your family been here?"

"Four days."

"Mr. Jamond, I think that we have taken care of your hypertension today. But you look like something else is on your mind."

"Uh yeah. I just don't know what to ask. Where do I begin?" He looked around for a moment, gathering his thoughts. Then he began, "There are some people we've gotten to know here who are from New Orleans. They're suggesting that we get an apartment here and just live in Houston."

"Sure. There's room for your family in Texas, that is, if you're OK with leaving New Orleans."

"Oh, sure," he responded. "We have to leave New Orleans. The houses are gone. The neighborhood's gone. The New Orleans we knew isn't there anymore. So we're OK with leaving. But," he finished, "apartments don't sound like a good idea."

"That's right, sometimes," I replied. "Some apartments can be bad, even unsafe for you and your family. But many apartments are safe, and might be a good idea for you to consider temporarily."

"Well, of course we would want to stay somewhere safe," he replied. "But they all require me to sign something. That's what I don't understand."

"They all require that you have to sign an agreement that says how long you'll stay there," I agreed.

"That's what I can't figure out. Why do I have to agree to stay for a given period of time?"

"It's called a lease."

"Well, why can't we leave the apartment when we want to?"

I tried to explain. "The owner needs to know when it will be available for someone else to use."

"Well," Mr. Jamond responded, "if I let someone move in with me back home, they wouldn't have to sign a paper to say that they are staying one week, or one month. They just stay as long as they need to," he replied, perplexed about the novel arrangement.

"It's different with apartments. The person who owns the apartment needs to be sure that he or she gets a certain amount of money each month to pay the bills. So, when the renter—that's you—agrees to stay for six months, the owner knows that he can count on six months of income from you."

"How do I do that?"

"You do that with rent. You pay rent every month."

"What's rent?"

What! I thought. *He doesn't know what rent is?* "Rent is the money you pay. The owner won't let you live there for free. You have to pay him."

"I have to pay?!" he protested.

"Uh, yes. Everybody who lives there pays him. That's how he keeps the apartment complex safe and clean. That's how he makes his money. That's how he pays the bills. Everybody who rents has to pay rent."

"I never heard of this!"

"Well," I asked, equally puzzled, "how did you live back in New Orleans?"

"We lived just east of town. My family had three houses. I mean, my sister, my aunt, and me, we each had a house."

"You didn't have to pay for the house?" I asked.

"Oh no. No. The houses were owned by my parents," he said. "We just lived there. We always lived there."

"How long have the houses been in your family?"

"Seven generations," he answered without any hesitation.

A generation is about twenty years, I thought. That means the houses have been in his family . . .

"Since about the end of the Civil War?" I asked.

"Yeah, the first owner was born a slave. His family worked the land to be able to live there after they were freed."

"They were sharecroppers?"

"That's right. Over the years, the house came into family hands. They built a second one, and then a third. All on the same land. That's how it's been. It's how it's always been.

"Handing down the houses always had to be done carefully," he continued, smiling for the first time. "I heard that it could be a real mess when the owner at the time didn't make their wishes clear. But, the houses were always, you know, given away. Nobody ever had to pay for anything. The house was given to you, and before you died, you wrote down who would get it next. That's how it was done."

I was stupefied. What I had just heard made perfect sense. Comfortable with a lifestyle that had been established decades before, this young man was struggling with the basics of modern living. How could I explain in clear simple language what would be required of him? I needed a few minutes to catch my emotional breath.

We agreed to meet in five minutes in the make-shift pharmacy. The hub of activity for days, it was now deserted. When I arrived, I saw Mr. Jamond sitting quietly. He was crying.

When he saw me, he said "I'm really sorry about this. But I'm just . . . lost. I don't know this world, this place. I can't do anything right here. I don't know what to do here. Josie," referring to his wife, "and my kids are going to need me, to lean on me, and, honestly, doc, I don't know what I'm doing."

"We came here as a last result," Mr. Jamond continued. "Because we had to. I've got nothing here. No job. No friends. No way to make any money. And I'm scared. Really scared. You know, back in New Orleans, I was thinking about trying to finish high school. Now, there's no chance of that. I don't even know what bills I have, much less how I could begin to pay them. The thing is, I need to do something. Not just anything. The right thing. But how do I find what that is?" he asked plaintively, the strain showing clearly on his young face.

"My family and I've been here four days," he continued, "relying on people to look after us. We didn't have much at home, but we relied on each other. And," he paused, "we knew how to get some answers. Things made sense. It wasn't much of a world, but we knew how it worked. I don't know how anything works here." He sobbed quietly for a few more minutes.

"You're seeing your problems right," I began. "I don't think you see yourself right, though, Mr. Jamond," I said, trying to comfort him.

"What do you mean?" he said, wiping his face, working hard to control the emotions that had finally overwhelmed him.

"Mr. Jamond, you didn't ask for any of this mess. It found you. The problems are in your lap. Just as your grandparents years ago provided for you, you now have to provide for your family. But you have to do it in new ways. You need some different skills."

We talked. Not about rent, but about the past and the future. "I can't say that it's been easy for your family in New Orleans," I continued, "but it sounds to me like it's been OK for you there. I mean you knew all the rules."

"Yeah," he replied, "like *you* know all the rules here."

"Yes. That's it,". I responded, warming to the conversation between the two of us. "But now, even though the rules have been changed, you can use that to your advantage, if you're willing. Don't get me wrong. You had some terrible things happen. Your life and that of your family has been altered in a horrible, unimaginable way. I know that it will never be the same for you. But, you know, maybe, ultimately it will be to a good end."

"What good? I don't see any good," he responded, his eyes cast down and voice choking.

"Yes. I know," I replied. "It's a little like being born."

"What?"

"Imagine what being born was like for your daughter," I continued. "You and your wife may remember it fondly, but if your daughter could remember it, she probably would describe it differently than you would. To her, it was unexpected, sudden, probably frightening. Cold. New. Loud, harsh noises. Some discomfort. Bright lights. Different, even alien, surroundings. That's what being born is like. The comfortable surroundings had changed. For all time."

"And there's no going back." he replied.

"That's right. Life had changed, and all she could do was to get on with it. And, even though she didn't know it, you and your wife would look after her. That's what happened this year to you and your family. You have been swept out of your old familiar world into a different, transformed, and frightening place. You had no say in the matter, but here you are."

"What do I do next?" he asked.

We talked on—about making money, about making plans, about thinking about goals. What should life be like in a year?

"How old is your daughter?" I asked.

"She's six," he replied with a touch more animation.

"When you were six, what did your dad want for you?"

"Hmm . . . what *he* had. That's what he gave me. His house, everything else he had, which wasn't much."

"Now, you get to do things differently. You can give your daughter more than you had. Ever think about college."

"For me? No way."

"Ok, but how about for your daughter?" I replied looking directly at him. She can have what you don't have if you want her to."

His gaze sharpened for just a moment. "She can do that?"

"If you think about it now, work for it now, talk to her about it, starting now, she has a great chance of doing it. Will you be president of this U.S.A.?"

"What? Shoot no. Will you?"

"Nope. Its not for me, and it's not for you, but it could be for your daughter, and your granddaughter after her. If you work for her, work with her, speak to her, she can do it.

"Look," I continued. "You have a second chance, really, for you and your family. Up until now, she has had the same opportunities for life that you used to have, which wasn't much. Now, that second chance just got much bigger. It's up to you."

"How can this be possible?"

I looked down, groping for an answer. "I think it's because, while you were safe in New Orleans, what made you safe kept you separated from these possibilities."

"I don't get it."

"To try something new, like getting your daughter a college education, back at home, would have been tough for you. It would put your life style at risk, as you tried to reach out for it. That's very difficult to do, because you would be choosing to give up a familiar lifestyle for a new unfamiliar one, and that's not a choice we voluntarily make.

"But now," I continued, "the change has been made for you. You've been pushed out. You have to change. So, now that you're out, take a good look around. Think about some new possibilities for your kids. For your children to see a new life of possibility, it would help for you to see it for them first. They'll see it best through your eyes."

We talked for about an hour—about taking tough days one day at time, sometimes an hour at a time, sometimes a minute at a time. We also talked about commitment.

"When you commit, you must commit it all," I said, as we sat together in the deserted area. Hold nothing back. You'll find in yourself strength you didn't know was there. It was never there for you as an individual. It's there for your family. Tap into it. Use it. Commit yourself totally to the betterment of yourself and your family. Make the best decisions you can, expecting that some will be wrong or won't work out the way that you hoped."

It was late. "I don't want to mislead you," I finished. "This'll be hard for you. But it will be different, and for the first time, you get to work not just to keep things the same, but to make them better."

"So, my children won't have to go through a flood like this?"

"No. So they will have the skills or the money along with the strength of heart to help those that do."

"Doctor, I had not thought about things like this before. I promise you I'll think on them. Josie, too. Josie and I will talk. She's pretty strong."

"Really?"

As we said our goodbyes, Mr. Jamond joked: "I hate going to the doctor; and look at me now."

"See the trouble it got you into!" We both laughed.

"Maybe it's not all trouble," he said.

There will be challenges and seemingly insurmountable obstacles for these people. The fraying social network across the United States makes it easy for people to fall through the cracks. They will need all of the strength they can muster. Despite their best efforts, they will continue to be viewed as waves of drug dealers or other social locusts descending on their new home areas by people who refuse to give them a chance.

People of good will among the Katrina survivors and among the ordinary folks in our society will have to organize collectively to help give these individuals and families a decent chance to enter the mainstream.

CHAPTER 9

Above and Beyond the Call of Duty

Houstonians appeared by the hundreds, and ultimately by the thousands to take part in the care of the evacuees. While it is commonly acknowledged that evacuees were uplifted by the generosity of Houstonians, the citizens of this large city recognized that, for several weeks, the evacuees transformed the city—not just by adding to its population but by appealing to its heart. If Houston helped breathe life back into the drained spirit of the Katrina survivors, then these survivors returned the favor by infusing the Houston civic spirit, a spirit commonly fractionated by competing urban needs, with generosity and unity. The urgent requirements of the survivors allowed Houstonians to shove aside our individual and neighborhood goals, needs, and problems. We chose to knock down the racial, ethnic, economic, and geographic dividing walls between us so that we could jointly come to the aid of struggling strangers. The Houston spirit was flooded with light. We were, for several illuminating weeks, a community with a clear commonality of purpose, on a single mission—the demonstration of compassion through self-sacrifice.

It started with the huge caravans of cars filled to overflowing with donations for the survivors. However, while this was a critical contribution, Houstonians also freely gave what is one of the most jealously guarded commodities of twenty-first-century urban dwellers—their time. Many, including myself, were asked to volunteer because of our skill sets, e.g., health care delivery, or electronic capabilities, or pharmacy skills. However, the vast majority had no such skills at all. They could easily have stayed at home and watched events play out on television. But thousands showed up simply to help.

These untrained volunteers brought a giving and open heart attitude. It was their generosity of spirit that made all of the difference because it was not passive, but active. Once ignited, it could not be readily extinguished. They insisted on being involved. Rather then sitting on the sidelines, talking among themselves, waiting to be called, they actively sought opportunities to help. They wanted and needed to make a difference. These volunteers were proactive, pitching in where they knew they had the ability and skill to make a difference. Knowing their own talents and abilities like no one else did, they found where they fit and put themselves in place. Like living pieces of a living jigsaw puzzle, they moved and circulated until they found their best spot, settling in and making a difference as only they could, bringing the entire human mosaic alive with kindness.

I saw Rose in a conversation with one of the janitors who was emptying the wastebaskets. Clinics generate immense amounts of trash, and the waste bins rapidly filled with gauze, wadded paper, instrument wrappings and so on. The cleaning crews worked hard to keep up, and they were doing a good job.

"What's up," I asked her when she walked back over.

"I needed to stop the janitor just to tell him how important his work was here."

"You mean, keeping the clinic clean?" I asked.

"Not really," she replied. "We have to have clean surroundings here, but there's something else going on. Something more subtle. It took me a few minutes to puzzle it through."

"What are you talking about, Rose?" I asked.

"Many of the evacuees have come from filthy conditions in New Orleans," she began. They didn't keep dirty homes, yet they were thrown into surroundings that were incredibly dirty. The survivors were simply told to just 'make do'. Papers, soiled rags, and slime were everywhere. That environment was despicable, and they couldn't get away from it. There was no way to get clean, and no clean place to stay. Even if they wanted to feel normal, they couldn't because they were existing in squalor.

"That's why the cleaning crews are so important here," Rose finished. "It's not so much what the result is, a clean clinic, but what that result signifies. It sends the message that things are getting back to normal and that they all deserve to be in a clean environment, a safe environment. I try to stop and tell every janitor I see how much their work matters."

"What did he say," I said nodding to the janitor I saw Rose speaking with.

"He said, 'I keep thinking that the only difference between them and us is three hundred miles. If Katrina had hit here, many of us would have gone to New Orleans and have had to rely on them.'"

Indeed, janitors and other care providers who were paid for doing their jobs performed above and beyond the call of duty. However, it must be simply and plainly acknowledged. Volunteers made the difference at the Katrina Clinic.

Rushing over to me, the young nurse's aide pulled me aside anxiously.

"Doctor!" she said, nervous and breathing rapidly, "you'd better get in Room Six—fast!"

Pulled away from my brief sidebar conversation with Rose, I quickly looked at the papers the nurse worriedly shoved into my hands. Two charts. The top sheets of each said simply, "sunburn." Scanning for the patients' identities, I saw the name—Meriwether.

Facing me were two adults whose flesh was so red and blistered that I couldn't identify their true skin color. Shredded clothes covered only the essentials, so it was easy to see that their distorted skin color varied with location. Each face was a dark, angry purple. Both of their backs were beet red, as were their shoulders and upper arms. Even the backs of their hands were blistered. They appeared exactly the way a child might imagine two partially boiled people would look.

On top of it all was the ever present thick layer of gray-black grime. The dirt itself looked like it was a permanent fixture of their skin, enameled on by a mix of dried sweat and continued baking under the hot Louisiana sun.

That's not sunburn! I thought, as I briefly introduced myself. *That's sun poisoning, and the torment must be unbearable.* Both patients were in their twenties, and both were clearly large people squeezed into chairs that were much too small for them. I estimated that the man was 6'4" and his female partner was almost six feet tall. Yet the Meriwethers each sat quietly on the woefully tiny chairs. Gauging by their ever shifting positions, they both were terribly uncomfortable. *Yet,* I thought approaching Ms. Meriwether, *neither speaks.*

I studied Ms. Meriwether closely. A faint and mournful moan lifted off her lips by her shallow breath. Looking into her swollen face, I saw that although she was crying, no tears ran down her face. As I had seen in one of my earlier patients, crying without tears would commonly occur at this clinic.

"It's . . . all right . . . now . . . baby," Junior Meriwether soothed, speaking with eyes shut, comforting his wife. The large man, his skin angrily inflamed by the sun-induced UV damage was careful not to touch her, for any physical contact was sure to inflame their discomfort.

"Please, Ms. Meriwether," I pleaded, noticing that her eyes were open, watching me carefully, "sit on the small cot, just over here." I pointed to the clean cot that went unused as both sat in the uncomfortably small plastic chairs.

Painfully turning their swollen faces to each other, they came to an unspoken agreement. Then the husband, opening his swollen eyes for the first time, responded for both of them, "Can't do that. We're too dirty, and that bed's clean and made up fresh. We don't want to ruin it."

What! I exclaimed to myself. Overwhelmed by this completely unexpected attitude of humility, I quickly traversed the small room, to the cot, pulling the tucked-in top sheet free. Then, tugging it down, I opened the bed sheet.

"This cot, Ms. Meriwether," I offered, "was made for you. It's been waiting for you. Please use it now for your own good and that of your family."

They looked at each other again, and finally, Junior Meriwether nodded his assent. She painfully stood up, and leaning on me, stumbled to the bed. There she lay on it crosswise, painfully stretching her legs out while sitting up. Belle Meriwether moved like her skin was contracting, pulling at her, transforming every exertion into tight, tender agony. After a moment, Ms. Meriwether gingerly leaned her burned dirty back against the cool wall.

As his wife worked to get "comfortable," I asked, "When did you last have anything to eat or drink, Ma'am?"

Belle Meriwether said nothing, looking over to her husband, who looked at me, inquiring, "What day's today, sir?"

"Friday, sir," I responded at once, a little more urgently. "When did you last eat or drink?"

"Must have been . . ." pausing for a minute, actually giving my question as careful attention as dehydration and sun toxicity would allow, ". . . Monday."

"Monday?" I replied, surprised, my questions stumbling out of me. "You've not eaten anything for four days? There was nothing on the bus for you?"

"No sir," Junior Meriwether affirmed. "We never got anything." After a quiet moment, he added softly, "We were just so glad to get out of the sun and onto that bus. I think we're beyond worrying much about food and water now."

"You didn't go to the Superdome, or the Convention Center?" I asked. "Where'd you stay?" I continued, quickly examining him. He had sunken eye sockets, dry skin covered by old sweat, and dizziness when he moved from a sitting to a standing position.

I turned to Ms. Meriwether, first asking, "I would like to do the same exam on your wife, sir," seeking his permission before I proceeded. "I really should check her first, before I choose a treatment."

They each nodded their approval, and I rapidly completed my assessment. The exam and their subdued behavior confirmed the intense dehydration from which they suffered. They needed nourishment, but, to save their lives, they needed fluids first. Both were beyond thirst, but each needed liquid—lots of salt and loads of water.

Working quickly with nurses, we set up two intravenous sets. The volunteers searched for and returned with clear bottles of sterile solution containing the right mineral content, and ten minutes later, clear salt water loaded with nourishing sugar was rushing into their veins, coursing through their all but collapsed circulatory systems. I stayed for a few minutes until they had each received a liter, ordering a second, and then a third bottle of the lifesaving fluid that would be hung for each of them.

Before I left, though, I turned to Ms. Meriwether, asking "Where were you this week that you couldn't get shielded from the sun."

"We stayed out on the roof," she replied, eyes closed.

"I understand," I gently countered, "but for four days? Surely there were rescue boats around, weren't there? Why not take one of them?"

Looking right at me, she responded softly, "Because they wouldn't take all of us."

I returned to see the couple an hour later. In addition to the salt and sugar enriched fluid they received, we also provided intravenous medicine to help reverse the destructive effects of the sun on their skin. The largest organ on the body, it had been badly damaged by the corrosive effects of the intense ultraviolet radiation. We also provided some much needed pain medicine, and began to treat the blisters.

I found Junior Meriwether quietly lying on the floor next to his wife who now lay on the cot, each with their own IV. Sixty minutes made all the difference. The smell of their decrepit clothes was intense, but the spark of life had returned to their eyes, or at least, to the eyes of Belle Meriwether. Her husband remained quiet, with no room for emotion on his huge, burned, grim face.

I'd seen this look many times that day. *He's grieving*, I thought.

"You told me," I began, sitting on the floor next to Ms. Meriwether, "that you were out in the sun for almost five days."

"Yes," she answered "and my name is Belle," she finished with the first smile I had seen from her.

"That's a long time without food and especially without water," I continued, giving her the opportunity to elaborate if she chose.

"Yes, but the two of us made it out of there," she said, the light in her eyes diminished by some new internal pain.

"Two?" I asked. "How many more were out there?

"Ms. Ziggs," she said, suddenly crying again. This time the tears flowed.

"If you'd like to tell me, I'm here to listen to you."

Gathering her strength, this young, articulate woman explained.

"We'd lived in New Orleans all of our lives, but the rains of Sunday and Monday were like nothing we'd ever seen. It was . . ." she fell quiet, struggling for the words. "It was like the heavens opened up, allowing a new lake to fall from the sky! It seemed like suddenly water surrounded our house. Like our house was going to drown.

"It was so strange, so sinister. The streets were rivers, and cars moved in those dark rivers that Sunday night, but no one was driving them. It was like . . . like demolition derby from hell! Cars pounded into each other propelled by the waves. Cars crashing into houses. Sometimes," she said, trying to lift her head from the cot's thin yellow pillow, "they slammed into people." Looking right at me, she said, "The world we knew ended that night, and a terrible new one began. What will happen to us?"

I stayed silent as she refocused her thoughts.

"We didn't know anything about the levees breaking. We just watched that water rise higher, and higher, and higher until it was up to the second story. We had a two-story house, but the water rose so quickly, there was no place to go but out onto the roof. That was Monday, when the rain was slackening off. Didn't even think to take any food or water we were so panicked," Ms. Meriwether added. "Ms. Ziggs handled it pretty well, especially for her age." At night we would take turns holding her. Sometimes crying."

"Crying?" I repeated.

"Crying." she said again. "Crying for everybody. For everything! You could hear the cries in the streets that first night. From all sides of the house, from everywhere in the city. The only lights were those of the occasional helicopter, but the night was full of cries. Anguish, Fear. Loss. The city itself was crying. Writhing in the agony of its loved ones. It was terrible," Ms. Meriwether said, crying again.

"But Ms. Meriwether," I asked again, "weren't there boats going by? Why didn't the three of you call out for one of the rescue boats?" not understanding her earlier answer to this same question.

"Sure we did," she said, raising her voice some, turning to face me again. "Called out until we were hoarse for those things. But every time, it was the same story. Nobody would take Ms. Ziggs. We could go. But Ms. Ziggs had to stay behind. And, well, we couldn't leave her."

"Please continue," I asked, puzzled, but not wanting her to stop.

"The worst day was Wednesday, I think," she began again, laying still, looking at the ceiling. Tuesday was my hungriest day," she asserted, closing her eyes as the memory overtook her. "But Wednesday, the thirst took over. Unbearable thirst. The sun was so unbearably hot, so unbearably yellow. We couldn't look at the sky, so bright did that yellow sun shine. But what could we do? The three of us stayed up there, beyond waiting, almost beyond caring. We took turns looking after Ms. Ziggs, making sure she was OK. But, we both knew she was dying. It was hardest on my husband.

"But," Ms. Meriwether continued, "we knew what was coming. She was old, and the hot sun, lack of food, and no good water wore her down. During the hottest part of the days, she just whimpered and cried. My husband would pull her into his arms, put his head on top of hers and just softly call her name over and over. 'Ms.ZiggsMs. ZiggsMs.Ziggs' he'd say until she would get herself settled.

"How'd the three of you get off that roof," I asked.

"The three of us didn't. Ms. Ziggs . . ."

"Doctor," a volunteer announced from the room's door, "one of the nurses needs to see you."

I hated to break off our conversation but needed to leave. "I hope to see you soon, Ms. Meriwether," I said, standing up. "I think you and your husband will be OK."

"Different, but OK." she replied, closing her eyes.

I returned in fifteen minutes. Walking into the Meriwether's room, I was surprised to see only Junior Meriwether in the small yellow room, lying quietly on the floor, the IV now removed from his arm.

Still grimy, his eyes now had a new light, the grieving chased away, at least for a short time.

"Got a cigarette?" he asked.

"Uh no," I responded taken a little aback by the question. "You can't smoke here anyway."

"Pity," he replied laconically, but softly. "I can smoke outside though, right," he asked, genuinely concerned.

"Sure"

"Well that's one more reason to get better," he replied, looking up at the yellow curtained wall.

"You appear to be feeling better," I pointed out. "How'd you finally get rescued from the roof?"

"Wife told you that, did she?" he responded, turning again to look at me.

"Uh, yes she started to."

"She tell you about Ms. Ziggs?"

I hesitated, not knowing what to say, "I don't know. . . . We never finished our talk."

Junior raised himself up on his elbows to look at me. "Ms. Ziggs was all I had before I married my Belle six years ago. I'm twenty-nine years old, and Ms. Ziggs was with me for eleven of those years. So pretty! Always there for me. No matter how busy she was, whenever I came in, she'd come around to check on me. When things went well and I was happy, she was happy, and when things didn't go right, well, she was right at my side no matter what."

"You all lived together?" I asked.

"Sure did," Junior Meriwether replied without hesitation. "Ms. Ziggs and I lived in my folks' house after they died. Then, when Belle moved in, well, Ms. Ziggs didn't make a fuss. It was like she understood from me that Belle and I were special. But she also understood that it wasn't just that Belle and me were special. The three of us were special. We all belonged together. She trusted me with everything. Even her life.

"But," Mr. Meriwether continued, sighing, "she was old, so old. It hurt her to walk. She almost fell off that roof twice. Finally, I had to take her in my arms and hold her, touching my forehead to hers.

That's what I was doing on Thursday when she died, rubbing her nose and eyes the way she always loved me to do."

The light finally came on for me. "Ms. Ziggs was your . . . pet? Your dog? You and your wife waited on that roof for two additional days because, even though rescue boats were available, they wouldn't take your pet with you . . . ?"

"That's right, doctor." Mr. Meriwether gently responded, "I could no more leave her behind, than someone could leave their parent, or a mother could leave her child. It's different with pets. You just don't own them. They become part of you. Ms. Ziggs was part of us.

"There was no leaving her out there by herself," he continued, new emotion filling his eyes. "She was so very tired, and she couldn't make it on her own. Without us, she'd fall off the roof into that filthy water and drown. Or other animals would get her. She lit up my life, and I was her world. I wasn't going to desert her because of some damned storm."

He went on to describe a precious relationship, one that had no room for abandonment or betrayal in the name of self-preservation. Those low emotions of desertion had been squeezed out over the years by a simple, sustaining devotion that guided the interaction between two loving owners and a loving pet. Over the long years, Ms. Ziggs showed the Meriwethers a part of their hearts that, without her, they would never have known they had.

His wife came back in, looking much better, without an IV, aided by a young woman volunteer.

We don't have to stay here in this room, do we?" Ms. Meriwether asked.

"No ma'am," I responded. "You each need a good meal, and could probably use some more to drink, but you don't need to stay in the clinic for that."

"Well, where can we take a shower?" Junior Meriwether asked.

"What?" I responded, nonplussed. I stared at them, having no clue how to answer. "Well, maybe . . . ," I fumbled.

"Don't bother doctor!"

I whirled to see the young volunteer, speaking up clearly and affirmatively. "They can come to my house!" Turning to face them, she said, "I've got a shower and some clean clothes for each of you."

The room was dead still, those words and their tender sentiment overwhelming us all, blocking any response.

"And," she said, looking carefully at Mr. Meriwether, "I have a dog. Her name is 'Twinkles'. She stays home all day by herself. How about if we give her some company today?!"

Huge tears suddenly welled up in Mr. Meriwether's eyes. Held first by his wife, then the small, young volunteer, the big man broke down—completely, utterly, and honestly.

A half hour later, the three were gone.

It took me several moments to settle down and complete these patients' paperwork, so moved was I by the generous offer of this volunteer. This was the enchantment that played out at the Katrina clinic each day. Unforeseen contacts seemed to work much too perfectly to be random. Volunteers and survivors fit together so flawlessly that you wondered whether the relationship hadn't been etched into their hearts in Houston and New Orleans years before, laying dormant, waiting for the terrible storm to bring them out. When exposed, they seamlessly meshed, and we marveled at it all.

There sat a patient, Mr. Wilson Sage, anxiously waiting to be seen as I arrived back from a break, five days into my Katrina clinic experience. He was remarkable, not because he was, at 6'5", the tallest patient I'd seen there, or at 370 pounds the heaviest patient I had seen there, or even because he was the first (and, as it turned out, the only) blind patient I saw. He was most memorable because he was happy. Not just happy—the man was positively ecstatic! We had seen all kinds of emotions at the Katrina clinic, but not unbounded delight. Life had shown him something so wonderful that morning, that he couldn't sit still! The only other patients I had ever seen with this joy of life were the nervous patients who had feared cancer but found out that their test results were completely negative.

This kind of joy was like the first fragrant flower after a long, dark, cold, northern winter. The small room was full of Mr. Sage and the sweet smell of new life.

After introducing myself, I said, "Mr. Sage what can I do for you?" I had caught his infectious cheer, smiling even though I didn't know why. There was also something familiar about him. I hadn't seen him in the clinic before as a patient. Something else about him struck me. *Where do I know him from?*

"Doctor," he said, his huge face turned to face me, his large frame threatening to collapse the wheelchair. "You can help to get me out of here." He smiled and clapped his hands together.

I gave up and just starting laughing with him. "You mean, out of the clinic?"

"No sir," he replied, clapping his hands again. "Out of this place. It's time for me to go home."

"I'll help you do that if I can. Let me just take a look at your chart," I said, smiling and touching his right shoulder with my hand. He reached his left hand over to grasp mine. "Yes sir. Yes sir! I am going home now. It's happening TODAY!"

Stepping to the side, I examined his chart. Although this was the first time that I had seen him, Mr. Sage had been to the clinic before, arriving on one of the first buses from New Orleans the previous Thursday night. In fact, he was one of the acutely ill patients that were in my instrument-less "clinic", although I didn't meet him on my first day at Reliant Park. *Oh! That was it! That's where I had seen him*, my stomach flipping for a moment as I recalled the experiences of that memorable afternoon. Seen by another first-line physician, Mr. Sage was diagnosed with diabetes out of control, hypertension out of control, and intense dehydration. He had been rushed to the county hospital for admission and emergency care. He had been discharged from the hospital just this morning.

"They let me out when I was better, and now I'm here!" he exclaimed. "How about if we just get me back to Louisiana?!"

"Do you have family here?" I asked, fearing that he didn't understand the complexity of the problem. He was blind, needed his medication, and had to have a wheelchair to get around. I just couldn't declare his medical problems resolved and wheel him to the street.

As usual, this survivor was way ahead of me.

"C'mon now, doc! They're not here! Why would they be here? They're in Louisiana, and they're coming for me!"

Wow! Family had found him and were coming to get him. I don't know how they connected, but the contact had been made. And, like a live wire, strong current was flowing. These versatile people surprised me all the time.

"Yeah. Yeah," he said, moving and jumping in his wheelchair that was already overwhelmed by his bulk. "We talked this morning on the phone. Everybody's been found." He jumped a little again. "We're going to be together tonight!" he shouted, shooting his right hand up in triumph.

"Well, where are they?" I asked, smiling, but falling far behind the reveling of my ebullient patient.

"We got split up trying to leave the city," he replied with a smile. "We'd been told that all of the buses had the same destination, but we were wrong. One sister went to Atlanta. Another wound up in Baton Rouge with my son. My mother and sister are in Alexandria." These details rolled off his tongue like a song. "We were all in New Orleans, but lost contact with each other in the scramble to get out of town. They're all heading to Baton Rouge today. I can't drive," he paused only to catch his breath, "but my son can, and is driving here to see me today."

I laughed as his smile grew. "To get me." It grew bigger still. "To GET me and to TAKE ME HOME!" Holding his head high, this huge man, with his large head, exposed me to the world's biggest smile.

"OK, then," I replied, still smiling. "Let's get you on your way." Looking at his chart, I saw that he needed to have his blood sugar checked, and that his prescriptions had been lost and required re-writing. I could do these, and do them quickly. There was no way that I was getting in the way of Mr. Sage's well conceived plans! Excusing myself, I walked across the cubicle's entryway to the open area to arrange for the test, absorbed by his chart, trying to find his last measurement . . .

"Owww!"

"Oh! I'm so sorry!" In my total immersion in the chart, I blundered right into a trim woman who was trying to enter Mr. Sage's room as I was leaving.

Reaching over to help keep her from falling, I apologized for my clumsiness again. I introduced myself.

"That's OK," she replied. "I'm Ms. Peterson, Mr. Sage's social worker."

"It's a pleasure to meet you," I replied." I just spoke to Mr. Sage. You're the one who helped him contact his family?"

"That's right. We were able to work that out."

That was it. It was Ms. Peterson who had made the family connections, who tracked his family down, who told the son that his father had been discharged from the hospital. That's how this family miracle had occurred.

Something was wrong. She had been the cause of his joy. But there was no trace of it on her face.

"Now," she said, lowering her voice, "I have to let him down."

Turning around, I re-entered the room behind Ms. Peterson. I had no idea what bad news was coming, but I wanted to be available to help. Or, at least share the responsibility of the failure.

"That's you, Ms. Peterson, isn't it?" the irrepressible Mr. Sage said at once. It wasn't a question at all. It was a statement of fact.

"Yes, Mr. Sage. I'm afraid that I have some bad news for you."

"What could that be?" he asked. Then, only an instant later, he asked "Is my family, my son, OK?"

"Yes, Mr. Sage. Your family's fine. In fact, I just got off the phone with your son . . ."

"He's a fine man," my irrepressible and irresistible patient said.

"I spoke to your son just a few minutes ago. Unfortunately, Mr. Sage, he . . . he can't come get you."

"Really? Why not?"

"He had car problems, and he couldn't find another one to drive. He was pretty upset about it on the phone."

I unconsciously steeled myself for the outburst that had to be on the way. This man had been through so much. Stripped of his dignity by his treatment in New Orleans, his family summarily broken up, he was transported to Houston, only to be forced to go to a hospital. Neither he nor his family knew how to contact each other. A man used to being surrounded by his family was now in the hands of strangers. He had endured so much. And now, this. After Mr. Sage's determination to reunite with his family, and the dogged persistence of this social worker, the plans for his discharge came crashing down. I tried to prepare for the intense emotional onslaught.

"Well then. What's next?" he said, simply, calmly, and evenly. The disappointment was palpable, yet he overcame it. *The smile was gone, but what remained was not anger, just steadfastness. Not fury, but fierce determination, fueled by an inner strength and a binding discipline.*

I left to let them talk while I had his blood sugar checked and wrote his prescriptions, thinking as I wrote. I realized that my instant reaction to the evacuees was almost always wrong. I thought Mr. Sage's plans had suffered a stinging defeat. That wasn't true at all. From his perspective, the ground shaking event of the day was not the car's failure, but the reconnection with his family. That was the victory that no one could take from Mr. Sage. Their rescue of him? Well, he was prepared to wait for that.

I continued to write, amazed by these people and their unshakable resolve. *They refused to live down to my expectations.* Yet, even with this revelation, I would within a few minutes realize that I had underestimated them yet again.

"Your blood sugar is fine," I reported when I returned after a few moments to see Mr. Sage. "Now it's time to get you out of the clinic area . . ."

"and with all the healthy people," Mr. Sage responded, completing my sentence for me, though not the way I intended. "Got it, Doc!"

"You're all set to go to the Astrodome to stay for awhile," I concluded. Turning to Ms. Peterson, I asked, "Could you step outside with me for a moment?"

Outside we found a quiet place to talk. That was difficult, because the clinic had erupted with a new force. Social workers were everywhere. The new word for the day was *disposition*, and the survivors were ready for it.

Physicians can't discharge patients from a hospital just because the patient is well enough to leave the hospital. There has to be a plan for the patient once he leaves; that plan has to be a formal part of the patient's chart. Is the patient going home? If so, who's picking him up? Is she going to another facility? Long term treatment? Specialized care? Hospice? Do the people at the receiving facility know when the patient is coming? Have they approved the transfer? Who'll pick him up?

These plans are known as the patient's disposition, and it's often a logistical nightmare to set them up. Commonly, they involve tough decisions that a family and the patient must jointly make. Phone calls have to be made and connections established and bills paid. It's just one of many non-scientific components of a physician's care that is essential and must be carefully handled. One invaluable service that social workers provide is to develop the patient's disposition.

Up to this point, we had all been involved in acute patient care; diabetes out of control, severe and dangerous high blood pressure, lacerations transformed by the toxic shock of poison sludge immersion, profound dehydration, debilitating hunger. All required urgent attention. And, of course, hanging over it all was their rending mental stress, emotional exhaustion, commonly attended by anguish over a lost loved one.

Treating these patients for their emergent medical needs, we gave no special thought to any special disposition. Patients were either sent to the hospital, or discharged back to the general area. However, the acute phase was coming to an end. No new evacuees were arriving, and the survivors, recovering from their acute medical problems, were now thinking in the long term. Social workers were everywhere at the clinic and in the arena to help them.

The social workers arrived by the hundreds from Harris County, the Red Cross and the Salvation Army to help with this. It was the social workers who were arranging for phones for the survivors, who contacted the churches about the need to consider long-term care. Their work was critical because, if carried out in a step-by-step manner, it could shape the direction and help create the momentum these displaced families needed to begin anew.

"Ms. Peterson, this is outstanding work you're doing," I began when we were out of Mr. Sage's earshot.

"I'm so disappointed about its outcome," she responded, now

visibly deflated. "You should have heard his family on the phone. They were so anxious to be with him again."

"Yes, but he can't go to the general area on his own with no vision. Also, he's still weak and can't push his wheelchair. He's going to need some help getting there."

We looked at each other for a moment, both thinking the same thing. She left the clinic for a moment, returning with a volunteer, Mr. Metcalf.

It was a complicated situation, and I didn't want to abuse Mr. Metcalf's charitable spirit. "Mr. Metcalf," I began, "we have a patient who needs help getting back to his area in the Arena." Taking him back to the treatment room, I introduced the two men, and as they began to talk, Ms. Peterson and I tried to work out the other issues involving this patient's care, hoping to avoid yet more delays or problems for this disappointed patient. We identified a small area in the Astrodome that was taking care of the sicker patients. The Astrodome was in the next building, several hundred yards away. It would be quite a trip, rolling the huge Mr. Sage to that building.

Mr. Metcalf came out of the cubicle in a moment. Frowning as he listened to our plans, he bluntly said, "Wilson," referring to the patient by his first name," needs more than that, though. He really can't eat by himself."

"That's right," Ms. Peterson agreed

"He can't take his medicines by himself either," Mr. Metcalf continued.

"Yes. That's right too," I agreed. "Ms. Peterson and I are trying to work this out as well."

"Well, I'll just stay with him," Mr. Metcalf responded immediately. "That way he'll get his meals, his water, and his medicine." This wasn't a question. "At night, I'll push him over to the Astrodome area to sleep, but for now, I'll stay with him in the Arena."

This was an astonishing act of selflessness. Typically, volunteers were used for *short-term* services e.g., helping to unload trucks, sorting clothes that were donated for the survivors. Occasionally they would transport patients. But Mr. Metcalf was offering much more.

"Mr. Metcalf," I responded, "this is a great service you are doing not just for Mr. Sage, but for us all. I wasn't sure just how we would work this out."

"This is what I'm here to do. I'm looking forward to spending time with him."

As final arrangements were made, I left the two gentlemen talking as the nurses ensured that he had all of the prescriptions and that the required paperwork had been completed.

When I returned, I saw Mr. Metcalf. Ms. Peterson was next to him, a look of surprise on her face. Leaving her side, Mr. Metcalf came right up to me.

I instantly knew that something had happened to Mr. Sage. Fearing that his diabetes had roared out of control again, or that he may have suffered a stroke, I rushed over to him. Again, I was dead wrong.

"Wilson told me he has family in Baton Rouge," Mr. Metcalf began.

"That's right," I responded, relieved that there was no medical emergency. "They were hoping that one of his family members could pick him up today, but couldn't work it out."

"Well," Mr. Metcalf said, "I can just drive him to Baton Rouge today!"

Stunned, I took a step backwards, trying to take the measure of this rock solid man. The willingness of the volunteers to extend themselves to the nth degree overwhelmed us all. This solution would fix the problem at once, yet we never thought to suggest it. Mr. Metcalf, seeing the problem for what it was, simply threw himself into it. He saw the gap, and plugged it. He suggested the six hour drive to Baton Rouge with the same ease as if he was just going to the drug store four blocks away.

"My car is here. We can just gather his belongings up, and I'll drive him to meet up with his family. Does anyone have his son's address?"

"I do," Ms. Peterson replied at once.

"If it's OK with you," Mr. Metcalf said, addressing me," I would like to tell Wilson."

"I would just like to be there with you when you do," I replied.

The small room was now crowded with an empty bed, an empty cot, the large Mr. Sage, and three happy caregivers.

"Ms. Peterson here," Mr. Sage said to Mr. Metcalf, unaware of what had been arranged, "explained that you would be taking me to my area today," he began.

"Yes, but let's do something else. Let's get you back to Louisiana," Mr. Metcalf stated.

"That'd be great," Mr. Sage replied, "but how can we do that?"

"Wilson," Mr. Metcalf began, "I'd be glad to drive you there."

"What!" Mr. Sage responded with astonishment. "Why would you do that? How can you do that?" He couldn't believe his ears.

I expected simply that Mr. Metcalf would just explain his devotion to help people in need. Wrong again.

"You're a great guy. I would love to talk with you. Nothing would please me more than the two of us spending time on the road for a day. You OK with that, Wilson?"

"Man! That would be just great!" Then the big man began to quietly weep.

Two hours later, Mr. Wilson Sage was wheeled out of the Katrina Clinic, the Reliant Arena, and Houston, for the last time. He hadn't been helped by a volunteer, but by a new friend. I guessed that before the day was over, Mr. Metcalf would have gained not just a new companion, but another family, as Mr. Sage's incredulous family greeted their loved one, returned safely to them.

The small number of superlative actions portrayed in this chapter are not exhaustive, but merely representative of the many acts of self-sacrifice and kindness that the workers and volunteers repeatedly displayed. The few elaborated here are like the brightest stars in the sky: they were most easily seen, yet with patient attention, many others become visible. One only need look for them.

CHAPTER 10

For Conduct Honoring Humanity . . .

Giving pity and sympathy alone to the Katrina survivors and those who did not survive desecrates their sacrifice. While many volunteers worked hard, it was the rare one who was expected to give up his or her well-being or life to save the evacuees. Yet evacuees themselves did this repeatedly. These heroic Katrina victims should receive medals with a new inscription . . . *For Conduct Honoring Humanity*. Here are my two living candidates for this award.

The idea that Katrina victims inflicted terrible and indecent treatment on each other had no more cruel target than that of parents. The estimates thrown out from the television all suggested that there were thousands of parentless children abandoned in New Orleans. Again and again, the question begged by the television commentary was "How could someone leave a child behind?" The picture that the media permitted to be painted was one in which parents abandoned their children to the elements, wild dogs, and alligators, as they fled in a panicked attempt to save themselves. My leisurely reacquaintance with Ms. Traylor revealed that the story was much more complicated and heartening.

"Ms. Traylor," I called, quickening my pace so she wouldn't get too far ahead of me in the crowded general area. Turning, and recognizing me, she made her way toward me and shook my hand.

I hardly recognized her at our reacquaintance. A week or so ear-lier, when I first saw her, she had just arrived from New Orleans on one of the early buses. Then, she could barely remember the check-in process; now she was alert with a smile that emerged easily. The filthy clothes had been replaced by jeans and a blouse. However, merely de-scribing this young woman as "well-groomed," doesn't do Ms. Tray-lor justice. A week before, she was "the walking dead." Today, her eyes were flooded with light. The child standing next to her was her daughter, whom I had met on my first day at the clinic. Ms. Traylor greeted me with a smile, and surprisingly, a handshake.

After saying hello again to her daughter, I stood up and smilingly asked, "Can you introduce me?" referring to the tall man standing next to Ms. Traylor, holding a six-year-old who just had to be the child she was so concerned about a few days before.

"Yes. This is the father of my other daughter, Greg Hayden," she smiled, "and this," she said, taking the six-year-old from Mr. Hayden's arms, "is Regina."

I leaned over, saying hello to this delightful child. No exam was needed as she smiled saying, "I'm R'gina," her rolling bright eyes driven by playful embarrassment. She was delighted with the atten-tion. Clutching a doll, this child was in love with life.

As she handed her back to Mr. Hayden, I turned to Ms. Traylor, stat-ing "You really look much better today. Is Regina the child who . . ."

"Yes. Yes. This is my family who were back in New Orleans," she replied at once.

"Well," I asked, trying to steer us over to the side, "can you tell me what happened? You know," I said, turning to Mr. Hayden, "I had the pleasure of meeting Ms. Traylor when she arrived the other day. She was really worried about you and Regina."

"I know, I know. I'm sorry it took us so long to get here," Mr. Hayden responded. "I didn't mean to worry Dawnie, here," he said, nodding over to Ms. Traylor. "I know she was upset about what hap-pened. I'm surprised that we're here in Houston at all. Actually, the bus driver didn't know where we were going!"

"Well, how could that be?" I asked.

He shrugged his shoulders. Smiling slightly, he explained. "It seemed like he was getting different directions. First, he told us we were going to Houston. Then, he said, we were headed off to 'some-place in the north in the state,' meaning Louisiana. One time he said we were going to a camp in Arkansas. After a couple of more hours, he said we were going to Houston after all."

"Well, how did you know you would see Ms. Traylor when you got here?"

"I didn't. There was nothing I could do, since it was the last bus, and I promised her that I would catch a bus that day. But I felt that I had to stay on back and help the others before Regina and I got on a bus ourselves."

"Help how?" I asked, looking down at Regina who was twirling around and around among the three of us, just living life.

"Well, it was such a mess," Mr. Hayden started. "You know, we had been waiting for days for buses to get us out of New Orleans. When they finally arrived, we all rushed over to them, across the grass, onto the highway. We were ready to begin boarding before they had even stopped. But then, things got, well, bad.

"What do you mean?" I knew what the media had suggested—more evacuee-led pandemonium. Now, I could hear whether that de-piction was true.

"Well," Mr. Hayden said, putting his hands on Regina's shoulders to calm her down some, "there was no real control and no information. When the first few buses arrived, no one knew if these were the first of hundreds of buses, or if they would be the only buses that arrived. But, given our experience of the past several days, everybody assumed no more buses would be coming, so there was a rush. Most people reacted just fine, but too many people were trying to get on at once. Only one person could board at a time, but two and three would try to board at once. It was like everybody knew that the absolute worst feeling would be that you were going to be left behind. Again.

"Also," he continued, "no one wanted their family separated. Sometimes, there would be a family. Say, a mother with three or four children, a grandmother, and two aunts. They all wanted to get on the same bus. When the bus was full, these families had to be split up." He was quiet for moment before continuing to speak. "After what they had been through, families refused to be split up. They wanted to board all together."

"So, tell me, then, why didn't you get on the first bus with Ms. Traylor?"

"Well, with all of the confusion, many of us were getting angry that we would be left behind. The emergency folks who were there didn't provide much help. They were supposed to explain the situation to us. That more buses were on the way. That we were all leaving. Instead, all they did was count people. When the bus was full, they stopped the boarding and told the bus to leave. They just counted," he said, shaking his head, "like you're not really there, you know."

I shook my head, not really understanding.

Mr. Hayden was patient with me. "It's like the clerk who checks you out at the food store. Sometimes, they don't treat you like a person. She counts your goods and takes your money, but she doesn't look you in the eye. They're there, but it's not like they're there for you."

I got it. "OK," I said.

"Well these people just counted us, but they weren't helping, and when some of us trying to get on the bus would get angry, they got angry back. If the worker thought that they were shoved, they would shove back. Hard. Some women got pushed around. Everyone had run out of patience, and it was getting ugly."

"So, what did you do?"

"Well, once I was sure that Dawnie was on, I just stayed to try to help sort out the mess a little bit. Regina," he said, allowing his hand to gently caress his daughter's hair, "would have to stay with me, because I don't get too upset when she's getting ready to have a seizure."

I was starting to get it.

"You mean that you stayed behind to help with the bus loading?"

"Yes sir."

"And your daughter stayed with you?"

"That's right. You never let your children out of your sight. Never! I stayed most of the day and the evening helping to load buses. I counted folks," he explained, "but, more importantly, I talked to people, joked some. Reminded them that we had all lived through this, and that now, *finally* we were getting out. We had made it. We were getting out. Maybe for just a time, maybe for all time. But, one way or another, we were finally leaving.

"What we all really wanted was the truth. That's what we needed. You have to understand," he explained. "By this time, we'd heard all of the lies that we could stand. Toilets at the convention center would be cleaned. That didn't happen. Food was coming that never came. 'The police are on the way', they said, but they never arrived. We couldn't believe anything anybody said. We just wanted some of the truth. And, that's what I tried to do. That," he said, "and treat people like people, not like suitcases."

"How was your little girl during all of this?" I ventured.

"Safe. Not too happy, but safe."

"Well where did she go while you did this?" I asked, trying to visualize this.

Stupid question! His scowl came from nowhere, rising to the surface at once. And he looked at me like I should have known better. "She was right with me! The whole time. Sometimes I would have to hold her. But she was with me as long as I was there."

How could I think anything different than that after all I'd seen! He kept his daughter close, like any parent would whose bond to his child was unshakable. That's what I would have done, and I'm a loving father. That's what he did. Ms. Traylor had never abandoned her daughter. She left her with the father, who was as devoted to her child as she was. And Mr. Hayden had kept his daughter right by his side, just like Ms. Traylor would have. Yet, even knowing this, Ms. Traylor was still worried about both of them.

"Yes. I understand," I replied, nodding. "Did your daughter have any trouble with her seizures on the bus?"

"No. I was sure to give her medicine. I knew the times she was supposed to take it, but I didn't have a watch, so I would always ask what time it was, and when the time came, I gave her the medicine."

Then he took out a sandwich bag, folded so many times it was more cloudy and creased than transparent. Inside, were the few remaining pills. Regina instantly made a face.

He put them away, then apologized to the child "Not now, sweetheart, Daddy's sorry." Looking again at me he said, "She doesn't like her pills much, but she'll do what I say."

I tried to picture this. Father, mother, and two daughters had been left stranded in New Orleans. Dirty, almost out of medicine for one child, definitely out of food and water, their turn, at long last had come to board a bus—to escape. Yet this man, seeing the growing chaos, had chosen to remain behind. *He let Ms. Traylor and one child go to Houston, and he stayed behind with the other daughter. And he did this just to help his fellow survivors.*

I hadn't heard anything like this in the past week. It was almost time for my break to end, and I felt the pressure to get back. But, I couldn't help myself, so I pushed a little. "You know, you and Ms. Traylor had waited a long time for those buses."

"Yes we did," Ms. Traylor responded. We waited day after day."

"But when your time came," I said turning to Mr. Hayden, "You let her go with one child, and you stayed with the other. Why?"

"I..I just needed to do that," he explained. "Things there were so bad. If I left, they were better for me, for us. But they would be worse for many others. I couldn't leave like that. I really wanted to get out of there, but not that way. I . . . I knew better. I had to stay. And Dawnie knows I would keep our daughter safe. So, that's what I did."

"Well, I'm glad your bus was headed to Houston."

"So am I" he shrugged, "but if not, me and R'gina would have gotten here one way or another."

I bid my goodbyes to this family. Then shaking Mr. Hayden's hand, I said what I needed to. *"Mr. Hayden, thank you for talking to me. It's been an honor to meet you."*

———————————

A sea of emotion flooded my heart. Sure, this was a common-law family. They had not been married, and would be criticized for that. I didn't know and it wasn't my business to know if both of Ms. Traylor's children were Mr. Hayden's. Yet, *he met the measure of what makes a father: steadfast, unshakeable devotion to his children and active self-sacrificing concern for others in distress whom he could help.* I was the one who had been to school for many years, yet *I needed to make room in my head and heart for Mr. Hayden's example.*

I walked back to the clinic through the entry area of the arena that was full of activity. People were eating. Families were finding themselves. I had thoroughly enjoyed the conversation with Mr. Hayden and Ms. Traylor. It wasn't that I was pleased, though. Nor was I happy, joyous, or glad. What I felt was much deeper. *I had been ennobled.*

On my first day at the clinic, the very first patient I attempted to meet was an older woman who appeared to be eighty years old but who I would shortly learn was fifty-five. "Hello, ma'am, I'm Dr. Moyé, and I'm here to help you. Can you please tell me your name . . ."

"Uh, you'd better let her get some rest," someone in the crowd called out to me. Tall and dirty, the new speaker wore badly torn jeans and a filthy T-shirt. Looking right at me, the same man repeated his comment, "Best that you leave her to sleep for a time," nodding toward the woman I had begun trying to talk to. He wasn't threatening at all. In fact, he delivered this unsolicited advice seriously but softly and politely.

"I can do that, but why?" I responded, turning to him, perplexed. The only reason that I started with her was because she was the closest. I could begin my evaluation with anyone. *But why couldn't I start with her?* I wondered. "Abby," he said, nodding toward that nearest woman, "was on our bus. She got no rest on the seven-hour ride out of New Orleans. She looked after us—made sure we were comfortable. There was no food on that bus, and the only bottles of water we had were what she brought along. She gave it to us," he continued, shaking his head. "Each and every bottle. Then, she stood for most of the bus trip," he went on, "giving her seat to a man who had to keep his injured leg up."

Looking around, I saw several of the evacuees nodding their heads in agreement with him. "She has to be dead tired," he finished, looking over to her, near the point of collapse himself.

"I'm happy to let her sleep and spend time among the rest of you," I responded, raising my voice so the entire group could hear me. "I'm simply here to help."

An hour had passed as I spoke with most of the evacuees. Some, sound asleep, I chose not to wake. Finally, it came time to return to the woman I was first told needed to rest for awhile. This is her story.

"My name is Abby Mantac, and I'm fifty-five years old," this much more elderly looking woman said. "You see," she smiled tiredly, "I've been listening to what you've been asking my friends here," she said waving her arm around. "I thought I would save you the trouble of asking me about my age."

"And I've heard much about you as well, Ms. Mantac," I replied smiling. "You have a spirit of sacrifice for . . ."

"No I don't." She cut me off at once with a fierce new energy that caught me off guard. "I've done nothing but try to repay a debt. One that I won't ever be able to," she finished.

"Who do you owe?" I asked.

"All of these survivors, and the ones I can't see, and will never know."

"I don't understand," I replied, "but first, tell me how you're feeling."

"My shoulder hurts, the same as yesterday, and the day before that," she replied.

"How tender are you now?" I asked, gingerly feeling along her shoulder inside her shirt for any sign of a fracture or a deeper internal injury. I was loath to do this type of exam in an area open with other people in plain view. But, with no privacy available, there was no choice. I completed the exam rapidly and as discretely as possible, deciding that she had a deep contusion but no broken bones.

"I think you have a bad bruise here. I'll get you some medication as soon as some becomes available."

She just nodded. I tried to make her as comfortable as possible, and I asked her if she needed to sleep. She simply replied, "I think that I've slept enough."

"Well, tell me then," I asked, "just who do you owe?"

"I ran an apartment complex north of the Superdome," Ms. Mantac began, speaking in short, tough sentences. "I was stubborn, and I know it. I didn't leave when we got the word to get out. We'd had hurricanes before, and I had stayed through every one of them! This one seemed no different. Most of my tenants saw it different though. Only one stayed," she said pausing. "Melvin stayed. Melvin, and his dad, Willard.

"Melvin had a lot going for him," she continued, allowing a new softness to enter her voice. "He'd finished high school and wanted to go to college. Was planning on it, too, but his dad had some strokes about a year ago that left him paralyzed in his legs and one arm. Melvin was his only family, and money was tight for them. So, Melvin just passed on the idea of college. Instead he found a job, and just lived with his dad in the apartment up on the second floor. He was trying to line up some kind of technical training that he could complete instead of college. It was hard on him, doing all that and taking care of his dad. I didn't make it easy for them, always in their face every month for the rent. I just didn't know . . ."

"Know what, Ms. Mantac?" I asked.

She just shook her head and went back to her story. "Since no one else was around, I visited them both a lot that weekend. The three of us spent Sunday and Monday together since we were the only ones in the building. We expected folks to return on Tuesday after the storm, and that things would soon be back to normal. It was the end of the month, and I started asking them about the rent. That's when Melvin said he'd given up school to make more money, and that paying rent wouldn't be a problem for him and his dad anymore. He was very pleasant about it, but it still made me feel bad. It hurt bad because I was the cause of it . . ." her voice faltering for a moment.

She sighed, strengthened up some and continued. "Anyway, Tuesday, the rush of water began. The first floor of my apartment building flooded out completely. This never happened before, but I was prepared for it. I'd set up a second floor apartment for me just in case, and that's where I was when it happened. Melvin was helping me to move some furniture back away from the windows and the bed.

"We were scooting a chest of drawers across the floor, when the world kind of tilted with a groan," Ms. Mantac said.

"What do you mean?" I asked.

"It seemed like there was a huge sigh that came from the apartment building. All that water had soaked into the walls of that old building. They were weak from age anyway, and pulling that water up into them didn't make them any stronger, you know? The walls began to shift and the upper floors started to give way. Suddenly the floor wasn't level and I fell hard on my back, and went sliding over to the wall. Melvin fell too, but he was holding on to the door so he didn't slide over. He was just laying there, one hand over his head holding on to the door stop at the bottom of the door and the other hand in my direction, kind of spread-eagle like on his back."

"I could use a cigarette about now," she inserted abruptly.

"You can smoke outside, but not in here," I responded.

"It's not going to be much fun around here, is it?" she replied.

I just shrugged, asking her to continue.

"There we were. The second floor room was now really tilted down. I was on the floor against the wall that was now the lowest part of the room. Melvin was laying on the floor, with his hand outstretched to me, the other hand holding the bottom of the door that had swung back into the room.

"We needed to get out of this mess. Melvin called to his dad in the next apartment room asking if he was OK. Willard said he was, but that he had fallen out of his wheelchair. Melvin suddenly started twisting left and right, scrambling around some with his feet, as he struggled to find something to rest against that would allow him to push his way up, closer to the door. I could tell he was nervous about his dad.

"We heard one more growl from the building, and the room shifted again. The slant in the room got steeper. The furniture against the wall on the other side started sliding over. First came the bed, slowly sliding down toward the lower wall. Next the chest of drawers started sliding. It began to pick up speed as it went by me, hitting the wall just over my head with a crash." The tough woman involuntarily shuddered for an instant, reliving the dreadful moment.

"That's all it took. The wall broke open, breaking apart in huge chunks and falling to the street below. A moment before I was lodged against it. Now, I was leaning forward over the edge of a floor that would spill me over onto the rubble. I could see the street below, full of debris-filled water rushing rapidly by. I was going to fall.

"'Grab my hand!' Melvin shouted. His one hand remained outstretched above him, holding tight to the doorstop on the back of the door that had opened into the room. His other was reaching down trying to find mine. I reached my left hand up, and grasped his hand as the floor tilted some more. Now, the only thing keeping me from falling was my hold on Melvin's hand. I was holding on to him for all I was worth!

"Without warning, we heard a crash then a cry from the other room. It was Willard. He was in trouble. The room he was in was right down the hall from mine. It had to be tilting forward as well. Willard was in just as much trouble as Melvin and I were."

"'Mel!' his dad called. I looked up at Melvin. I thought I knew what must be going through that young man's mind. Both me and his daddy needed him to save us. But he couldn't save us both.

"You know," Ms. Mantac said, looking right at me, "I started to forgive him for letting go of me. What else could he do? That was his daddy calling for him. Melvin had given up college for him, had chosen to stay with him when many folks these days give their parents over to strangers. Of course Melvin would let me go. It was the right thing to do. I began to let go of him, getting used to the idea that I would be dead in less than a minute.

"'Ms. Mantac!' Melvin called to me. 'What are you doing? Hold on tight!' I looked up. He wasn't letting go! I wasn't just beyond words. I was beyond all thought, save one—hold on tight!

"He called to Willard, 'I'll get there as soon as I can, Dad!'"

"'I can't stay like this for much longer!' Willard yelled back." The entire building was groaning and crying as it died.

"I'm holding Ms. Mantac now,' Melvin shouted.

"I braced for what I feared I would hear. I knew what I would say if I was Melvin's dad. 'Why're you doing that? She never did much for us!' That's what I'd have said. But, I didn't hear that. What I heard instead was 'Then look after her first, son. I know you'll be here soon.'

"I couldn't believe this!" Ms. Mantac said to me. "How could this man put me between him and his son? I wouldn't have done it. Not in a minute! Yet, he did that.

"Melvin worked hard to get me turned around some. Slowly he started to pull me up toward him. I thought my arm was going to come right out of its socket! The pain was shooting lightning right through me. But, he pulled me toward him. In a few minutes, I was able to grab his elbow with the other arm. I wanted to rest but he told me to keep going. Soon, I was all the way up. Up, and out of danger.

I put an arm over his chest. He then rolled up, forcing me over him and up to the door. A couple of minutes later, I was laying on the floor in the tilted hallway. Safe. I tried to help to pull him, but he didn't need my help. He hauled himself into the hallway too. We got up and quickly walked to the next room to look for his dad. We didn't find him. We only saw the hole in the wall through which he had fallen.

"Melvin didn't cry or anything. He headed at once to the stairs, heading down to find his dad. I followed. Melvin knew to be careful, but knowing wasn't good enough. One of them gave way, and he fell. I still see that. On the way down, he hit his head on the tilted banister. When I finally got down there, he was dead. Water was everywhere. I called to Willard, but I never saw him. He died too.

"Awwrgh!" Ms. Mantac cried. "Why couldn't that banister have fallen all the way over? Why did he have to die like that? Two men, good men, dead. For me! I never did much for them. I treated them badly over their rent when I knew they would pay eventually. But, they died for me. Worse than that. They chose to die for me. Willard could have called for his son to come for him. What son would ever refuse that? Family was everything to Melvin. Yet his father told him, basically, it was OK if his son let him die to help a woman who was never any good to them. I just don't know. I'm so ashamed of my life.

"You know," Ms. Mantac continued, "they treated me like I was their family. The only thing I can do is to treat these folks here who left with me from New Orleans as part of my family. That's the only thing that makes the pain stop. So, doctor, I don't think there's much you can do for me. I have to do this for myself."

She slowly got up and went in the back to sit for awhile with the needy Ms. Tyler (discussed in Chapter 2). To treat herself, she was going to treat another. The death of Willard and his dad was tragic—but their self-sacrifice resonated in the new heart and soul of Ms. Mantac. *Courage is contagious.*

These brave evacuees will receive no medals. The graves of Willard and Melvin go unadorned, remembered by and memorialized in the conduct of the landlady that they had died to save. Their sacrifice was not made to honor those of greater value, but in the affirmative recognition that they themselves possessed high value, regardless of their educational level or net economic value. It was because of that high value, not in ignorance of it, that these victims of the storm sacrificed themselves for others.

This spirit of self-sacrifice was there, in the core of survivors like Mr. Hayden and Ms. Mantac, quiet, but vibrant. It did not spring up *de novo*. It was not practiced. These Americans saw the gap whose presence would destroy the life of another and they plugged it—with themselves. The strength immediately welled up from within, instantly becoming an unstoppable force. This strength resides in each of us, lying dormant, waiting for its time to rise. The story of the Katrina survivors is filled with living epistles of compassion. To read it, we only need listen to the evacuees with open hearts. To learn about them is ultimately to learn of ourselves.

However, now, we can do even better. Perhaps the best honor we can bestow upon these heroes, some dead, others distancing themselves from us as they move into their new lives, is to marshal their force, yoking it to our own latent, untested power. We must do this before the next major public tragedy strikes. Neighbors must protect neighbors. *To take the best care of our own family, we must care for the family of man.*

CHAPTER 11

Conclusion

The Katrina clinic operated for only ten days, and, when it closed, thousands of us Houston first-responders and volunteers returned to our day jobs. For me, that meant going back to my research and teaching obligations at the University of Texas. However, although my academic responsibilities quickly consumed my time again, I now saw the world with "new eyes." The compassion that I shared imbued me with new vision, while the kindness that I received elevated my perspective.

It's both tempting and foolhardy to simply generalize a limited number of personal observations, however emotionally-gripping, to an entire nation. Therefore, I offer the following commentary in the spirit of "hypothesis-generation," hoping to spark dialogue rather than snuff it out with premature and perhaps even hasty conclusions.

Dual-Pronged Attack

The Katrina survivors sustained a devastating, dual-pronged attack in August and September 2005. The first was the more obvious and also the more short-lived—the *physical* assault of Katrina. Physical injury, dehydration, and acute malnourishment each took a terrible toll on the storm's victims. Of course, stress was the screw that tightened the pressure. Added to the strain of fighting for their lives was the stress induced by loss of family members or ignorance of their family's whereabouts, fear for their personal safety, knowledge that their homes were gone, and the unanswerable question of whether they would ever be able to return home to New Orleans again. The added burden of property destruction, lost wages and jobs, and separation from home still defy calculation.

We now know that this terrible debacle was only the first punch of a devastating one-two combination; it represented the short left jab that precedes the knock-out uppercut. For the Katrina survivors, this second, demolishing shot was the spirit-smashing realization that their experience simply didn't matter to the United States government. In fact, the belated response of the government was not ignited by the need to help the struggling, abandoned survivors, but was initiated to appease the world-wide criticism of their incompetent inaction that bordered on the criminal. *To the survivors, it appeared that government had measured them, and determined that they were worthless.*

The effect of this realization on Katrina's survivors went well be-yond physical or emotional pain—it was a sensation that carved out the human soul. The Katrina victims' collective reaction to this spiritual savagery was neither anger, nor protest, nor outrage—those would come later. The first reaction was overwhelming shock and stupefac-tion, not unlike the numbed reaction of a wounded soldier whose eyes tell him that the two mangled, amputated legs splayed on the street in front of him are his; the mere possibility is just too big for the spirit to understand. *The spiritual evisceration of the Katrina victims required life-restoring surgery that only humane human contact could provide.*

Houstonians: Part of the Solution

In my view, this was the most important contribution that Houston provided for the evacuees' well-being. Many Houstonians watched the ghastly catastrophe unfold just three hundred miles to the east. When they learned that their city would be involved, its citizens chose not to add to their neighbor city's disease but instead contribute to its cure.

Earlier chapters detail several of the many sacrifices Houston's den-izens provided. Their material donations quickly overwhelmed many organizations' abilities to organize them.

However, while substantial, these material contributions were dwarfed by the unique response of Houstonians that provided what the survivors who arrived by the thousands needed *first*— validation and the reestablishment of their dignity. This response was not administratively crafted; it was generated at the citizen level. Volunteers flooded both the George R. Brown Convention Center and the Reliant Stadium complex, ready to sacrifice for strangers with little thought to themselves. Many Houstonians, be they equipped with specialty training or not, recognized that the desperate people coming to their city neither meant nor brought trouble with them. They wanted simple human decency. This, Houstonians ladled out in huge dollops.

The survivors needed physical attention, but they also required respect. Respect for their endurance. Respect for their courage. Respect for their sacrifice. Respect for their losses. Respect for their value. The evacuees responded positively to the sense that they were welcomed, and that their lives were perceived as valuable.

The Houston Katrina experience was a success because of attitude. As crucial as skills sets are, it was not the technical expertise of the volunteers, but our mind-sets that made the critical difference. The good will of the volunteers who opened their homes and lives to strangers of whom they knew nothing but their desperate need for help overshadowed the falsehoods that had developed a life of their own. We discarded "by-the-book" solutions that failed, instead embracing new and untested ideas that worked. Time and time again, our desire allowed us to successfully jump the intercultural gap that pundits said was un-crossable. Unlike FEMA and the government bureaucracy with their secret, selfish agendas, we wanted our efforts to work so we made them, we *willed* them to succeed.

America's Dirty Little Secret

While serious, the survivors' medical problems were by and large easily predicted and treated. The new and unanticipated psychological burdens defied standard therapy because they were novel—the corrosive effect of American citizens being treated as aliens, excommunicated by the government in their own homeland.

Arguing that institutional racism was over in this country, dashed to pieces in the 1960's, locked away forever by ironclad legislation against racial discrimination, many Americans initially reacted in genuine shock and outrage when they heard survivors complain about the inherent racism in the government response. They responded reflexively, even understandably. In fact, many of us sincerely believe that American crusaders of culturally diverse backgrounds sacrificed their freedom and sometimes their lives throughout the 1950's and 60's to avoid precisely the act of institutional racism of which this country now stands exposed.

African-Americans and others quickly came to understand that, when push came to shove and their livelihood and lives were at stake, the response of the strongest nation of the world to a predicted disaster in a city known for its vulnerability was a pathetic pyramid of incompetence at the municipal, state, and especially the federal level. They knew—as all America knows—that this incompetence would not be tolerated if Katrina struck luxuriant Fort Lauderdale, or profitable St. Petersburg. Believers in the American dream themselves, the storm's disenfranchised, poor victims could not fathom that such a reaction could be due to lack of preparation. The strongest nation in the world could not be so inept in a predicted time of crisis; therefore, the answer must lie elsewhere.

In a very real sense they're right. It's not that politicians would shout louder from a storm-struck wealthy, non-African-American, non-Hispanic port. In fact, that strong political protest wouldn't be necessary at all. In these scenarios, the government's response would be immediate, coordinated, and effective because it had to be. Politicians understand that in America, white middle-class and wealthy citizens vote in greater proportion than impoverished minorities. The needs and desires of the rich are the gravity wells that attract political action. Thus, in this country, even in life-threatening circumstances, power derives not from the governed, but from the influence of the powerful. Disenfranchised and impoverished populations are passed over, their condition given only occasional, cursory attention. *The competence of the response tracks not with the needs but with the political power of the community.*

This was America's dirty little secret—institutional racism, not just ineptitude, determined the tenor and speed of the government's response. The world was astonished by this conclusion, yet its revelation was on full display for all to see during the dog days of summer, 2005. As the Katrina debacle played out, Americans, Nova Scotians, Brazilians, and Europeans asked themselves, their families, their friends, and their colleagues, "How could this happen in America?"

The answer is now self-evident. The American corpus held a built-in susceptibility. The Katrina disaster revealed this deep institutional and cultural weakness, an infirmity held over from the days of slavery that permeated the government's support structure. The tepid response was preordained, the debacle's roots deeply hidden in America's bones.

As political power grids and influence lines bypassed indigent communities, poor neighborhoods (like the Ninth Ward in New Orleans) were left for decades to wallow in early twentieth-century (and late nineteenth-century) substandard homes, schools, and services. The vulnerability of these communities to a storm was obvious, yet the American culture, as well as its government at all three levels, bypassed these poor "leftover people" for generations. It was no surprise that it took the authorities more than twenty-four hours to even pay attention to what was happening.

This culturally acceptable community vulnerability was amplified by the inchoate bureaucratic response of the government, an ineptitude that staggers the imagination to this day. The devastating effects of poorly-conceived plans were magnified by poor execution. Warnings for years that the storm of storms would arrive, followed by acute warnings that it would make landfall in first 48, then 24, then 12 hours produced a signature-inaction on a multibillion dollar national scale. This was no sudden terrorist threat. Nature telegraphed her pitch, and the three tiered municipal/state/federal government complex not only missed it, but missed it repeatedly.[1]

The physical damage will be repaired, but the emotional desolation, like radiation, will affect an entire generation of America's urban poor. It is only the strong character of the victims and volunteers that protected them from more grievous effects of this governmental abandonment.

Miscommunication, inertia, and a hyper-concern of government bureaucracy to first serve itself and its corporate sponsors didn't just

---

1. An incisive contemporary review of the government's inept reaction to the Katrina debacle is Dr. Michael Eric Dyson's book entitled *Come Hell or High Water: Hurricane Katrina and the Color of Disaster*, published in 2006 by Basic Civitas Books.

blunt its own response—it poisoned the well-intentioned response of others. For example, while the clinics were under local municipal control, volunteers like my wife, daughter, and many other concerned Houstonians could mingle freely with the shell-shocked victims of Katrina, providing their first compassionate contact with fellow human beings in days. Yet, when federal responders descended on Houston, they chastised the volunteers for their meritorious conduct, and warned them to keep their distance from the victims. Volunteers who insisted on coming in were told not to talk unnecessarily to the Katrina survivors, while providing their material needs. So in order to comply with the new rule, volunteers fell all over themselves and each other sorting socks and organizing underwear.

Once the federal responders arrived, the volunteers were denied the opportunity to provide what many were driven to do, why they volunteered, *and what the survivors needed*—the display of simple human dignity that comes from mutually respectful interpersonal contact, beginning with the words "How can I help?"

After the series of edifying, personal face-to-face conversations and interactions I had with the survivors, I was outraged at this new, insipid edict. The rule not only denied the execution of common sense whose balancing influence can be so stabilizing in a crisis, but conveyed the message to the struggling survivors that they were too alien (and of too little value) to engage in conversation. *Survivors were to be treated like specimens to be observed rather than people to be engaged.*

My one repeated act of open defiance was to tell the volunteers, for the sake of the survivors they volunteered to serve, to blatantly disregard this anti-litigious, organization-protecting, *and* spirit-destroying rule. I fully concede that the volunteers were not trained mental health specialists. But I also assert that the Katrina survivors didn't need what FEMA couldn't provide anyway—thousands of trained counselors. They needed what FEMA had and wouldn't release—contact with people who treated the survivors with respect and honor. FEMA's rules simply did not fit the needs of the time, and they didn't have the sense to get out of the way. Incredibly, some FEMA representatives actively discouraged volunteers from coming into the complexes at all, claiming falsely that the facilities already had all the volunteers they could use!

The local volunteers who knew the area and had come to know the victims should have dictated what FEMA would do—not the reverse.

Many U.S. citizens have reacted by slamming the government, quite appropriately attempting to startle it into action. While this may appear to work for a time, the bureaucracy suffers from the poisoned belief that power and right flow from the wallet. With this toxin deep in its system, attempts to stir it back to life are futile, much like a poisoned man slips back into his stuporous state when temporarily aroused.

It is not the government that must wake up—it is the rest of us. We must provide our own solutions to local and regional crises, adapting the old Russian adage "Pray to God, but row to shore" as we craft our own solutions. These solutions can start with identifying *local* organizations as the focal point for supplies, with *national* chapters and organizations funneling material and personnel to the local groups and local affiliates for their most effective dispersal. What we need are resources, and those resources flow from political rivers. Now is the time to divert them to us. We require political power, as that is the tool from which we will forge strong safeguards for our communities.

We have the right, the authority, and the responsibility to insist that, in times of national emergency, political face-saving and self-serving decisions will not be tolerated. Any local official who does not petition for state support in a clear emergency must be immediately fired. State officials who can but do not deploy needed resources with dispatch to afflicted communities must be summarily discharged. Federal officials in the line of command who do not respond immediately to a state's request for urgent aid must be fired, impeached, and removed.

Katrina survivors repeatedly intimated to the workers and volunteers who chose to speak with them the shock of being U.S. citizens, born and raised in this country, but being treated as if their lives, concerns, and crushing problems were meaningless. They began the week as Americans, giving little thought to what that meant. They ended it with the clear sense that, while *they* knew they were U.S. citizens, their government would neither portray them nor treat them as such! With every broken promise of rescue, or food arrival, or healthcare delivery, the survivors got the message loud and clear that they were not worth taking seriously. The consequences for all of us of ignoring the destructive effects of the government's mistreatment of other Americans is too terrible to contemplate.

Geographic vulnerability and bureaucratic incompetence, aggravated by the greed of the powerful, joined together to tear the heart out of New Orleans. There was one missing piece that was supplied by the media, completing the tragic Trifecta, creating the Perfect Storm. It remained for corporate-owned media, appealing to the base instincts of the public, to sensationalize the tragedy and *blame the victims.*[2]

This circumstance of conflicting perspectives begs the question, in a news event where there are hundreds of stories simultaneously occurring in one specific locale, who decides which stories should be broadcast? Local, on-the-scene reporters commonly don't choose their stories. While the American public may believe that these stories are identified by freewheeling local journalists reporting representative events, in fact, the reports are carefully identified and selected by local producers. These producers respond to the demands of general managers, who in turn respond to corporate executives, who worship at the shrines of ratings, insatiable profit, and corporate political dicta. Thus, like the army, corporate executives determine policy from the top down.

However, this reverses the established reporting paradigm of the twentieth century, in which reporters report what they find (whatever they find), and senior journalists allow opinion to be shaped by the facts, as opposed to shaping the reporting of the facts. As an African-American myself, it is curious to me that, with the exception of Oprah Winfrey and Anderson Cooper, no one seems to have maintained this journalistic integrity.

Hopes for A Better Future

Dynamism animated the Katrina clinic. During the ten days of its operation, we saw people whose changing circumstances required their growth and cultural evolution. These individuals were not merely pa-

---

2. Getting the media's message, churches around the country carried the story that the victims somehow deserved their fate because they lived in a "sin city"!!

tients, moving slowly and predictably along the natural history trajectory of their disease. They were instead travelers. Some knew where they were headed. Others changed course rapidly and sometimes erratically.

This emotional, kinetic energy made the interactions at the clinic unpredictable. After resolving their acute medical problems, the evacuees were absorbed by the process of self-transformation, moving to the business of getting on with their lives. Twenty-five thousand survivors reacted in twenty-five thousand different ways to the changing landscapes of their lives. The universe of new future possibilities opened wide, and the evacuees changed and adapted as their circumstances required them to readjust to the challenges they faced.

Our interactions with the evacuees changed and matured during the ten day operation of the center. Conversations with patients that were both necessary and appropriate for the first two hours at the clinic were no longer helpful a week into the clinic's existence. The requirements of the evacuees changed as they moved from the helpless, passive state to an active one. And the knowledge they required changed as well. Like any other group of people, they simply needed the facts to make the best decision.

It was a delight to see the evacuees get their feet on the ground again, turning their eyes to the future. Many of the survivors were sought after, and reveled at their new status as cynosures. Prospective employers looked for them. Churches engaged them in conversation. Charitable families opened their homes to them. This attention was a new experience for the evacuees, especially for the poor. In their years of poverty, these survivors had always been the seekers. Their government never sought them out or wanted their opinions before. Now, for the first time in their lives, they were sought after by some of their generous fellow citizens.

Dealing with competing opportunities was a new experience for the Katrina evacuees. Some of the survivors clearly struggled with the dizzying array of choices that confronted them, like a Russian or African immigrant does when shopping at an American supermarket for the first time. Others simply chose the first opportunity that came along. Collections of survivors could be seen trading opportunities with each other, looking for the best one, while giving up what was best for others. There was energy, and sometimes the arena was electric with the feel of opportunity.

The United States itself faces a great time of opportunity. If we embrace the displaced survivors, educating them while easing them into the mainstream of American culture, America benefits. The survivors have great strength of heart and character. More than one well-to-do volunteer worker questioned whether they would have what it took to survive as the evacuees did. An infusion of that strength of heart back into the U.S.A. would produce wonderfully new and strong fruit.

It is much easier to reach a hand out to the survivors if we see them with "new eyes." They are not merely poor and African-American people from a part of the country that many of us have never seen, who speak "strangely." These superficial differences hide the fact that they are much like each of us.

In fact, Katrina, a storm, moving at random, not even identifiable a month before it struck, shattered the lives of some of the rich as well as the poor. Not only the impoverished were ruined. Bank managers found that they were in charge of banks that no longer existed. Some lawyers, physicians, dentists, dry cleaners lost their livelihoods and practices. Many New Orleans residents, cruising comfortably financially, smashed into ruins on August 29th when the storm hit. They are among the new disenfranchised and can learn much from the flexibility, adaptability, and heart strength of their impoverished fellow victims.

Finally, the rest of us who do not live along the Gulf Coast are not as far from disaster as a casual glance at the map might suggest. Recent insurance cancellations, in the wake of Hurricane Katrina, as far away as New York City and Cape Cod, Massachusetts, because of concerns about more frequent serious hurricanes and floods due to global warming, can unleash its own financial storm. The communication from your physician that your child, or parent, or spouse, has a serious disease can be just as crushing as what the Katrina survivors experienced. And there are many other forms that devastation can take both at the personal and the community, regional, or even national and global levels.

My experience with individual survivors at the Katrina clinic was not unique. As we volunteers gathered again at work (after the fears of Hurricane Rita scattered us throughout Texas) sharing our different accounts, it was clear that many workers had experiences as gripping and moving as mine. We shared stories, adventures, and our interactions with each other. However, it was no longer with the open-mouthed astonishment that characterized our first interactions with the Katrina evacuees. It was now with a deeper, affirmative understanding and appreciation of the survivors' convictions.

We had done more than provide emergency health care. Instead, we discovered our unwitting enrollment in a ten day civics course in which the evacuees were the teachers and we were the students. They taught us that in the most despicable of circumstances, breathing an atmosphere superheated by horrid lies, compassion still made sense. They taught us that people of character rise above decrepit conditions and that the impoverished react to uncivil situations with civility. They reaffirmed our belief in the unshakable bonds between husband and family, between mother and child, and between citizen and community.

Finally, the deep character of the survivors remains well beyond measure. This is the life-lesson of the Katrina survivors to the world: economic and ecologic disaster are trumped by strength of character.

Appendix:
The University of Texas School of Public Health

As soon as the busloads of Katrina survivors began arriving less than a mile away from its main campus, the University of Texas School of Public Health (UTSPH) at Houston found itself at the epicenter of a national crisis.

Rarely does a U.S. school of public health have the reaction to a national disaster occur in its own neighborhood. Established in 1969, UTSPH publicly demonstrated its devotion to the creed of community service during several critical weeks in September 2005. Suspending its regular didactic and research activities, it released its faculty, students and staff to help lead the Houston response to the Katrina disaster.

As its physicians treated the Katrina survivors, UTSPH public health specialists provided indispensable support for the evacuees' transition to Houston. Its epidemiologists rigorously tracked down any sign of epidemic development, and its students carefully interviewed and cataloged the chronic health needs of the survivors. Most importantly, UTSPH staff volunteered their personal time to meet with the survivors, providing the precious human interaction that so many of the evacuees needed.

The school's wholehearted commitment to this national public health crisis exemplified Texas' dedication to the well-being of Katrina survivors. It provides an outstanding model for the other public health institutions around the country to emulate.

About the Author

Born in New York City in 1952, Lemuel A. Moyé, MD, PhD, attended public schools in Queens. After graduating from The Johns Hopkins University in 1974, he earned his medical degree at Indiana University Medical School in 1978. He then earned an MS degree in statistics at Purdue University, after which he completed a Ph.D. program in Biostatistics at the University of Texas School of Public Health in 1987.

Working as a staff physician, he saw hundreds of patients at the Harcourt Clinic in Indianapolis, Indiana. In addition, Dr. Moyé was a treating physician at the U.S. Steelworks Plant in Gary, Indiana in the early 1980's, a first responder at this huge industrial complex. After moving to Houston, he was first a staff physician, then associate medical director, then chief medical officer and owner of a Physicians' Association in Houston Texas, responsible for supervising physicians at seven urban clinics. During this time, he diagnosed and treated hundreds of patients in general and family practice in the multicultural and multiethnic setting of Houston.

A diplomat of the National Board of Medical Examiners, he is Professor of Biostatistics at the University of Texas School of Public Health in Houston where he holds a full-time faculty position. During the Katrina crisis, he was chair of the faculty. Dr. Moyé has served as a clinical trial consultant with Berlex, Proctor and Gamble, Marion Merrill Dow, Pfizer, Hoerst Roussel, Aventis, Key Pharmaceuticals, Coromed, Dupont, Bristol Myers-Squibb, Novartis, Medtronics, Astra-Zeneca, CryoCor and Vasogen pharmaceutical companies. He is a National Institutes of Health Investigator, working with both the

National Heart, Lung and Blood Institute, and most recently with the National Institute for Neurologic Disease and Stroke. In addition, Dr. Moyé has served for six years on both the Cardiovascular and Renal Drug Advisory Committee to the Food and Drug Administration (FDA) and the Pharmacy Sciences Advisory Committee to the FDA. He has served on several Data, Safety, and Monitoring Boards that oversee the conduct of clinical trials, and formally reviews research grants submitted by fellow scientists for federal funding. Dr. Moyé is a consultant for the National Medical Association (NMA). In addition, he has served on the National Research Advisory Committee (NRAC) overseeing the Research Centers in Minority Institute (RCMI) program at Texas Southern University, chairing that committee for four years. He has been an expert witness in both state and federal court.

Dr. Moyé is sole author of three science books: *Statistical Reasoning in Medicine: The Intuitive P value Primer* (2000), *Multiple Analysis in Clinical Trials: Fundamentals for Investigators* (2003), and *Statistical Monitoring of Clinical Trial: Fundamentals for Investigators* (2005). He has also co-authored two published texts in mathematics (2002 and 2005) and has published 125 manuscripts in the peer-reviewed scientific literature. A second edition of *Statistical Reasoning in Medicine: The Intuitive P value Primer* appeared in summer 2006. He is currently writing *Elementary Bayesian Biostatistics—Fundamentals for Investigators*, which is scheduled to appear in the summer of 2007.

He and his wife Dixie live in Houston, Texas, with their two daughters, Flora and Bella, and his mother, Florence.